Adirondack Timber Cruising

LOGGING TALES AND LUMBERING DAYS MEMORIES

Including Mart Allen's Recollections

Adirondack Timber Cruising

LOGGING TALES AND LUMBERING DAYS MEMORIES
Including Mart Allen's Recollections

Written, Edited and with Biographical
& Historical Commentary by William J. O'Hern

First Paperback Edition, May 2020

Cover image: Daniel M. Christmas, president/owner
of Christmas and Associates and Christmas Farm and Forestry.
Dan is a forestry graduate of Paul Smith's College.
Photograph courtesy Christmas and Associates Marketing Department

Published by
In the Adirondacks
P.O. Box 526
Camden, NY 13042
www.adkwilds.com

Printed in the United States of America
by Patterson Printing

ISBN 978-0-9890328-5-8

Adirondack Timber Cruising

LOGGING TALES AND LUMBERING DAYS MEMORIES
Including Mart Allen's Recollections

The History of the Men and Women
Who Manage the Vast Northern Forest
with an Eye on Conservation,
Substantiality and the Logging Industry.

William J. O'Hern

TABLE OF CONTENTS

To Mart Allen,
Who is Proud to Have Been
a Part of the Culture
and Spirit Embodied and
Exemplified by the
People Who Helped Build
the Character of his
Adirondack Community.

EPIGRAM

An Inexhaustible Supply of Timber

That a greater appreciation of the forest has developed has been evident since about 1919. In earlier times when lumber and pulpwood were abundant, few thought about the future supply. As forest resources became somewhat exhausted, men began to think in these terms, and to plan perpetual lumbering programs. By using selective cutting methods, better fire protection, better pest control, and a more effective program of reforestation, foresters sought to provide an inexhaustible supply of lumber—a renewable resource adequate to supply the needs of coming generations.

Courtesy Hamilton County Historical Association

PREFACE

To Talk to Mart Is to Talk To a Legend of the Adirondacks

Being asked to write a short essay on my association with Mart Allen is certainly a privilege. Because I've had a camp in the Old Forge area for many years, I'd heard about Mart and enjoyed reading his thoughtful and well-written articles in the local paper.

Bob Sauer, Harden forester. Sustainable forestry is a goal of the American Forest & Paper Association.
Courtesy Mart Allen

Mart, like me, is a retired forestry professional, and we have a great deal in common as far as forest management is concerned. When Mart was general manager of the Adirondack League Club (ALC), he was heavily involved in the management of their woodlands, and he has a knowledge of good forestry practices few can match.

My first meeting with Mart was set up by a friend of mine, also a forester, who was working at the Adirondack League Club. We met Mart at the Bisby Lodge, and had a great visit on a wide array of forestry-related issues. I realized I was talking to a man who had a great deal of knowledge on just about everything related to the woods. Actually, I did more listening than talking, knowing full well that Mart had a wealth of experience that I could only hope to someday match. It never happened.

Mart, throughout his career, told it like it was. He wrote many articles on forestry practices and on other topics from his point of view. He wrote about both the past and present. To talk to Mart is to talk to a Legend of the Adirondacks and know what he has to say is well worth-listening to. Mart is the Man!

—Bob Sauer, January 2019

FOREWORD

Mart Allen's Un-sugarcoated View of Logging's Past

Mart Allen, with his roots in the past and his eye toward the future, gives people today a chance to glimpse into the way things used to be. I was lucky enough to edit Mart's column in the *Adirondack Express* for many years, and his breadth and depth of knowledge on forestry always astonished me. He is one of a vanishing number of people who could make your woodlot work for you, dowse a site for a brand new well using a forked stick, and tell you stories about the men and women who worked and lived in the woods long ago.

Early 1960s 8 hp., 4-cycle Skidoo loaded with beaver with Nancy and Marty's children with their dad. Marty remembers, "My son trapped, but not long, just long enough to catch seven of everything. Then, that was enough." Photo by Nancy Allen. Courtesy Mart Allen

Many people today decry the state of the world and long for a kinder, simpler time. Take a listen to Mart's stories and you find that the world, even many years ago, was a harsh, dangerous place. Mart celebrates the times and people of his youth, but he does not sugarcoat what a difficult world it was when men had to wrest their living from a forest that, in many cases, was very willing to fight back.

Mart Allen. *Adirondack Express*

Mart's stories take you back to a time when you did what you had to do to get a job done, and whining or giving up weren't options. You hear about hard work that was done before the prevalence of modern machines and you're in awe of the people that undertook those jobs.

Mart Allen was one of those people.

—M. Lisa Monroe, editor, the *Adirondack Express*

"Forest Engineer" might be a better title than "forester" to describe the profession. The job of a forester includes so much more than timber cruising. For instance, there are surveying, map making, and forest management; camps need to be planned, stream beds improved and in this Mart Allen photo, a road must be laid out where this trail exists. Courtesy Mart Allen

Part One

FOREST ENGINEER

A Forest is Far More Than Trees. The object of forestry is to discover and apply the principles according to which forests are best managed. The forest is the most highly organized portion of the vegetable world. It takes its importance less from the individual trees which help to form it than from the qualities to it as a whole. Although it s composed of trees, the forest is far more than a collection of trees standing in one place. it has a population and plants peculiar to itself, a soil largely of its own making, and a climate different in many ways from that of the open country. Its influence upon the streams alone makes farming possible in many regions, and everywhere it tends to prevent floods and drought. It supplies fuel, one of the necessaries of life, and lumber, the raw material, without which cities, railroads, and all the great achievements of material progress would have been either long delayed or wholly impossible. The forest is as beautiful as it is useful. The old fairy tales which spoke of it as a terrible place are wrong. No one can really know the kindliest and strongest parts of nature. From every point of view it is one of the most helpful friends of man. Perhaps no other natural agent had done so much for the human race and has been so recklessly used and so little understood. —Gifford Pinchot, from *A Primer of Forestry*, 1899

Adirondack TIM-Berrr!

Chapter 1 | William J. O'Hern and Barbara K. Bird

TIMBER CRUISING

TIMBER CRUISE. A sample measurement of a woodlot used to estimate the amount of standing timber that the forest contains. These measurements are collected at sample locations called plots, quadrants, or strips.

"WASTING AMERICA'S SUSTENANCE" read the headline in the *New York Herald* on December 9, 1906. The full-page story quoted an unidentified writer saying, "This [Pacific Northwest] timbered area is the richest natural treasure of the American continent, compared with which the gold mines of Alaska and Nevada are of picayune value for this and for coming generations. It is so wonderfully rich a treasure that its owners are squandering it like drunken spendthrifts. A billion feet of lumber is wasted every year; enough to build 100,000 comfortable American homes."

A new log road that extends through private timberland. It was laid out to minimize excavation and filling that would otherwise disrupt water flow. Courtesy Mart Allen

By 1906, outraged voices were saying America was "squandering its precious natural resources "like drunken spendthrifts." Courtesy John Fram

The writer was one voice among many of the day who was critical of what was seen as a rising awareness that America's prosperity and success was being achieved by the "useless extravagance of nature's gifts."

One of those natural resource "gifts" was America's forests, considered the largest in the world.

An early timber cruiser who became a convert to Gifford Pinchot's principals of selective harvesting. Courtesy John Fram

Fingers were pointed at wanton cutting, wasteful culling and burning, the introduction of steam-powered machinery, timber companies' lack of concern for conservation and America's ingenuity at turning forests into cash as fast as possible.

Log-hauling from a skidways in the woods to a river that would soon be choked with logs. Today's foresters plan logging activity to minimize the area disturbed by operations. Courtesy John Fram

The National Hardwood Lumber Association estimated in the same article "a possibility of the destruction of the forests of the United States in thirty-five years. The association estimates that there are now (1906) standing in the United States in the neighborhood of 1,475,000,000,000 feet of lumber, but 45,000,000,000 feet is being cut every year."

This was the era of the rise of Gifford Pinchot and his legions of supporters who were passionate about raising public awareness of the wanton abuse of the country's natural resources. Pinchot became a convert to the practice of selective harvesting of forest resources and lobbied to put his knowledge to practical use.

Working initially as a forest cruiser, his silviculture models later gained the attention of President Theodore Roosevelt, who named him Chief Forester of the redefined United States Forest Service. A close friendship developed between Roosevelt and Pinchot, resulting in a collaboration that put into practice Pinchot's guiding principle that forests could produce sustainable timber and still be maintained for the use and enjoyment of future generations.

As a result of this newfound sense of conservation and sustainability, forest (or "timber") cruisers became more informed, and through education became some of the frontline defenders of the forest.

But first, a little background that includes interesting recollections of Barbara Kephart Bird in a witty article, "I Married a Forester," that appeared in *North Country Life's* Spring 1951 issue. Bird later converted her remembrances into a delightful book, *Calked Shoes, Life in the Adirondack Lumber Camps* (Prospect Books, 1952). The book relates her experience of lumbering as seen by a "forestress" over a period of four years as she shared all the labors of her forester husband, Robert Royal "Roy" Bird, on arduous cruising tours and long winter months in lumber camps. He had long been associated with the Gould Paper Company, of Lyons Falls, New York.

Logging was rugged work. River drivers Wally Wager and Jim Craig.
Courtesy Hamilton County Historical Association

Mrs. Bird learned the Tug Hill country the hard way—by cooking for a cruising team with such facilities as tent life could afford. Miles from a food supply, it was she who took to the trail when the larder ran low, toting in a pack-basket load at a time. Such hours as remained after these activities were spent in studying bird and animal life, the ways of the weather, logging techniques, and such.

A student of forestry learns more than how to plant tree seedlings. These Port Leyden high school girls are developing the skill of peeling bark with a spud. Courtesy Lyons Falls History Association

When not on Tug Hill, the Bird team was stationed in Gould Lumber Company camps in the mountain terrains of Ice Cave Mountain at the head of North Lake and the upper Moose River country. Here the author gained what Roy called "a Bird's-eye view" of lumber camp life, the activities that made the camps click, and such-all from a feminine point of view.

All of this came as second nature to Barbara Bird, daughter of Horace Kephart, who for an earlier generation wrote inspiring books for campers and lovers of the trail. Back then, no man or boy ever thought of preparing for a hiking expedition without studying the Kephart books and once in the woods as a tent-site was selected, the tent erected, a fire built and a meal cooked, the same eloquent authority.

A lot of understanding of the outdoors, and of the men who harvested the trees and got them from skidway to mill, went into the writing of *Calked Shoes*, and a lot of men and women who would have never known of backwoods lumber camp life will in a vicarious way gain deep pleasure in reading Bird's experiences. pleasure in reading Bird's experiences.

★ ★ ★

Many years ago, when waterways were filled with moving logs, there seemed to be an endless need for lumber to meet American's requirements for wood.

Small local mills and large commercial sawmills could be found everywhere. Flood dams were built on small streams to help the movement of logs to market, and river-driving camps were manned by lumbermen who used to mark and measure every log before sending it down the rivers. Most older Adirondack and Tug Hill men, at one time, could claim they had been engaged in lumbering at one time or another in their lifetimes.

Logging was rugged work. The lumbering schedule called for log-peeling in the spring and building tote roads in the summer and fall in advance of log-skidding until Christmas; the work continued for three more months before the 'jacks were paid and left to celebrate St. Patrick's Day at some saloon or dance at one of the many local hotels. But there was an unsung job that came in advance of all the more flamboyant logging jobs: timber cruising.

A team of Port Leyden high school girls on a field trip to learn general forest management skills.
Courtesy Lyons Falls History Association

Barbara Bird tells how she became involved with cruising when in the early 1920s she hefted a pack basket on her back and worked her way along a "faintly blazed" foot path following her forester husband to a Gould lumber camp in the middle of a 25,000-acre tract of virgin timber known as the White Tract on Tug Hill.

It was thirty years ago when extensive forests of virgin timber were to be found in the Tug Hill country of Northern New York and in certain sections of the Adirondack Mountains which have since been burned over or lumbered. Access to the forests was by train, boat, horse, or on foot. Most roads were impassable for autos, even at a time when cars were built high over the roadbed. A snowmobile was an oddity; skis were not in vogue in 1920; and whenever the forester made his rounds in winter, he did so on snowshoes unless he could catch a ride on a tote sleigh or a load of logs. Under such circumstances the wife of a forester defied convention if she followed her husband into the woods. A lumber camp was definitely thought to be no place for a woman; and as to living in a tent and cooking for a gang of timber cruisers—a lady in 1920 did not do such things! But I did.

America's rising prosperity resulted in the invention of massive machinery that helped grow the United States economy throughout the 20th century. Courtesy John Fram

The life of a forester proved to be so interesting that I put up with many inconveniences and discomforts in order to be with Roy on the job. I liked it, but I would not advise any young man to take up this profession unless he is a hardy enthusiast and immune to the rigors and tediousness that a forester's life entails.

If you doubt the need for rugged fervor, just imagine yourself with us cruising timber. Come with me, as a tenderfoot, into the deep woods. Spend week after week in the virgin forest and get the feel of it under your skin. Make your bed of balsam boughs under a pup tent and sleep thus under the stars, the moon, the rain. Have the rising sun for your alarm clock; make "bucking the brush" your daily toil; cook your supper of speckled trout and corn-bread baked in the ashes; and have as a lullaby, the yapping fox.

The Kemlock Special was a mid-western competitor to Holman Harry Linn's break-through Linn Tractor machine. Courtesy John Fram

Tune your life to the rush of water over stones, the sighing wind in the balsams, the chatter of squirrels at noontime, and the soft animal noises of the night. Accustom your eyes to the lace carpet of speckled sunlight, the soft gloom beneath the spruce trees, the tangible blackness of a starless night. If then you are filled with joy, if such pleasures satisfy you, if the arduous tasks of the day and the petty necessities of living do not lessen your ardor for life such as this—then, and only then, may you know what the life of a forester means.

What is a forester? What are his duties?

In my capacity as wife of a forester I have been bombarded through the years by questions as to the nature of my husband's

First Linn Tractor used by the Gould Paper Company in 1918. Softwood logs were transported over haul roads to landings to await the spring thaw log drive. Dewitt Wiley stands atop logs in forefront.

Photo by Dewitt Wlley. Courtesy Leigh Portner

work. In town and country alike there seems to be a distorted notion among laymen that a forester "plants trees" for a living, fights forest fires in dry seasons, and works on blister rust control as a side line.

Swing log loaders such as this Raymond design made work safer and easier. Courtesy John Fram

The student of forestry does learn to plant trees, but his education also involves a study of the mature forest as it stands: its history, its composition, its extent, its natural enemies, its protection, its harvesting, its uses. The proportion of planted acres to acres of standing forest is obviously small and relatively unimportant. It is the mature timber that is most liable to attack by insects and disease. It is in over-mature timber that we find the worst windfalls. A forest tree, like a man, grows from a baby to an adult and to hoary old age. In the last stage its resistance is lowered and it often falls prey to some insect or fungus. Sometime prior to that event, the tree may be cut, and when scientifically done, such cutting leaves a parent stand to reproduce the forest or provides artificially for its continuation.

Forest management, then, involves cutting trees as well as planting them. The difference between the forester and the ordinary logger is that the forester is primarily interested in perpetuating a sustained yield by appropriate cuttings for which various systems have been evolved to meet the requirements of the forest. He does not exploit the present timber crop at the expense of possible future crops. He knows that these methods of forestry have proved to be both conservative and profitable.

Visualize America's great Northern Forest in 1820. Imagine a sea of continuous forests comprised of a mix of softwood and hardwood trees. Miles upon miles of spruce, balsam, pine, birch, maple, beech, cherry, oak, chestnut and other tree species spread across a great expanse.

By 1850 logging companies were actively harvesting America's forests from the Great Lakes to the Atlantic seaboard. Twenty years later, logging companies that cut hardwood trees loaded them onto flat cars and transported them to sawmills by train. Courtesy John Fram

Mechanical log loaders were an important development. Once the stems have been bucked into a series of log lengths, logs are sorted and stacked into piles. Once enough logs of a specific sort have been accumulated, and a truck arrives, they can be loaded onto the truck and transported to their destination. Courtesy John Fram

The young forester must study the fundamentals of botany, soils, geology, plant pathology, forest entomology, surveying, silviculture, logging, history of forestry, uses of wood, and so on. In addition to his school work, he must spend months of actual experience in the woods. Then he should familiarize himself with details of whatever branch of forestry he intends to follow, for already we see that the profession of forestry is not so simple as mere "tree planting" suggests.

If he decides to take up general forest management, rather than some of the more highly technical work, such as pathology, he must make up his mind that for years he must live most of his life in the woods. His home life must be secondary; and if he acquires a wife, she must abide by such conditions philosophically.

One of the first jobs that falls to the lot of the forest manager is cruising timber.

This is how it happened with us. We were eating supper one Saturday evening. Roy was paying one of his infrequent visits to our home at Forestport during the summer of 1922 when he was cruising on Tug Hill.

"Do you know, Barbara, you could be a help on this cruising job."

"Good heavens! How?" I asked. "I don't even know what cruising timber means, much less how you go about it. How could I help?"

"You can cook," cannily responded my spouse, "and a good cook is an important asset in any camp. We three men don't have time for cooking good meals, yet we cannot go on bucking the brush day after day, unless we get good food. How about it? Did you ever cook over an open fire?"

"Some," I answered dubiously, "but I don't know if the results of my limited experience along that line would suit you."

Roy reached for another biscuit and smiled reminiscently. "The last batch of biscuit we had in camp was all right—except Carl forgot to put any baking powder in them. Perhaps we could stand YOUR cooking, if we tried hard enough."

The result of this conversation was that Roy spent the rest of the evening giving me a short course in timber cruising.

"And what, may I ask, is meant by cruising timber?"

"It means timber estimating. In other words we get an estimate of what a given stand of timber will yield in merchantable material."

"You mean you take a sort of inventory; so many cords of spruce, so many board-feet of maple, etc. is that the idea?"

"Well, yes and no," was the hesitant reply. "There is more to it than that. We have to survey the tract of timber first so we know the area of the entire tract. Then we count and measure the trees in quarter-acre plots at specific distances across the tract, thus getting what we hope is a fairly accurate average of what may be found in the entire stand. This is known as the circle-plot method of estimating.'

Patiently and in great detail, Gould Paper Company timber cruiser, Robert "Roy" Bird explained his method to his wife this way in her *Calked Shoes: Life in Adirondack Lumber Camps* (Prospect Books, 1952).

After we find out the area of the tract, we determine the amount and nature of the timber in numerous fractional parts or sample plots and can then compute what must be in the entire stand. For convenience in measuring, these quarter-acre plots are circular. Hence we call it the circle-plot method.

By the 1840s pioneer families that immigrated to America were pushing westward from New England. Land was changing. America was becoming industrialized. Booming cities were calling for more and more lumber for homes, offices and such. Wood was in high demand.
Courtesy Lewis County Historical Association

We use a surveyor's chain 66 feet long and made up of 100 links. Actually we use a steel tape graduated in links. It's lighter to carry. Starting at our base-line, I lead the party, taking off at a definite compass bearing and following a line straight across the tract by means of a staff compass. Frank and Carl [assistants]

> follow right behind me, measuring with the chain. We halt every ten chains. One man stays at the stake marking the tenth chain. The other two men pace off 59 feet radially from the stake in opposite directions. They measure each tree in their return path with Biltmore Sticks,[1] calling off the measurements to the man in the center, who writes them down in a notebook—spruce, 16 inches; beech, 19; hemlock, 24; etc. Returning to the center, each man takes another radius, and thus we continue until we have measured every tree in the plot.

Today, the understanding of "cruising" has expanded to incorporate the process of measuring forest stands to determine stand characteristics, such as average tree sizes, volume, and quality. The primary purpose of cruising remains to obtain a volume estimate to appraise and prepare timber sales. Timber cruisers provide technical expertise in statistical sampling, measurement protocols, and volume estimation procedures. They stand between an uncut forest and the awning blade of the sawmill.

There is a litany of support for the 21st century forest cruisers in the form of software, educational documents, training, and technical support. There is also a National Cruise System that includes a set of software tools developed for timber cruisers to design a cruise, collect cruise data, and produce statistically defensible volume estimates for timber sale contracts.

The following accounts are from a woman and three men from different generations. Barbara K. Bird accompanied her husband, Roy, on timber cruises and lived in lumber camps on Tug Hill and in the central Adirondacks. Byron Cool operated in the nineteenth century. Joe Conway's telling comprises his memories of assisting a timber cruiser on Tug Hill in the Depression era. Mart Allen shares some of his more recent cruising experiences, and in doing so helps to educate lay readers who might otherwise be unaware of the occupation and duties of a timber or forest cruiser.

Adirondack TIM-Berrr!

Chapter 2 | Barbara K. Bird

Barbara Bird's 1920s Life in a Virgin Forest

Life in the Tug Hill and Adirondack forests is not limited to hiking, fishing, hunting, and skiing. While countless visitors to the mountains are deriving pleasure from these recreational activities, logging operations are being carried on along numerous Adirondack lakes and rivers.

The men who engage in these more essential enterprises wear calked shoes of one kind or another while on their jobs, and forsake this type of footgear only in winter, when the nature of the work and the severity of the weather obviously call for warmer boots.

Calked shoes are strictly men's attire, and their use is confined to certain activities in a man's world. They are worn by lumbermen, foresters, surveyors and lumberjacks as an indispensable part of their costume during certain pursuits, the kind of calk depending upon the type of work at hand.

Calks are metal devices, like nails with pronounced or pointed heads. They are driven into the heavy sole of a woodsman's shoe by means of a special tool. The calks project downward from the sole and prevent slipping. Some calks, or hobnails, are short with snubby heads and are often used by hikers on rough terrain. The forester, while cruising timber, may have hobnails in his shoes, but the log-driver's calks are long, pointed and sharp to assure him of good footing on floating logs.

A riverman is as particular in the selection of his shoes and the supervision of the calking as milady is when she chooses evening slippers. And please do not accuse the log-driver of vanity, for his life depends on his footgear and his ability to use it. Breaking a log jam is a procedure that is neither easy nor safe unless the driver has good calks on his boots.

The world in which these men live and the work they accomplish became part of my live after I married Roy Bird, an Adirondack forester. I followed

Timber cruising on Tug Hill, ca. 1920s. Photo by Dewitt Wiley. Courtesy Leigh Portner my husband into the woods, where we lived the better part of four happy years in isolated lumber camps from Tug Hill above Boonville to Red River, a tributary of the south branch of the Moose River.

Barbara Was a Tenderfoot

Until our marriage in 1920 my knowledge of the Adirondack Mountains had come largely from the colorful descriptions with which Roy and my brother, a fellow forester, had regaled me during their student years. Their summers in Forestry Camp and in lumber camps, working for the experience, had infected them with an enthusiasm which I readily absorbed. When, during a vacation in Ithaca the second year of our marriage, I received a letter form Roy saying he had accepted a position as Forester for the Gould Paper Company of Lyons Falls, I was eager to join him. Glory be! We were to live in the Adirondacks!

The work boots of log drivers gave traction on slippery logs. Croghans had a pronounced instep and high heels. The soles were half an inch thick and heavily studded with calks. Courtesy Donald Wharton

First came an introduction to Tug Hill, a new name to me. I was familiar with Utica and Watertown but was unaware that to the west of the highway that connects those two cities lies a high rolling plateau, devoid of towns and uncrossed by highways—Tug Hill.

At that time extensive forests of virgin timber were to be found in the Tug Hill country above Boonville and in certain sections of the Adirondack Mountains which have since been burned over or lumbered. Access to the forests was by train, boat, horse or on foot. Most roads were impassable for autos even at a time when manufacturers built cars high over the roadbed.

River driving was a serious business. Courtesy Lyons Falls History Association

In the Adirondacks, unless fires have damaged the forest, there are usually enough seedlings to replenish the stand when they have been released to sunlight by the removal of the large, old trees. Planting is necessary only when the young growth has been destroyed by fire or other means.

Cruising the White Tract

"How do you measure the trees?" I asked Roy on my first day timber cruising.

He replied, "With Biltmore Sticks. I'll make one for you. And I'll show you how to pace distances. You can come out on the job with us some day, if camp life gets monotonous."

"You don't seem to question my capacity for rough going." I said, "You don't need to tell me what it means to follow a compass line straight through alder swamps, over windfalls and across streams, to say nothing of climbing rocks and pushing my way through witch hopple and striped maple and every other kind of brush. What do you think I am, an elephant?"

Robert and Barbara Bird. Courtesy *North Country Life* Summer 1952

"Humph," grunted Roy. "You must have acquired some stamina along that line. You scrambled over the hills and gorges at Ithaca with your brother. Don't I know what it means to climb Buffalo Street day after day?"

"Old Buf is a pretty good developer of leg muscles and wind," I admitted, "and I seem to recall wetting my feet once or twice in the waters of Cascadilla Creek. But I don't remember ever meeting any bear there and you can't deny there are bear on Tug Hill."

"Well, you may stay in camp if you prefer," said Roy. But of course I knew I would do no such thing.

Lost on Tug Hill

A week later, with a small pack basket on my back, I worked my way along the path to camp, which was situated in the middle of 25,000 acres of virgin timber known as the White Tract. I graciously label the route a "path" whereas in actual fact it was merely a trail, faintly blazed, from which brush had been made to improve the path underfoot. I had perforce to climb over logs, bark my shins on stones and mire myself in oozy mud. The blazes were inconspicuous. Property lines and the main trails were clearly marked, but temporary trails were blazed lightly.

An aerial view of the Gould Paper Company's plant in Lyons Falls, New York. Ca. 1945. Courtesy Harold Link

Roy went with me this first day or I would surely have become lost. Subsequently, however, I often made the trip out alone for supplies and I became wise in sighting blazes. I made one such expedition in the pouring rain with twenty pounds of provender in the pack basket on my back.

Traveling alone through dense forest, relying absolutely on your own resources, is a broadening experience. It is so easy to mistake a deer-run for the trail or to enter one edge of an alder swamp with confidence, only to pick your way out uncertainly at the further side; so simple to strain an ankle but not so easy to get to camp, hampered by ankle strain. You must always keep watch of the time in order to reach camp surely before dark. It is no fun to find yourself lost in the woods at nightfall with the chill of an evening rain soaking you to the skin.

Barbara never forgot the feeling of being lost. Courtesy Roy E. Wires

I have reason to believe the native residents when they say, "Tug Hill is a hell of a country to get lost in." The country has no distinguishing landmarks such as guide the traveler in the Adirondacks. There are no lakes, river, high mountains or rocky cliffs. One hardwood knoll succeeds another, each alder swamp duplicates its predecessor, every little stream looks like its brother and a towering hemlock has its counterparts scattered throughout the forest.

I shall never forget the day I accompanied the cruising party and the compass went wrong. Roy did not become aware of this inaccuracy until two o'clock in the afternoon when, instead of reaching the western base-line, he discovered that we were crossing the northern boundary. He had been puzzled all that cloudy morning because the topography was not what he thought it should be, but of course he did not question the accuracy of the compass.

Roy consulted his pocket map and determined what must be our approximate position. "Our best bet is to make for the eastern boundary line at Fish Creek," he said, "and follow the trail down to the fishing club. We'll have to use our pocket compasses. Go single file. Observe your own compass and, if you find that the man in the lead is deviating from our course, step ahead of him and lead until you are supplanted by a fresh guide from the rear. In that way we won't go far astray. We must get to the trail before dark or we'll have to spend the night in the woods."

The Fish Creek Club that Roy and Barbara were nearing by moonlight. Courtesy Joanne Sattler

We started out with Roy in the lead. There were not many stops for rest. As it grew late, the sky clouded over and rain added to our discomfort. Our wet clothes soon hampered our speed and hunger emphasized our fatigue.

Then came black night. When I say black, I mean black! There was a tangible quality to that darkness. I was oppressed by it as by a weight and felt inclined to cut it and push it back with my hands. I walked abruptly into Frank, who had come into sudden contact with the roots of a fallen tree. The luminous dials of our compasses added their weird ghostliness to our apprehensions. We began to distrust them and to compare one compass with another. The uncertainty of our footing necessitated a grotesque goose-step, now high to avoid obstructions and then low into muddy hollows. Blindly we forded streams. Profanely we fell over rocks. We walked finally with left hand on the shoulder ahead of us, holding our compasses close with our right. Blackness! Blackness everywhere!

I remembered stories of men being lost for days in these woods. I fought against these gloomy recollections and tried to concentrate on my compass. There was no need to watch for good footing. I could not see my hand, much less the ground under my feet. That black darkness became a physical pain.

Roy guesses our distress and called a halt. With fumbling fingers he struck a match, safely dry in his waterproof box.

What relief! What joy to see human faces, no matter how bedraggled and streaked with mud! Courage came back. Tiredness vanished. All was right with the world.

The match went out!

But the courage remained. We knew we could master this black monster any time we wished, hence it no longer filled us with awe but became merely annoying, like the rain and the rocks and the mud.

The warm Fish Creek Clubhouse was a welcome relief to the Birds. Courtesy Joanne Sattler

Roy soon bade us stop again. "If you feel over your heads," he said, "you can break off some of these dead branches and we'll build a fire."

We welcomed the suggestion and set to work. When we had a small fire going, Roy started alone on a short trip of reconnaissance, saying, "Hear that water rushing? I think we must be near Fish Creek. I'll see if I can find it, now that the moon is coming out so I can see."

In no time at all he was back again. "The trail to the club is fifty feet ahead," he announced. "We will have to feel of the blazed in order to be sure we stay on the trail. It's pretty well trodden underfoot, but we ought to be able to follow it fairly well by moonlight."

Fish Creek Club House porch is as comfortable to rest on and listen to the birds today as it was in days gone by. Courtesy Joanne Sattler

Fish Creek Club farm. Courtesy Joanne Sattler

We scraped the embers of our fire into the bed of a small stream and started out again. In half an hour we came out of the woods into a clearing where lights shone from the windows of the Fish Creek Club.[2] How good it was to be under a roof again with friendly walls shutting out the scene of our miseries! Here were chairs to sit in, a carpeted floor underfoot, a warm fire and dry clothes and a refreshing smell of bacon and coffee.

The next day I went cruising again. It doesn't pay to let tired muscles grow stiff.

Linn tractors pulled great lengths of log sleighs. Photo Jim Fynmore. Courtesy Black River Canal Museum

Barbara Bird watched many Linn tractors during her days on the White tract.
Courtesy Lyons Falls History Association

The whistle from the "G-Whiz" or Glenfield and Western railroad made by the locomotive as it hauled logs from Michigan Mills was a familiar sound that echoed across Fish Creek Club's meadows.
Courtesy Lyons Falls History Association

Adirondack TIM-Berrr!

Chapter 3 | William J. O'Hern and Barbara K. Bird

LUMBERMEN, FORESTERS, AND THE PUBLIC

An 1899 decision of New York State's Court of Appeals in what was known as the Moose River case[3] was a very important judgement that was deemed to have an important effect on the preservation of the forests and protection of trout in Adirondack streams.

It placed the pulp manufacturers and lumber companies at a serious disadvantage as it declared unconstitutional every law that made Adirondack streams public highways for floating logs to mills.

Highpoints of the case were reported in the June 17, 1899 issue of *Forest and Stream*:

> "The ground taken by the court is that these laws are not passed for the general public, but were mere subterfuges to get around legislation so that private individuals may enjoy special rights in the use of the specified waterways. This view of the court is strictly in accordance with the facts in every case where the Legislature has passed a bill for the benefit of the lumbermen, who drive their logs through the Adirondack streams, and often kill large tracts of timber by building dams to provide sufficient water for their purpose.
>
> "This practice kills the trout, and has been so destructive, especially in the Ausable River, that once-excellent fishing grounds are no longer available. Trout not killed by the logging are destroyed by the sawdust that is boldly emptied into the streams by the mills in defiance of the law.
>
> "The law just declared unconstitutional was passed in 1894 for the benefit of the lumber firm of Thomson & Co., in which

Lemon Thomson, John A. Dix and Senator Curtis N. Douglas, of Albany, N.Y., are interested. This firm had legal trouble with W.S. DeCamps, who objected to the [Thomson & Co.] lumbermen going across his property. They then got the bill through the Legislature, but were enjoined, and the case was stubbornly fought until the present decision was reached.

River of pulpwood logs. Courtesy Eric Johnson, The Northeastern Loggers Association archives

"Under the decision no logs can be floated down a stream without consent of the owners of the riparian rights, which means that these owners can charge such tolls as they see fit for the use of the streams for the floating of logs. This will increase materially the cost of getting lumber out of the woods, and in some cases practically will put a stop to lumbering on account of this increased cost. In the case of Thomson & Co., the firm can get its logs out by rail from its lumber tract to its mills at McKeever on the Adirondack & St. Lawrence Railroad by hauling the logs a short distance.

"The pulp mill men claim that it is unwise for the State to ignore such large business interests simply to benefit a few sportsmen; that the value of all the trout in the Adirondack streams is infinitesimal in comparison with the value of the pulp mill interest. This State's pulp industry is three times as large as that of any other State in the country. There are [in 1899] ninety mills, representing an investment of over $25,000,000, and a very large number of men are dependent upon pulp manufacture for a livelihood. The claim that they were denuding the watersheds of the rivers that take their rise in the Adirondacks the pulp men deny, and say that they are exercising great care in the cutting of trees for the protecting of their future supply.

"This claim is not admitted by those who have been working to secure better protection for the Adirondack forests."

A half-dozen half-frozen whitewater 'jacks are riding logs on flood water, wresting the raw material for next Sunday's newspaper from its lodgment on the bank of an Adirondack river.
Courtesy Lyons Falls History Association

Two decades later, following the Moose River case, lumberjacks were still logging across America's landscape but timber operations had changed. Gasoline-fueled tractors chugged and swayed over Tug Hill and throughout the Adirondacks. Day and night, over snow and ice-prepared roads, they tugged bobsled trains loaded heavily with logs.

Opponents of logging claimed the thunderous motor tractors were doing more than hauling logs; they were leading a noisy march back across 300

Lt. to Rt. Barbara Bird and Hazel Todd. Circa 1924. Bird, a forestress, shared all the labors of her forester husband, Royal, on arduous cruising tours and, long winter months in lumber camps. Mrs. Bird learned the Tug Hill and Adirondack country surrounding Ice Cave Mountain the hard way—by cooking for a cruising team with such facilities as tent life could afford. Miles from food supply, it was she that took to the trail when the larder ran low, toting in a pack-basket load at a time. Such hours as remained after these activities were spent in studying bird and animal life, the ways of the weather, logging techniques and such.

When not on Tug Hill's White Tract, the Bird team was stationed in Gould camps 7, 9 and 10 in the mountainous terrains of the upper Black River and Moose River country. It was there that Barbara gained what Roy called a bird's-eye view of how lumber camps get that way, the things that make them click and such-all, from a feminine point of view. Courtesy Dorothy Payton

The Gould Paper Company's lumber camps were designated by numbers. This is the Headquarters, Camp 7 (1920–1930). Fred Worden said he remembered that the day he snapped this picture "the temperature was 40 degrees below zero." The camp was snugged in the valley between Ice Cave and Canachagala mountains. Courtesy Fred Warden

years of forest devastation—"a great desideratum in America," a reporter for the Lowville, N.Y. *Journal and Republican* claimed in "Wood Crop Cut By Little Falls" on March 28, 1929.

"How can this be, it may be asked, when the cargo of these winter caravans is composed of trees that have been cut from their foundations and their lives ended?"

On the flipside, supporters claimed the lumber industry now followed a plan of management that would not destroy the forests permanently yet would permit the logging companies to take the maximum benefits of the yield of wood.

Little Falls was the first municipality in New York state, the article said, to "work its municipal forests extensively on a sustained yield basis, from seeding to harvest.

"All the trees will not be cut. The younger generations will be saved. A forester who knows how to obtain from the woodlands the highest commercial values goes through the forest marking only those trees that are to be removed."

By 1929, Little Falls and progressive logging companies, such as the Gould Paper Company, were applying scientific methods to logging. Planting, maturing, and harvesting the forest resources had begun to become a science. Extensive logging operations recognized tree slaughter was wasteful.

This scene of a Linn tractor with log-loaded sleighs headed out of Gould's Camp 7, located on east side of Ice Cave Mountain seven miles from the foot of North Lake, Atwell, N.Y. would have been a familiar one to Barbara Bird. Courtesy Dorothy Payton

Progress had come about. New logging operations instituted by trained foresters, the report went on to say, were diametrically different from those carried on hardnosed "loggers in the time in 1850 when New York was the leading timber devastating state. Forests were then cut with no thought of preserving them for future generations; total destruction of the wilderness was considered a triumph, and the public mind was deluded by the fallacy of 'inexhaustibility.'"

The writer continued to point out the positive benefits of forest management. There are "other areas in New York [state in 1929] that have been cut over two or three times and still have on them forests representing values equal to the original cost of the forest. These results are accomplished simply by the forestry plan of allowing trees of only a certain diameter to be cut…."

Little Falls decided that if their municipal forest was to be raised to its highest efficiency as a source of water supply and made continuously profitable, professional foresters would have to be called in on problems of management. Foresters from the New York State College of Forestry were consulted. Advice from them and from other state and federal agencies resulted in the city's plan for control of the forest on a sustained-yield basis.

Harvesting only mature timber on the stump, that is, as the trees stand in the forest, made good economic sense. Young trees were protected from injury as much as possible when mature timber was cut and hauled. This was an important factor in the newfound economic logging.

★ ★ ★

Logging has been the Adirondack region's principal economic activity. Peaveys, jamboats, bucksaws, log markers, sprinkler wagons for icing the log roads, loaded sleds hitched to Barienger brakes, and huge steel drums wound with cable that controlled the load on steep grades were only the tip of the list of tools and equipment used by the men who worked in the woods.

Camp 7. The Bird's cottage was a two-story log building built on a hill that overlooked the Gould Lumber Company's big water tower at the foot of the hill across Ice Cave Creek. Courtesy Fred Worden

The Adirondacks played a major role in making New York the leading lumber producing state in the nation after 1850. Within two decades, however, concern over the cutting methods of the big lumber operators and the resultant forest fire problem began to mount. By 1885, the added threat to the state's water supply, since most of its major rivers originated from streams in this region, helped to wing public opinion in favor of establishing the Forest Preserve and developing methods of scientific forestry.

This pattern, from the period when logging dominated the lives of the region's people into the 20th century, when over-harvesting and the removal of large tracts through public ownership combined to limit the industry, has been well-documented in literature.

Winter of 1927. Camp 7's water tower where sprinkler tanks were filled.
Photo by Asa Philips. Courtesy Robert Adner

Continuous protection of the forest also led to the development of firefighting techniques and equipment, including the fire tower. The Adirondack Museum at Blue Mountain, now called The Experience, was gifted a fire tower for their exhibition in 1973 by the Department of Environmental Conservation. The tower was erected in 1919 on Whiteface Mountain, which was the site of the second observation post established by the state in 1909, an action prompted largely by the extensive and severe fires of the previous year and 1903.

However, for all the changes in logging, I believe there is one change in the industry which no one, no matter how beset with nostalgia, can fail to welcome. It was this: Every logging outfit worthy of the name had begun to have on its payroll graduates of accredited forestry schools. Those industrial foresters advised which cutting practices should be followed and were responsible for the care, protection and reforestation of company and private lands.

Pump house in background of Linn tractor. Courtesy Dorothy Payton

Barbara Bird's husband, Roy, was among these early foresters. A portion of the third installment of her memoir titled "I Married a Forester" that appeared in *North Country Life's* fall 1951 edition tells about the forest engineers and the men who cut the tall timber.

From "I Married a Forester"

> The term "forester" has been so generally misinterpreted that I prefer the title "forest engineer" as being more adequately expressive of the profession. Much engineering knowledge and skill go into the proper management of a forest. Not only does it involve much surveying and map work but roads must be laid out and camps built; stream beds must be improved; machinery and equipment must be cared for intelligently; and the logging operations must be planned and supervised.

Water from Ice Cave Creek filled big tanks with water. In winter water from sprinkler boxes was sprayed on roadways to ice and harden the main haul road following their being rolled and packed.
Courtesy Dorothy Payton

Cruising and map-making are not annual performances, of course, but are the first steps in the management of a tract of woodland. Once the data are acquired and maps made, the working plan is based on them. The working plan must satisfy two demands: (1) the commercial needs, and (2) the silvicultural requirements of a given tract of forest. The first is settled by the volume of pulpwood required by the mill and the most practical diameter limit of the trees to be cut. Studies made by forest engineers have shown that it is more costly to log trees of small diameters than those of large diameters, so the problem becomes one of removing merchantable large-size trees and leaving the smaller ones to make the future forest.

The solution of the second factor depends upon the specialized silvicultural training of the forester, which enables him to designate the trees to remain as a nucleus for the next crop. He marks the trees which the lumberjack is to cut. The diameter limit is often variable, particularly among our native spruce, a shallow-rooted tree and liable to windfall. The forester must use his discretion. It is considered good forest practice to leave large trees for aesthetic purposes along highways and lake shores.

The marking is done with a special ax, equipped with a "die" on the head. A blaze is made on the tree, and a check blaze is made on a root swelling, below where the tree will be cut. The blazes are stamped.

Spruce and balsam are the trees commonly used for pulp wood in New York, although some hemlock is cut along with them. The felling and peeling take place during the growing season, between May and August. It is the only time the bark can be readily removed from the trunk. Peeling is much less wasteful of wood than the old method of removing the bark by machinery.

Mingling with lumberjacks, horses and early mechanized logging machinery helped Barbara Bird gain an understanding of the outdoors, and of the men who harvested the trees and got them from skidway to mill. Courtesy John Fram

The felling is done with ax and saw, commonly on a piece-work basis with two or three men working together. One man with an ax makes a wedge-shaped notch on the trunk of the tree in the direction in which he wants it to fall. The felling cut is started with the saw on the opposite side from the notch and slightly above it. It takes two men, of course, to operate the saw.

When the saw has buried itself, a wedge is driven in behind it to prevent binding. The wedge is driven further in as the sawing progresses. When the tree begins to fall, one sawyer removes the saw and both men run to safety, calling "Timber-r!" as a warning to others.

Spruce and balsam are the trees commonly used for pulpwood in New York.
Courtesy: Lyons Falls History Association

After several trees have been felled in this way, one man takes an ax and trims off the branches, while the other peels off the bark with a tool called a spud. When the trees are very limby, a third man helps with the trimming. In the old days they used to leave large tops of trees rather than do much trimming. Such tops, held up in the air by their branches, created a great fire hazard. We now have a "top-lopping law" which requires that the trunks be trimmed to a three-inch diameter. This leaves a small top and makes use of more of the stem.

The trees are trimmed and peeled the same day they are felled. Care is always taken to fell the trees so they do not interfere with each other on the ground and can be handily reached for sawing into log lengths.

When the trees have been felled, peeled, and sawed into logs, the skidder comes and snakes the logs, with a horse, along rough skid trails to a place by a nearby logging road. Here the logs are rolled onto skidways. A skidway is a skeleton log bed upon which the logs are piled parallel to the road. Here they are stored until winter.

It is fascinating to watch one of these horses skidding. They are intelligent beasts, not too heavy to be quick, and they show an understanding of what is expected of them which astonishes the onlooker. They are well cared for and sometimes live to a good old age.

It's easier to guess the age of a skidding horse than its driver. Courtesy: Lyons Falls History Association

It is easier to guess the age of one of these horses than it is to estimate that of its driver. Lumberjacks have no specific age: they are active, or they are inexperienced, or they are old-timers. Years do not seem to figure much. In general they are a roving lot with no great sense of loyalty or responsibility. They will work for a while, and then suddenly they will conceive the idea that they want to go out to the front. They return, after a spree, broke, and ready to work again. Few have had any schooling to speak of, and have the disinterest common to the ignorant. I once saw a crew of lumberjacks who kept right on with their work during a total eclipse of the sun. Birds started to go to roost, animals were all agog, but the lumberjacks did not even bother to look up at the sky. Some of them do not believe that big trees grow from little ones or that you can tell the age of a tree by counting the annual rings. I have heard one of them argue that the world is flat.

The lumberjacks lead a life of danger. A foreman told me of an accident that happened at his camp when cutting was in progress. Two men were sawing a spruce and had not noticed that there was a large loose limb lodged in a fork of a nearby beech tree with the upper end of the limb leaning on the spruce. When the spruce fell, the loose limb crashed down on one of the men and knocked him to the ground, crushing the eyes out of his head. Such a loose limb is known in logging camp vernacular as a "widow-maker."

Lumberjacks lead a life of danger. Courtesy: Lyons Falls History Association

The lumberjacks have their own idea of humor, as evidenced by such expressions as "widow-maker" and "school marm." Their courage and skill are noteworthy, and any one of them can stand more exposure, more hard work, and worse liquor than ten ordinary men.

It is sometimes difficult to understand the patois of the French Canadians. If you address them in American Army French, they laugh and say "Frenchman from France!"

Lt. to Rt. Unidentified Gould supervisor and Louie the road monkey at his station on the sand-hill that led down to the Moose River Landing.

Barbara Bird recalls the day she "flopped down belly-buster" on her snowshoes near Louie's rusty chewing tobacco can that hung on a limb of a sapling where a dark pool of liquid dripping from the bottom had splattered the snow. She wrote in *Calked Shoes, Life in the Adirondack Lumber Camps* (Prospect Books, 1952), "I was enjoying my first good mouthful [of snow] when a voice hailed me. 'Don't you know you'll get goiter if you drink lying down like that?' Goiter? This was a new one to me. I felt like asking Mr. Road Monkey what he thought I might get if I drank out of the only drinking vessel available, but I merely glanced with distaste at the rusty Velvet can at my elbow."
Courtesy Lawton L. Williams

One winter there was a French Canadian cooking at Camp No. 9. In previous years he had cooked in partnership with his wife, and he evidently missed the aid of her skill in certain respects. Pancakes are a staple breakfast dish in a logging camp, and Pierre could not make "panicake" fit to eat. The men grumbled. The cook was in despair. Finally he asked [my husband] Roy, "Madame—she mak' panicake?"

"Yes, my wife makes good panicake," said Roy.

"She tole me, mebbe, how she mak' panicake, non?"

"Yes, I will bring you the recipe."

Breakfast at 3:30 in the morning. Reporter Wells learned from one 'jack named Bert that once, when the thermometer hit a deeply disturbing subzero temperature, Ben Snyder lit four dozen candles. When the flames froze, Ben broke off the colorful cones and packed them twelve to a box to be sold as Adirondack strawberries. Snyder claimed he made about four hundred dollars. Eating and storytelling were serious business in a lumber camp. Courtesy Lawton Williams

The next morning when Roy went to work, the men were all happy and laughing. Roy made a point to go up to the cook house and see the cook. "How were the panicakes this morning, Pierre?"

"Ba gosh! Wat you call heem?" he asked, pointing to a big kettle.

"That is a kettle."

"Oui, I mak' heem full. Dey eat her all up!"

Lt. to Rt. Barbara Bird and Hazel Todd at Camp 7, circa 1920s. Hazel was the wife of John B. "J.B." Todd, Superintendent of Woodlands for the Gould Paper Company. J.B. was Barbara Bird's husband's (Royal) immediate boss. Courtesy Dorothy Payton

The day before New Year's, Pierre came up to our cabin to bring me a pie, the like of which I have never seen. It was a large, double-crust pie, filled with finely-minced pork. It was deliciously seasoned and the crust was as near perfect as a crust can be. Pierre may not have understood pancakes, but he certainly knew his pastry. He told me that at home they always served such a pie for New Year's.

Herb McGee was among those towering men who earned the reputation of "having the bark on."
Courtesy Lyons Falls History Association

I appreciated the gift very much. Endeavoring to make friendly conversation, I asked him if he had any children. Proudly he stuck out his chest and raised his chin, while quite unabashed he said, "Oui, Madame. I haf one an' a half."

I suspect that the average lumberjack is best known to civilization when he is on his least civilized behavior—that is, when he is in town on a spree. He is an all-too-evident object of contempt at that time, and unfortunately the contempt persists in the minds of most people who run across him. Hence he has acquired a bad name for himself. It is undeniable that the lumberjack drinks. It is also undeniable that when he is under the influence of liquor, he is promptly fleeced of his hard-earned cash by creatures who prey on him. If any contempt is warranted, it might better rest on the human vultures who make their living by enticing men to drunkenness and then robbing them. The lumberjack earns his pay with sweat and skill and hard work. He is in no sense malicious. At his worst, he is not so bad as the parasites that exploit him and consider themselves smart in doing it!

Although they earn their money so arduously, lumberjacks spend it freely. That is their idea of real fun. I know of one lumberjack who labored for months to earn $800. At the end of ten days in town it was all gone. I have seen another lumberjack who had three twenty-dollar bills wadded around some greasy pliers in his hip pocket. He bought a watch for eighty dollars when he first came to town; and two days later, while drunk, he gave it away.

Few lumberjacks die a quiet death. Accidents on the job, illness from exposure, unfortunate incidents while on a spree, or death by all these are common occurrences. They work hard, live hard, and die hard.

Of course, with the advent of machinery in the logging business, lumberjacks had less exposure to danger, but that is not to say that dangers didn't exist. The danger to the forest itself, however, was considerably lessened by the work of foresters like Roy Bird.

Adirondack TIM-Berrr!

Chapter 4 | William J. O'Hern

BYRON COOL CRUISED TIMBER

From before the turn of the twentieth century until the end of Prohibition, Byron Cool enjoyed sharing the experiences of his timber cruising days. The Rev. A.L. Byron-Curtiss was one interested listener. Cool and Byron-Curtiss met following The Reverend's move to Forestport in 1893 to take over leadership of the thriving lumber community's Episcopal Church.

Cool told of timber cruising during all seasons—from being stung by yellow jackets in the summer to trekking on snowshoes for weeks at a time. He did a considerable amount of timber cruising over forest snow to estimate the amount of timber of certain tracts, the best methods of getting it to the mills when cut, and what the timber was worth in dollars and cents

The Rev. Byron-Curtiss at North Lake. The Reverend and Byron Cool were often fishing partners.
Courtesy Tom and Doris Kilbourn

This timeless view of the foot of North Lake in Atwell, N.Y. has changed little since the time when Byron Cool and The Rev. A.L. Byron-Curtiss lived there. Author's photo

In cruising, he would say, he started out in a party of four, "all on snowshoes, of course, as the snow was five to six feet deep." Two experts, maps in hand, would start out estimating the timber after having given instructions to the others to begin setting up a camp. On one occasion, the first day Cool was out the party walked sixteen miles to reach the point from which he was to begin work.

The only known image of Byron E. Cool, an influential Adirondack conservationist. December 15, 1943, "Byron E. Cool Dies; Noted Camp Operator," Utica *Daily Press*

Vast tracts of virgin forest stuck the view on every hand—mountains, hills and valleys heavily wooded with spruce and pine. One wonders how men could ever make camp, but Cool would say, "A sense of direction seems born in every good woodsman. Then there was always loaded pack baskets, the map and the compass. But none of these cover the long journeys through the snow which must be made on foot."

Cool's winter repertoire included winds that howled and deep drifts, and freezing temperatures "when the mercury climbed as high as twenty below zero." The old-time woodsmen did not seem to mind the cold, however, except "for the feet, [on account of] the straps of the snowshoes which become somewhat cumbersome after one has climbed over hills and down into valleys for a day, only to meet another hill at the bottom."

And, Cool acknowledged, "out in the Adirondack Mountains, the smoke still curled at times from a carefully hidden still or jerk camp." It was not unusual for a shot to ring out as a moonshiner or jack hunter would exchange "pleasantries of the forest" to ensure the "shine" and "mountain lamb" would continue to trickle into Forestport, Boonville and other nearby towns. This was the not unusual sort of stuff that went with traditional backwoods Adirondack-style hospitality.

A timber cruiser sees backcountry areas of beauty seldom visited by trekkers such as this stream running through a typical bog that corresponds to a muskeg of the North. Courtesy Dick Wood

Timber cruiser Byron Cool shared these and other stories with the Rev. A.L. Byron-Curtiss, about the good old liquor and illegal venison days when stills and jerk camps were often found in the heart of the Black River Country.

A Summer Cruise in Highmarket

Joe Conway tells about his first job as a timber cruiser.

In the summer of 1933, Joe McDermott asked me if I would like a job on a timber cruise for the summer. Jobs were real scarce. The pay was excellent—sixteen dollars a week and "grub." I was about twenty, needed the money, and thought the cruise would be a good experience. It was.

The cruise was to provide an estimate of the timber on the White Tract, a large timbered area located for the most part in the Township of Highmarket. Gould Paper Company of Lyons Falls owned it; Joe was their forester, and now they were going to find out how much timber they had there. "Billy" Empey, a phenomenon among the lumberjacks, that is, a lumberjack

A windfall is a typical impediment encountered by past and present-day forest cruisers. Courtesy Mart Allen

who saved his money, was the estimator. By his calculations, he would tell Gould Paper Company, quite accurately, the cordage of each type of timber on this tract. I was the "mule," carrying the big pack-basket with the week's "grub," the utensils, and the blankets. My other duties were limited to lugging the firewood to the campsite each night, assisting in the cooking, and washing the utensils. I never did cut any of the firewood, for Billy thought that I was too inexperienced to use his razor-sharp, double-bitted axe. I didn't question his judgement; I just relaxed while he did the chopping.

Time-worn log shanties were not uncommon structures that Joe Conway would come across.
Courtesy Northern Logger archives

The first morning that we started the cruise is as clear to me as if it were yesterday. We went into the woods near the Fish Creek Club House. Shortly thereafter we stopped for lunch: cold cuts, beans on paper plates with bread and butter, and a cup of water from the spring brook by which we rested. That meal was a big disappointment to me, and I finally deposited my paper plate and its contents in the brush. I couldn't stand still long enough to eat. Black flies and mosquitoes—both were vaccinating me. I was on fire and had forgotten to bring any fly dope with me. That first week was tough, believe me. After that, I didn't need fly dope; I was completely inoculated against any discomfort from flies. From then on they left me strictly alone. As the fellow on the Alka-Seltzer ad says, "Try it. You'll like it."

Backcountry camps required an ample supply of firewood for winter heating. Courtesy Dick Wood

The first day in we went by some big skidways of spruce logs that Elmer Bernier was "putting up" for Goulds. They were real big logs of virgin timber. Doc O'Brien told me later: "Phil Joynt used to go into Moore-Meadow Pond with my dad fishing. Half the time, instead of fishing, he'd be looking at the spruce trees growing in there. And he'd say, 'My God! You could cut a twelve by twelve a hundred feet long out of that tree.' He was a carpenter and knew what he was talking about. A twelve by twelve, a hundred feet long! Those were some of the spruce that were hacked up into pulp.

As I recall, we started from the south line of the White Tract and headed by transit compass south toward the north line, with Billy estimating timber as he went. When we reached a border line, north or south, we would proceed a certain distance (which I have forgotten) down the line, heading by compass again toward the other boundary. Every so many feet, stepped off by Joe, we would stop, Joe would get out the account book and pencil; I would rest a basket on a stump or log to relieve the strain of the harness and to prepare myself for Billy's performance. He was a small, lithe man, gray-haired with pale blue eyes, pleasant-faced and extremely neat. He scanned the timber as he slowly turned in a circle. As he guesstimated, he grasped his chin between thumb and forefinger, assumed a serious and thoughtful stare, and began to meditate. Shortly, he'd call out the cords that were within his range: "Three and a half cords of beech, four cords of maple. No, make that six and a half. Did you ever see hemlock as big around as them? Twenty-four cords of hemlock," and on until all the timber visible in Billy's gyration was accounted for in the notebook. The notebook went into Joe's pocket; he took another compass sighting, shouldered the transit, and strode off. Billy followed with his double-bitted ax on his shoulder, and I plodded in the rear—off to the next cordage entry. This continued from early morning until lunch time, which we took around noon and usually when we were near water. We carried no water with us, for there were plenty of springs and brooks scattered throughout the woods.

Just before dusk, Joe would halt operations, again at a brook or spring. I would start lugging the wood, which Billy was chopping, for it got chilly on some of those summer nights, and Billy would rouse up and add firewood. After a meal from the cans that I packed, we would wash up the frying pan, coffee pot and other utensils. Then we'd lie back on the blankets, talking until sleep overtook us. Up again at daybreak, a quick breakfast, and away through the woods to the tune of, "Six cords and a half of birch. Eight cords of maple. What hemlock..."

Some of the other little incidents: I recall that we broke out on the upper line one afternoon near the old Glenfield & Western Railroad, and we came upon some large skidways of half-rotten hardwood, apparently "put up" with a lot of back-breaking labor and cost, and through some misfortune,

An early Linn tractor heading toward a Tug Hill backcountry camp. Photo by Harold Linck. Courtesy Dick Ulrich

left to rot. One morning we got caught in a terrific storm, thunder and lightning, a heavy rain, and a gale-force wind. All the ingredients of a perfect blinger! We could see and hear the trees crashing up in the hardwood knolls; we worked our respective ways down into a dry swamp, standing there under the alders for about two hours, until the storm let up. We were so wet our hair flowed out from under our hats. We went up on higher ground to a stand of spruce, built a fire, shucked off our clothes, and stood in our birthday suits until our clothes steamed out a bit. Then Billy, with a homemade spud manufactured from a limb with his axe, began to peel the bark off some of the spruce, and soon he had a bark shanty erected as shelter against the anticipated return of the morning's storm. Although it did not return, we laid around the rest of the day, and we slept that night in Billy's deluxe bark bungalow. This was the only day that we didn't work and the only one in which we were caught in a storm. Otherwise, our days were quite uneventful. All the time we were in there we saw one animal, a doe, which quietly slipped over a knoll to confront our campfire and then retraced her route. We found George Colvin's young bird dog a ways back in the woods where he'd become hung up on a bush with his chain. Probably he'd still be there if we had not heard him barking. We came across a tremendous windfall. It appeared to be about twenty feet high, and was impassable; we had to circle it. On the Osceola side, we saw where lightning had set a muck fire which had burned deep and steadily for quite some time without starting a forest fire. Joe pointed out stumps of trees that had apparently been cut during the original survey which he had read. Then they had real mules carrying the equipment. And the rum casks.

Probably the most excitement we had was when we were staying in a camp on the Osceola side. One night as we climbed into our beds, Joe winked at me and said, "I've been thinking that Roosevelt was one of our greatest presidents." Then he blew out the oil lamp. It was then that I learned of another talent Billy possessed—the ability to swear loud and long while seldom repeating himself. Billy not only disliked Roosevelt; he profanely disliked him.

The last morning in camp, I mixed up a batch of pancake batter from a new package of pancake flour. I noticed that they were not rising properly on the griddle and that neither Joe nor Billy were eating the first batch. In fact, they suggested that I need not bake any more. A look at the package showed why. It revealed, "Pastry Flour."

The summer and the cruise soon ended. I was about one hundred dollars richer, was completely impervious to any type of Tug Hill biting insect, and probably had the best developed back and legs in the North Country, yes, even New York State.

Now both Joe and Billy are gone; Gould Paper Company as such is gone, and all the timber that was appraised by Billy and noted in Joe's notebook has long since been pulped, made into newsprint, read, and discarded. But think again of Phil Joynt back on Moore-Meadow Pond looking up at those lofty spruces and exclaiming, "My God! You could cut a twelve by twelve a hundred feet high out of that spruce."

Adirondack TIM-Berrr!

Chapter 6 | Mart Allen

MART ALLEN'S TIMBER CRUISER TALES

***The following cruising recollections were written by Mart Allen and first appeared in his "To Make a Long Story Short" weekly column that appeared the* Adirondack Express.**

The essence of this column began many years ago in the heart and mind of a young man from the Catskills. His love of the outdoors and remote wilderness led him to the Adirondacks. There, near Schroon Lake, he and three companions indulged their passion for hunting and fishing from a semi-remote hunting camp. They ranged about the area sampling the sporting life and whatever else the area had to offer.

A logger's peavey usually has a four-foot wooden handle with an iron hook on the bottom and a pointed spike at the end. Courtesy Mart Allen

The longing barely sated, he continued to cast about for the more complete wilderness experience that the Adirondacks still offer. The search and the dream finally culminated this past year with the purchase of one of the last remote tracts of woodland left in New York State. Consisting of 1,600+ acres, it sprawls along and across close to five miles of the West Canada Creek. Bordering the State's West Canada Lakes Wilderness Area, it truly represents the ultimate in true wilderness east of the Mississippi.

Lt. to Rt. Joe Kriwox and Patrick Kriwox. Allen said, "the picture shows the beginning of a log bridge and access road to harvest timber in the township of Ava through property of Camp Kingsley Boy Scout property from the property of Mrs. Allen. It was a marked timber sale I managed for Mrs. Allen and sold to the Ethan Allen Lumber Company in Boonville, New York." Courtesy Mart Allen

It remains nearly as inaccessible today as it did in the days of legendary French Louis, hermit of West Canada Lake. The early foot trails that paralleled West Creek gradually transited from horse traveled tote roads to today's modern all-wheel-drive nightmare.

Access begins with an exemplary 2.6 miles of Town of Ohio gravel road from Route 8 north along the West Creek. Things go downhill from there. Driver and passengers alike are compelled to focus their entire attention on the roadbed and the dangers posed to both vehicle and occupant as you lurch from one boulder or depression to another.

At the end is the southern end of the property called the West Canada Preserve by owners Tom Williams and Mike Ostrow. A well-built two-story frame camp sits on the south bank of the stream. A smaller, less modest accommodation sets on the north shore of the creek at the far end of the holdings. It can only be reached by floatplane, all-terrain vehicle, snowmobile or shanks mare. The first options is the one most preferred by all, especially yours truly.

A comprehensive management plan of the property includes a forest inventory and timber sale in which I am an integral part. The inventory was completed in September 1999, and the preparatory plans for the timber sale were finalized in July 1999.

On August 18, the marking of the trees to be selected for harvest began and it is the subsequent events since then that will be reported in this space, inspired by a man named Ed Maunton years ago. I was impressed by his story on his exploits, entitled "Diary of a Beaver Trapper."

Forever at a loss for topics, it occurred to me that there may be many who would be interested in what a timber cruiser does. I will attempt to enlighten those so included starting with next week's missive titled, "Diary of a Timber Cruiser."

October 17, 2000

Up at 4:30 a.m. Put on the coffee and fix a good breakfast of pan sausage and eggs from the Lowville Meat Market. Make two ham sandwiches, toss in a couple of Payday candy bars and a Dr. Pepper six-pack and two cans of beer in a cooler.

Paint guns, a case of paint, tally book, tally sheets, marking stick and packs sit waiting in the garage from the night before. Ten after six Mike Black, forester friend from Long Lake, pulls in the yard ready to go. We load up, checking with each other to be sure that we haven't forgotten anything essential.

The hour-long ride down to Nobleboro is spent reviewing the work and talking about deer hunting. At 7:10 we are on our way into the woods and spend the next hour enduring the rigors of one tough woods road.

At 8:30 a.m. I mark the first tree, a 16-inch diameter breast-high red spruce. It's a tree close to the adjoining property line and two eye-level blazes are facing into the sale area on the stump before we tally it by specie, log height and diameter breast high (DBH) in the tally book.

A logger's axe and a logger's V-paint mark in a yellow birch veneer log. Courtesy Mart Allen

The boundary quarters up and across an ever-steeper slope through a mixed hardwood stand. Mike leads off following the boundary facing his paint marks toward the sale area where they are followed by me. I would be kidding myself if I thought I could stay ahead of a guy slightly more than half of my age.

By 10 a.m. I am ready for a rest and a drink of water. Mike has been back and forth checking to see if I am still coming. On one check he has to help me locate my markings stick, which I had left on a creek bank when I filled my canteen.

By noon it's hot. I am wringing with sweat and my legs are aching along with my shoulders. We eat lunch with our backs against a tree and discuss the quality of the wood we are marking. I give Mike one of my sandwiches—too hot and tired to have much of an appetite. We get up to begin again and I can hardly get my old legs working again.

The afternoon finds us with a strip along the boundary close to as far as the furthest end of the sale will go for this year. It's a long walk back out over the old tote road we hit on the way out, but like the old horse headed for the barn, my tired old legs find new energy and I am looking forward to one of the two beers I brought along.

Back at the truck we find Tom Williams and four fishing buddies getting settled in camp for some trout fishing. The ride back out to the main road doesn't seem nearly as bad with my mind on the hot meal and shower ahead. It's 6 p.m. by the time Mike drops me off and he still has over an hour to his home.

Supper is ready and so am I. The shower feels great and my pajamas and easy chair even better. By 10 p.m. I am ready for bed and I ease in, careful not to promote leg cramps. Before I fade away I lie there asking myself if I am up to the job, and why am I even trying?

Lumberjacks are men you'd like to know. A sturdy, hardworking lot with hearts of gold, men who would give you the shirt off their back if you needed it but show you no mercy if you tangled with them." —Conse R. Delutis. Courtesy Town of Webb Historical Association

Adirondack TIM-Berrr!

Chapter 7 | Mart Allen

All That Timber Cruising Culminates in a Contract

In another one of his columns, Mart Allen wrote:

> **As I returned from an overnight trip from the upper reaches of the West Canada Creek last Sunday night I was warmed with the feeling of relief and satisfaction. It was the culmination of several days of arduous work cruising and marking timber for a timber harvest.**

Following the marking of 2,818 trees of six different species, several days followed showing prospective buyers the sale area and pointing out conditions they will be charged with carrying out.

Harvesting timber following a forester cruiser's marking. Author's collection

There are several standard operating procedures connected with any well-planned and carried out timber sale. They are documented and incorporated in a timber sale contract which the seller and purchaser mutually agree upon. Each has specific responsibilities spelled out in the document.

The owner guarantees the timber to be sold to be his or her property and free from any encumbrance that questions their rights to transfer ownership. The responsible owner also shows the buyer the boundaries of the property on which the timber is located. Finally, the seller gives the buyer the right to enter the property to complete the harvest.

A landowner's harvested logs. Courtesy Mart Allen

The buyer agrees to all of the conditions spelled out by the contract that the forester feels are necessary to protect the landowner's interest. They are many and vary with each individual owner's wishes and concerns.

First and foremost is the amount and payment for the timber to the landowner, which is preferably arrived at by open competitive bidding. Normally, there is a lump sum payment tendered prior to starting the harvest. A performance bond should also be posted at the same time to ensure special conditions of the harvesting operation are complied with at the completion of the work.

Some of the conditions may be: how the log landing areas and yards are to be left free of debris and ruts; how high stump heights may be left; how high tops of felled trees shall be allowed to remain; in what area the operation is to be started; where log landings, skid trails and access roads will be located; which trees shall be harvested; and how slopes, watercourses and erosion control measures will be addressed.

Certificates of both liability and compensation in the landowner's name should be provided and kept in effect throughout the life of the agreement. They should be for specified amounts. A starting date and termination date should be included. Provisions should be made for either party to terminate the agreement should a reason arise that may call for the same. An arbitrator may be designated to act as a judge in case of any disagreement.

The contractor should agree to abide by all state and federal laws and to protect the property from fire. Provisions should include the right to temporarily limit operations when adverse weather conditions persist that, in the opinion of the forester, would unduly affect the property.

Both parties to the timber sale agreement have certain rights and obligations, both written and unwritten. Some are based solely on common respect for each other and what is "right" and may not necessarily dictated by law.

Contracts contain many legal terms and gobbledygook, such as "in a workman like manner." It all boils down to how honest and willing both parties are in working with each other. The forester's basic responsibility is to the landowner, but one would indeed be remiss in not ensuring that the timber harvester's rights as well are not abrogated.

Experience often has taught the forester who those operators are best able to carry out their prescribed obligations. That, and price consideration as well, may call for a provision included in the timber sale Request for Bids that reads: "The timber will be sold to the highest bidder, but the landowner reserves the right to refuse any and all bids."

The sale, like most I have been a party to over the past several years, has been a rewarding and learning experience. It has given me a sense of accomplishment knowing I am partly responsible in bringing two parties together in what, I hope, will be a mutually rewarding business venture, one that ultimately will lead to the best use of a renewable resource in a manner that conserves both it and the environment.

Part Two

MART ALLEN'S LOGGING TALES AND MEMORIES

Our memories give us voice and bear witness to history, so that others might learn. So they might celebrate our triumphs and be warned of our failures. —Mohinder Suresh

Mart Allen loves the Adirondack mountains and forests. He's proud to call himself an Adirondacker.

Steve Bick wisecracks in the foreword to Allen's book *Adirondack Character Builds A Community* (MHA Press, 2013), "This Mart Allen fellow has some hard bark on him. He's not an easy man to get to know. Friendly, outgoing, generous, and approachable...." Bick continued with a list of adulations, admitting "Most folks figured out a long time ago that his bark is worse than his bite. He's a kindly old grump...."

I probably became a fan of Marty Allen when I read his first weekly "To Make a Long Story Short" in the Adirondack Express some twenty-five years ago.

Columnist Mart Allen, of the long-running "To Make a Long Story Short" in the *Adirondack Express*. Allen witnessed the development of new technologies applicable to all points of the logging production process. Mart is holding the hat-stretcher he invented. Courtesy the *Adirondack Express*

My favorite Allen columns have been profiles of Adirondack old-timers and stories about area history, logging, and forest-related stories.

Years after I first began to read Mart's columns, I had the privilege of meeting him. I enjoy the opportunity to chat with him. Lately our conversations have been about logging and, if you will, seeing the forest for the trees. We enjoy old-time lumber-related subjects and we both believe the woods are a resource that isn't there to be exploited and used up in one generation.

Part Two of *Adirondack Timber Cruising* is an assortment of Mart's stories that share his admiration of logging and loggers, his connection to logging with horses, and memories that keep history alive through his telling.

All of the following are from Mart Allen's column, "To Make a Long Story Short," which appeared weekly in the *Adirondack Express*. This selection spans a period of nearly a year, from October 10, 1995 to August 27, 1996, and are representative of the kinds of stories he covered and of his famous quick sense of humor.

Mart Allen spent many nights in portable shanties such as this one. Courtesy Mart Allen

Adirondack TIM-Berrr!

Chapter 8 | Mart Allen

C.J. STRIFE: SMART FORESTER AND MAN OF STRONG CHARACTER

Adirondack Express, October 10, 1995

I wish I had known C.J. Strife. No one I have ever heard of has intrigued me more.

First of all, I admire his strength of character, self-reliance and faith in people. As a forester, I envy his knowledge and skill in the logging business. It has had no parallel that I am aware of throughout the Adirondacks.

He was born in 1887, in Belfort, N.Y., and described his education as attending school but three days and the teacher not being there for two of them.

His first work was on area farms until, at the age of 14, he started his career as a logger.

An aptitude for the business and boundless ambition eventually culminated in his becoming, perhaps, the largest individual logging contractor in New York State.

At the peak of his activities, in the late 30s and throughout the 40s, he directly employed upward of 800 people. He built, staffed and operated from 15 to 20 logging camps from Tug Hill to Lake Placid. Much of the activity was spurred on by the war effort in the late 1930s and '40s.

Almost all the large, private tracts in the Adirondacks were operated by C.J., as he was popularly known.

One of many celebrity clients he worked with was Kate Smith on her property near Lake Placid. Whitney, Brandreth and the Adirondack League Club were just a few of the larger private parks on which he conducted extensive logging operations.

International Paper, Finch Pruyn and Gould Paper were some of the commercial holdings on which he carried on harvesting operations.

Clarence J. "C.J." Strife. Courtesy Mart Allen

His work sometimes found him traveling to New York or other major cities to negotiate contracts with corporate attorneys. At other times it was at someone's kitchen table, as was the case with Kate Smith. He seemed to manage that aspect of business with no problem, but it was in the field with the men where he was most at ease. They respected him and would go the extra mile for him when the chips were down.

He resented government intrusion and complained bitterly of the increasing regulations, which he insisted stifled business. A man of his word, much of his business was conducted with a handshake.

Leo Villiere worked for him for years and he illustrated the point with a personal experience. Leo and four other local men were driving log trucks for C.J. when C.J. decided to get out of the trucking business.

He offered to sell them all five trucks and hire them to work for him as independent contractors.

Homes in Brandreth, N.Y. Courtesy Town of Webb Historical Association, P003887

After agreeing on a price for the trucks and the terms of the contract, the question arose as to how the trucks would be paid for. C.J. agreed to have them work off the price for a set amount each month. When they asked if C.J. wanted them to sign an agreement, his reply was typical: It would not be necessary; if their word was no good their paper wouldn't be either.

In 1920, C.J. and his wife, the former Arlean Company, moved to Brandreth Station to start his journey into the real world of logging. It was to be a real learning experience, although not always profitable, as we will soon learn.

Mr. & Mrs. C.J. Strife. Courtesy Town of Webb Historical Association, P003545

C.J. Strife, a man of strong character. During Strife's career in northern New York his total cutting program included about 500,000 cords of pulpwood and 125,000,000 feet of hardwood.
Courtesy *The Northeastern Logger*

Lt. to Rt. Clarence J. Strife, Rev. Frank Reed and unknown logger believed to be Joe Lindsey, C.J., camp clerk. Courtesy Town of Webb Historical Association, P6546.

C.J. Strife, McKeever Camp, 1952. Strife like other successful logging operators provided top-notch food to his crews. Courtesy Lyons Falls History Association

Adirondack TIM-Berrr!

Chapter 9 | Mart Allen

ONCE BRANDRETH STATION LIVED; TODAY IT'S ONLY FOUNDATIONS

Adirondack Express, October 17, 1995

Brandreth Station was located a short distance above Beaver River on the M & M (Mohawk & Malone, later part of the New York Central) Railroad. In 1920, when C.J. and Arlean Strife moved there, it was a bustling community with 25 to 30 structures.

A large sawmill and hot pond to hold logs was central to various support buildings. There were some 20-odd two-story homes in which the families of the mill and woods workers lived. A commissary, bunkhouse for the single men, and schoolhouse completed the gathering along the railroad.

Mac-A-Mac homes in the forest, Brandreth Lake. Courtesy Town of Webb Historical Association, P002424

C.J. Strife's job was to supply logs to the sawmill. The logs, for the most part, were hauled to the mill via the Mac-A-Mac Railroad. This was a private railroad placed strategically through the 30,000 plus acres owned by the Brandreth Corporation. It terminated at the station where either logs or lumber from the mill could be loaded on cars of the M & M to be shipped wherever.

Annex-Boarding House-Office and Depot, Brandreth, N.Y. Courtesy Town of Webb Historical Association

Helen Codega was one of the five Strife children of four girls and one boy. When it came time for Mrs. Strife to deliver one of the children, she would leave a month before for Croghan. The last child was born in Tupper Lake after a trip there by railroad handcar.

Dr. Robert Lindsay made one regular trip a year to Brandreth and everyone saved their aches and pains until then. All the children had a physical and inoculations. If necessary, Dr. Bob would spend two days to care for everyone. The rest of the year he came for emergencies only.

Lyle Campany, C.J.'s cousin, was the teacher at the one-room schoolhouse that served students through the sixth grade.

The schoolhouse also served as a community center. On Saturday nights the desks were cleared out of the way and a dance was held. Early Sunday morning, Catholic Mass was held, followed by a Protestant service. Monday morning it was back to school. Helen recalled as many as 15 children attending school at one time.

There was no liquor at Brandreth, but it was just a step to the Beaver River Hotel, if you were so inclined. After long, hard days in the woods, many of the lumberjacks, in particular, made the trek.

There were several trains a day and it was the only access to much of the area. Helen recalled the station agents calling ahead on up the line when Joe Jenkins, the game protector, was on patrol.

Unique and unusual old-time method of skidding logs. Courtesy Lyons Falls History Association

C.J. learned much of his expertise in the logging business during his years at Brandreth, which I am sure shaped much of his success in later years.

He also learned a bitter and hard lesson. In 1930, he ended up loading and shipping logs that had cost $28-a-thousand to cut and put up, for $19-a-thousand board feet. In short, he went bankrupt to the tune of $1 million.

There is no doubt that this had to be the low point in his life. The timber was exhausted and Strife moved with his family to Big Moose, determined to pay back his bankruptcy debt.

The mill burned at Brandreth, and today nothing remains except some cellar holes and foundations of a once-proud little Adirondack settlement.

C.J. Strife and a worker at Brandreth. Courtesy Lyons Falls History Association

Houses at Brandreth. Courtesy Lyons Falls History Association

Adirondack TIM-Berrr!

Chapter 10 | Charles E. Herr

Brandreth (Lake) Station

Brandreth Station was about 3½ miles north of Beaver River Station. In 1851, Dr. Benjamin Brandreth purchased Township 39 (Totten and Crossfield Purchase) and cleared land for brewing hops to use with nearby Beech Lake water for a brew project that later failed.

His family urged him not to sell the tract, and Brandreth family camps started being built in the 1870s when the lake would be renamed Brandreth Lake When Dr. Webb's railroad was completed in 1892 to the west of the tract, a flag station was established, connecting with a new eight-mile wagon road to Brandreth Lake. In 1895, a small depot building was added.

In 1912, the Mac-a-Mac Corporation formed to log the Brandreth tract. From a switch at Brandreth Station, a nine-mile logging line was laid to Brandreth Lake. At Brandreth Station, a village developed that included a general store, post office, boarding house, engine house, houses and other buildings. This line operated until 1920. In 1925, the Little Rapids Lumber Company built a sawmill at the station and used the Mac-a-Mac buildings. Instead of Mac-a-Mac's rails, this company used Linn tractors to load New York Central cars. The company and sawmill ceased operations in 1931.

Whitney Industries' origin was the purchase in 1897 of 68,000 acres by William C. Whitney, who established Whitney Park. Whitney and his descendants would practice selective forestry lumbering methods in the ensuing years. In 1934, the park's manager, a grandson of Dr. Brandreth, contracted with John McDonald, who had managed the 1912–1920 line operations to use the same Mac-a-Mac rail bed with new track and some of the original engines through the Brandreth tract to the Whitney lands. Its owners paid a fee to the Brandreths. This line and its extension operated until 1939.

The Brandreth Station depot later burned.

Mac-A-Mac Corporation, Brandreth, N.Y. Courtesy Town of Webb Historical Association, P01848

Brandreth Station was about 3½ miles north of Beaver River Station. In 1851, Dr. Benjamin Brandreth purchased Township 39 (Totten and Crossfield Purchase) and cleared land for brewing hops to use with nearby Beech Lake water for a brew project that later failed. His family urged him not to sell the tract, and Brandreth family camps started being built in the 1870s when the lake would be renamed Brandreth Lake When Dr. Webb's railroad was completed in 1892 to the west of the tract, a flag station was established, connecting with a new eight-mile wagon road to Brandreth Lake. In 1895, a small depot building was added.

In 1912, the Mac-a-Mac Corporation formed to log the Brandreth tract. From a switch at Brandreth Station, a nine-mile logging line was laid to Brandreth Lake. At Brandreth Station, a village developed that included a general store, post office, boarding house, engine house, houses and other buildings. This line operated until 1920. In 1925, the Little Rapids Lumber Company built a sawmill at the station and used the Mac-a-Mac buildings. Instead of Mac-a-Mac's rails, this company used Linn tractors to load New York Central cars. The company and sawmill ceased operations in 1931.

Whitney Industries' origin was the purchase in 1897 of 68,000 acres by William C. Whitney, who established Whitney Park. Whitney and his descendants would practice selective forestry lumbering methods in the ensuing years. In 1934, the park's manager, a grandson of Dr. Brandreth, contracted with John McDonald, who had managed the 1912–1920 line operations to use the same Mac-a-Mac rail bed with new track and some of the original engines through the Brandreth tract to the Whitney lands. Its owners paid a fee to the Brandreths. This line and its extension operated until 1939.

The Brandreth Station depot later burned. [Sources: Compiled by Charles E. Herr, author of *The Fulton Chain, Early Settlement, Roads, Steamboats, Railroads and Hotels* (HerrStory Publications, 2017), based on "The Mac-a-Mac Railroad" in *Logging Railroads of the Adirondacks* by William Gove (Syracuse University Press, 2006).]

Mart Allen holds a great admiration of logging and loggers such as these old-timers shown unloading logs at one of Mac-a-Mac's lumber camps at Brandreth Lake. From a historic postcard

Blacksmith and his assistant. Blacksmiths kept the horses going in demanding winter weather. They made a variety of horse shoes with cleats or spikes for dragging logs on icy roads.
Courtesy Lyons Falls History Association

Adirondack TIM-Berrr!

Chapter 11 | Mart Allen

"GEE" AND "HAW" GUIDED LOGGING HORSES AT WORK

Adirondack Express, October 31, 1995

I have long been an admirer of logging horses and the men who worked them. Growing up in the 1930s and 40s in a farming community, I gained a general knowledge of the farm horse.

My first exposure to logging horses came about in 1950. It was on a Ranger School field trip to a logging job near Tupper Lake.

I witnessed that day a demonstration of teamwork between man and horse that I have never forgotten.

The crews consisted of two men and a horse. The men were French Canadians, who spoke little English, and a roan mare that understood French.

They were cutting spruce on 30+ degree slopes. Tools consisted of crosscut, bucksaw, ax and peavey. The horse wore a collar, tugs and a whiffletree to which was connected a short piece of choker chain. She wore no halter or reins and was directed by commands of "gee" and "haw"— gee for a turn to the right and haw to the left.

One man remained in the woods limbing the trees and hooking them one at a hitch to the horse. The horse made her way down to the landing adjacent to a truck road. The other man stayed on the landing, bucking the tree into four-foot lengths after unhooking the hitch. He would then place the harness over the horse's rump and send her on her way back up the slope for another hitch.

All went well until one particularly large stem started picking up speed on the slope and began gaining on the mare's heels.

Suddenly, the butt rolled in behind a stump and the horse was thrown headfirst on her side. As she struggled to gain her footing, the lumberjack hurried to her side, pouring out words of encouragement in French.

Oxen were the beasts of burden loggers relied on before the introduction of draft horses. Charles Carpenter, Rt., used oxen as late as 1905 in his extensive logging operations. Courtesy George Stevens

As soon as she heard him, she lay her head back on the ground and relaxed. The logger sent one of our group for a peavey, which was used to roll the tree and relax the tension on the tugs. The horse was then gently coaxed, trembling in fright, to her feet.

The Bucksaw Era produced a number of woodsmen who could saw and pile 8 to 10 cords per day. This era also produced some excellent teamsters—men who took great pride in their fine horses and treated them almost as friends. Courtesy Lyons Falls Historical Association

After she had completely settled down, her master pretended to hook her back to the tree. On command, she bolted ahead, obviously afraid of a repeat of the incident. She was scolded with a sharp rebuke, and after she had settled back down again, the process was repeated with the same results.

Finally, on the third try, she actually was hitched to the tree and moved off smoothly down the slope and to the landing.

Sheltered inside from inclement weather, Mart Allen often reflected about the mechanization of forest extractions and how that revolution has meant the need for fewer workers in the logging industry. Courtesy Mart Allen

The remarkable teamwork between teamster and horse becomes all the more remarkable when you realize both man and horse are in a temporary partnership. In most cases, they work together for only one season.

In many instances, the horses were better trained than their masters. C.J. Strife was once heard to remark about a teamster who was having difficulty with a horse, "The horse was smarter than he was."

I gained a real measure of respect for both man and horse that day in 1950. I was to learn later that not all mishaps ended as well for man or beast.

The logging industry eventually replaced animals with mechanized vehicles that relied on power derived from internal combustion engines rather than relying on old-fashioned oats-and hay-powered horses and oxen. Courtesy George Shaughnessy

Adirondack TIM-Berrr!

Chapter 12 | Mart Allen

MEN AND HORSES TEAMED UP TO CUT ADIRONDACK TIMBER

Adirondack Express, November 7, 1995

Both man and horse shared the many dangers of woods work, and accidents were common to both.

Unfortunately, more of them proved fatal to the horse than to its master. Occasionally, a horse was injured to the extent that it would have to be euthanized. The remote areas and time constraints on at least two occasions led to unusual methods to carry it out. The gun was the accepted method at the time, but their possession on many of the large private parks was prohibited.

Mickey Freeman told me of a situation that occurred on the Nehasane Park when a horse suffered a broken back after a tree accidentally fell on it. Its suffering was ended by a stick of dynamite being tied to its head and detonated.

Horse-power provided the best way to twitch logs through demanding conditions. Courtesy Mart Allen

Story has it that legendary woodsman Herb McGee tried the same method with an ailing horse. The horse was led a discreet distance from camp, the dynamite attached and lit. Herb made for the camp in haste, but forgot to either tie the horse or he got loose and came hard on his heels. Herb was said to have just made it into the nearest camp building when the dynamite did its job.

In any event, the whole thought of putting a noble animal such as the horse out of its misery in such a manner is repugnant. I do not relate the story to shock or make light of the practice, but only because it at times did happen.

A teamster and his reliable horses. Courtesy George Cataldo

Lest you get too sorry for the horse, it should be remembered that some of them gave as well as received. Many an unwary teamster was seriously injured or killed by an ill-mannered animal. It paid to know your horse and to respect both ends of the animal.

I well remember old Duke, a very large workhorse my uncle Mart once owned. He was the kindest, most gentle giant imaginable. His sense of humor, however, was something else. Once when I entered his stall to grain him, he nonchalantly pinned me against the wall with his huge hindquarters.

I was about 12 years old at the time, and talk about a desperate feeling! After that, I would pretend to saunter on by and then quickly dash by his hindquarters and up to his front by the manger before he could get me. You had to reverse the procedure to exit the stall. He knew better than to try it with my uncle.

Loggers with modern equipment and machinery. Forest and paper people have a keen self-interest in making certain that woodlands remain healthy and productive. Courtesy Mart Allen

C.J. Strife, like most of his teamsters, knew horses and respected them. Bill Marleau relates an incident in his book, *Big Moose Station*, in which C.J. halted a runaway team and averted possible disaster.

The early logger and the logging horse were for the most part replaced by modern loggers with modern equipment and machinery. Today, one man can do the work of ten, and much more safely.

Like everything else, the entire logging industry has changed and is changing at an ever- increasing pace. Since it is still an important part of the Adirondacks, maybe I will dwell on the subject a bit longer.

Adirondack TIM-Berrr!

Chapter 13 | Mart Allen

WW II MACHINERY DEVELOPMENT INFLUENCED LUMBER INDUSTRY

Adirondack Express, November 14, 1995

For the most part, the logging horse has given way to the machine in moving logs and other wood products from stump to mill.

Horses are still used where esthetics and minimum surface disturbance are critical. As in most commercial operations today, cost dictates the way in which trees are harvested, and in this respect the machine is the only way.

The change occurred gradually and for the most part after the end of World War II. The technology used to develop machines of war played a big part in the development of specialized equipment for woods work.

C.J. Strife was one of the first operators to take advantage of this technology, and he modified some surplus prime movers to his woods operations.

Early 1950 advertisement. Courtesy *The Northeastern Logger*

Industry has made giant strides in the past 40 years in developing timber harvesting equipment, and Strife, who died in 1953, would be truly impressed with today's harvesting methods. One man today does the work of ten in Strife's era.

The one constant in the business since its inception has been the intense physical demands on the logger. The person who fells and skids the tree to the landing bears the brunt of those demands. He may produce many times the production of his early counterparts, but his energy output and risks remain the same.

Caterpillar's Traxcavator was an early 1950s answer to the logging industry. The new "cat" machines changed the landscape of logging all over the world. Courtesy Town of Webb Historical Association, P5261.

The successful modern-day logger has to be a better-trained worker. Mechanical skills are necessary to keep present-day equipment well maintained and running for peak performance.

There are many more uses for wood today, and species and material that were not merchantable a few years ago find a ready market today. The logger must be well versed in this aspect of the business as he ultimately determines the final end result of the wood and its price. Many a poorly-trained logger has cost his employer an amount equal to his week's wages with one wrong cut.

Oliver-Cletrac Crawler Tractors

GASOLINE OR DIESEL POWER

18 to 120 H.P.

OLIVER—Industrial Wheel Tractors
HEIL—Full hydraulic Bulldozers
DROTT—Twin Controlled Tilting Bullangledozers
DROTT—Hi-Lift Loaders
CARCO—Winches-Logging Arches
B & B—Preformed steelcore wire rope
BYERS—Shovels and Cranes
DAVEY—Air-cooled compressors
LULL SHOVELOADER—Log Forks
WARE—Hydraulic loaders
TORO—Power mowers
TORO—Tractors-gang mowers
SPEEDEX—Garden tractors

Complete Parts and Service Department—Crawler track service, all makes—Welding and steamcleaning service.

To better serve our logging customers, we have moved to a new 12,000 square ft. building, with greater parts and service facilities. Prompt day to day service will be available for tractor repairs, which will include complete motor overhaul.

KINNE - EQUIPMENT

416 BROAD STREET, UTICA 2, N. Y.
Two Blocks East of Utica Post Office
Telephones: 4-2179 — 2-3159
Open all day Saturday

Courtesy *The Northeastern Logger*

Safety training plays a much bigger role in present-day woods operation than it did in years past. Insurance costs are predicated on accident history of the operator and this sums up the statement, "Safety pays."

Modern timber harvesting equipment is tailor-made to fit the terrain and product to be harvested. This has also changed the forester's role in managing the forest. Generally speaking, the trees harvested and methods used to harvest them are ways to determine what the next crop will be. This is particularly true here in the Northeast where we depend primarily on natural regeneration for our next harvest.

Logging, like farming, is one of the few professions that generally face a labor shortage. The work hours, risks and extreme energy demands parallel each other, but they also share the same incentives. Few young people today are willing to accept the challenge; the few that do are a proud group and well they should be.

Old trailers moved from worksite to worksite served as shelter for foresters and loggers.
Courtesy Mart Allen

A young person today who likes working outdoors, is in good health and does not mind hard work should have no trouble finding a challenging career.

One last thing, men, the changing role of women in the workplace will have little effect on your career.

PULP WOOD CUTTERS
LOG CUTTERS – FARMERS
WOOD DEALERS

There is a chain saw awaiting you
which will increase your profits
and ease your work.

The Universal One Man Power Chain Saw

A REAL ONE-MAN SAW—Light in Weight.
Low in Cost. Economical in Operation!

For further information address:

F. H. HADLEY

BLACK RIVER, N.Y. Phone 2791

—Demonstrations by Appointment—

Courtesy *The Northeastern*

Adirondack TIM-Berrr!

Chapter 14 | Mart Allen

Remembering Norm Villiere, A First-Class Woods Worker

Adirondack Express, November 21, 1995

Old Forge has had its share of first-class woods workers. It also experienced its share of sorrow and tragedy as a result of accidents in the woods.

Felling the trees contributed to many of the fatal accidents connected with logging. Norman Villiere was only one of at least three area people that I knew who suffered such a fate. At the time he was killed Norm was living in Utah.

Norm did not die because of lack of experience. He was one of the most capable men around with a chainsaw, a man who was proud of his ability to put out a high rate of production.

I remember him telling me how he cut off his little toe with the saw and never felt it. He was bucking a big spruce and leaned over the tree to make the cut, not realizing his foot was under the saw tip. His first clue was when he noticed his sock was wet and soggy. Looking at his foot he saw the cut in his boot. It scared the hell out of him to take his boot off and look.

Norman was a well-known skier and lover of winter sports, with one exception—he hated snowmobiles with a passion. It was this dislike that ultimately prompted his move to Utah.

On one occasion he achieved a certain measure of revenge for the lost sleep because of late-night bar-hoppers. One Sunday morning, he got up at 5 a.m., parked his truck outside of the Forge Motel and tuned up his old XP100 Homelite saw.

He was a flamboyant, colorful character much like his dad, Reg. His snappy repartee entertained one and all, usually at one of the local diners. Upon hearing me addressed as "Honey" by my wife, he quipped, "If that's honey, I am selling my bees."

Norm Villiere was a first-class woods worker. Courtesy Mart Allen

His sense of humor carried over to his guiding activities; his hunting parties were always interesting.

While making a deer drive near the Adirondack League Club line, Norm came across a fresh track that could only be attributed to a poacher. To warn the interloper of possible capture, he started to call out, "Watch out L.L. Bean!"

Felling trees contributes to many fatal accidents. Courtesy Mart Allen

He was famous for lighting stackers. A stacker (to the uninitiated) is a tall hollow dead stub. A fire is started in the butt and with the right draft, the resultant fire is impressive; it is done only while snow is present.

Advertisement in a 1950s *The Northeastern Logger* magazine

A stacker he started on the Green Lake flat turned into a forest fire two days later when the snow melted. The guides knew how it started.

While he was crossing the Moose River on the ferry rope to retrieve a boat, his Uncle Leo shook him off into the river. Mr. Hunter, whose party they were guiding, was a little perturbed about interrupting the hunt while Norm dried his clothes in the camp.

Adirondack TIM-Berrr!

Chapter 15 | Mart Allen

BAD ACCIDENT 17 YEARS AGO ENDED BUD'S LOGGING CAREER

Adirondack Express, November 28, 1995

I have discussed at length and in some detail the dangers of logging as an occupation. There is no question that the importance of safety training cannot be overemphasized.

As in every way of life, there are pitfalls that can never be controlled or anticipated. I submit the following real-life example to illustrate some.

It's September 7, 1978, and Clayton Gribneau Jr., better known as Buddy, is cutting standing timber on International Paper Company lands near Woods Lake. He was far from being a novice, although he had little formal safety training. Like many of his contemporaries of that era, he had been well trained under the tutelage of his father, an experienced logger.

Safety cannot be overemphasized enough when harvesting logs. Courtesy Mart Allen

Pat Gagnon was running the skidder, moving the merchantable stems to the landing. Pat was a capable and experienced logger in his own right, which played an important part in the outcome of the incident that occurred.

The terrain they were working on was steep and laced with rock ledges. Bud had just dropped a large hard maple when he caught some movement out of the corner of his eye. The movement was the top of another tree that was tumbling off the ledge above him. He was struck across the back by a large limb, which drove him into the ground.

Lt. to Rt.: Norm Wilday, Bernie La Roque, Rod Carlson. Norm was an independent log buyer. Bernie was his helper. The men were scaling hard maple veneer logs they had bought from the Adirondack League Club. Wilday sold the logs to Carlson for the Gutchess Lumber Company in Cortland, N.Y.
Courtesy Mart Allen

His face was imbedded in deep mud and he was unable to breathe. Fortunately, one arm was free and he was able to dig away the mud so that he could breathe once more. As he lay there, he realized there was little he could do to help himself. The real danger was that when Pat returned for his next hitch, unaware of his dilemma, he might attempt to push the tree out of his skid trail.

Bud lay there patiently listening to the sounds of the skidder as it made its rounds to the landing and back. When he heard the machine approaching, with his one good arm he was able to grasp a protruding limb and shake it as vigorously as possible.

Pat Gagnon's experience enabled him to quickly analyze the situation and he immediately saw the movement of the branch. Halting the skidder, he quickly cut the tree, freeing Buddy. He then made him as comfortable as possible before heading to Big Moose for help.

It took the Big Moose ambulance crew nearly three hours to get Buddy off the steep hill and out of the woods.

All of Buddy's ribs were broken on one side and two on the other; in addition one lung had been punctured. His right leg, which had been pinned up under his chest, was shattered in several places below the knee. He spent a month in the hospital and several years recuperating before being able to work at some other occupation.

Load of logs heading out of the forest. Courtesy Mart Allen

As I interviewed him 17 years later, the strain and anxiety of the event was still evident in his voice. He realized how fortunate he was to be alive.

When asked if his ordeal had dampened his enthusiasm for logging, his reply reinforced my faith and admiration for all loggers:

"If I still had two good legs I would still be logging."

Falling trees kill Boonville logger

By ROB BOOTH
Observer-Dispatch

PARISH — In June, Boonville logger Gerard Hoage found the body of one of his co-workers who was killed in a logging accident. Tuesday, Hoage's body was found in the same forest by another co-worker.

Hoage, 43, of Gulf Road, died of massive head injuries when he cut down a 45-foot beech tree and it fell into a nearby rotting tree, resulting in both trees landing on top of him, state police said.

Hoage, an employee of O.F. Failing and Sons of Boonville, was working alone about one mile into the woods off a winding logging road in Parish, which is about 30 miles north of Syracuse in Oswego County.

Federal Occupational Safety and Health Administration officials said Hoage's accident and the June accident are under investigation. In June, O.F. Failing and Sons' employee Scott Wendt, 18, of Boonville, was killed in a logging accident in the same area, police said. Hoage found his body.

"We do have rules and regulations for logging operators," said Ron Williams, assistant area director for safety at OSHA's Syracuse office. "What type of equipment they were wearing, if there were any dead trees around him."

Williams said OSHA also will review procedures used and the training involved at O.F. Failing and Sons. The company could not be reached Wednesday.

Hoage, who graduated from Adirondack Central School, was married with two daughters. Funeral arrangements are being handled by Fitch-Mills Funeral Home, Boonville. There are no public calling hours. Funeral services will be Saturday, at a time yet to be announced.

October 23, 1993, Utica *Observer-Dispatch*

Adirondack TIM-Berrr!

Chapter 16 | Mart Allen

LOGGER BRUCE MARTIN SURVIVED PORT LEYDEN BRIDGE COLLAPSE

Adirondack Express, December 19, 1995

This is a story about Bruce Martin, a long-time acquaintance and experienced logger. Bruce started working in the woods when he was 13. His father was a combination farmer and logger in Croghan.

There were sixteen children in Bruce's family; eight girls and eight boys. Six of the boys are loggers, and it was a natural step for Bruce to follow suit.

Our story starts on November 13, 1985. Bruce was trucking logs with his brother Mahlon's new GMC tri-ax truck.

The route took him across the bridge over the Black River in Port Leyden. It was his 120th trip, but for some unexplained reason, Bruce was filled with apprehension and trepidation. He soon had reason for his uneasiness.

Careful as truck drivers were, accidents were common. Courtesy Lyons Falls History Association

The front of the truck rolled easily across the bridge onto the middle abutment. Suddenly, the bridge behind him let go with a horrendous roar. Bridge and truck plunged backward, dragging the cab off the abutment and downward to the cold swirling waters twenty feet below.

There was no time to react. Stunned, Bruce could only hang on to the steering wheel, bracing himself for the inevitable. With a tremendous roar the windshield was blown out and the cab was immediately inundated with water and fuel oil. In total darkness he found himself pressing his face against the roof of the cab, trying to take advantage of the three or four inches of air trapped there.

Flipflop! Courtesy Lyons Falls History Association

Swallowing both water and fuel oil he realized he had to get out and to the surface. Groping his way to the windshield, he worked his way out and up through to the surface 30 feet above. Surfacing, he quickly swam against the current to the nearest shore.

As he pulled himself up onto the bank, cold and shock set in and Bruce was unable to stand. Help was there almost immediately and he was quickly whisked off to the hospital. He was treated for the fuel oil he had swallowed. After a couple of hours of recuperation, Bruce was pressing to go home.

Bruce was well equipped to survive such an ordeal. He is one of the most rugged individuals I have ever met. Anyone who puts the chains on and off

This is a precariously-loaded truck approaching a narrow bridge. Courtesy Lyons Falls History Association

his truck all winter in a tee shirt has to be tough! When I first heard about the accident and the circumstances, I was not surprised he survived.

The Martins have always had a strong and abiding faith in the Lord, and Bruce gives credit for the outcome to that faith.

The next time you cross that bridge, think of Bruce and what might have happened if the bridge had given way with a loaded school bus. Perhaps the Lord does work in mysterious ways.

Again! Photo by Harold Linck. Courtesy Dick Ulrich

Adirondack TIM-Berrr!

Chapter 17 | Mart Allen

Loggers Flopped More Than One Truck While on the Job

Adirondack Express, January 2, 1996

Please bear with me for one more episode on the subject of log truck drivers. Frank Ritz Jr. assured me that it was very hard to make a living at it in the early days. As he put it, "It was hard to make any money, but it did put food on the table."

Most drivers were paid by the amount of logs or pulp delivered to the mill, so they were constantly pushing their trucks to the limit.

The old bridge at McKeever had an overhead structure much like the one on Route 28 in Forestport. The cross members on either end were so low it was impossible to clear them with a full load.

Frank and many others would pull up to the bridge and pass the top of the first two tiers back on the rear tier, pull up to the rear tier and transfer the top of that to the front.

The whole process was repeated again at the other end of the bridge. They were able to carry one half cord more pulp by operating in this manner.

One driver would park his truck under the loader and sleep most of the night so he would be the first one loaded in the morning. With luck, it was possible to haul an extra load some days.

Frank agreed that a real log trucker had flopped a few trucks. On one bad stretch of road that was breaking up in the spring, he put one over three times before hitting the main haul.

Bob Pashley was riding with Frank when he had two close calls. One was at Burdick's Crossing near Grieg, when they rounded a turn in a snowstorm and a car was coming at them on their side of the road. Frank took the right shoulder and the truck lay over on the snow bank with the snow barely keeping it from going all the way.

Harold Linck of Boonville, N.Y. saw many truck accidents during his logging career.
Self-portrait by Harold Linck. Courtesy Dick Ulrich

Another time they were heading back into the job on a steep woods road when the truck started to spin out and head back down the hill.

Bob had the door open ready to jump when Frank reached across, grabbed him by the belt and pulled him back into the cab. He was able to throw the truck in reverse and bring it under control at the same time.

Frank was driving for Oliver Scouten and had to be pulled uphill to the landing with a cable on the loader and let down the same way. Finally, Oliver suggested that Frank try it without the cable to go back down the hill. Frank wanted no part of it until Oliver said he would ride down with him. It was Oliver's truck so Frank figured if he was willing to ride with him he would give it a try.

Ooby Dooby! Another truck summersault. Photo by Harold Linck. Courtesy Dick Ulrich

They started down the hill, Oliver bailed out of the truck and Frank was on his own. There was a right turn at the bottom of the hill and Frank put it this way: "You might just as well have not turned the wheel at all." The truck and Frank ended up out in the brush none the worse for wear.

It is a tough life and takes a special breed of man, but they know they stand in a class by themselves. You don't need to be told or try it to know it's true!

Again! Courtesy Lyons Falls History Association

Nothing left to do but wait and have a picture taken. Courtesy Lyons Falls History Association

Almost Over! Missing death by a split hair was all in a day's work for log drivers. Courtesy Howard Wieman

18-foot load of logs piled on a Ford V-8. Courtesy Eric Johnson, Executive Editor of *The Northeastern Logger*

Chapter 18 | Mart Allen

TALES OF LOGGING TRUCKERS

Adirondack Express, December 12, 1995

I have covered many aspects of the logging industry to date. Log truck drivers were another aspect brought into focus during a lively discussion at Walt's Diner last Friday.

As usual I was sitting quietly, enjoying my coffee, when Walt proceeded to chide me about the time he ran me off the Camp 9 Road. He was on his way back to the landing for another load of logs, pedal to the metal, and there was only one path left for me.

He was bearing down pretty hard so I was forced to bite back. My retort was that if I were ever in need of a brain transplant I would want one from a log truck driver. I would want one that had never been used.

A fully loaded truck headed to Canada. "A large percentage of log trucks on this job were Canadian." —Mart Allen. Courtesy Mart Allen

I hasten to add I was not serious, as I do admire anyone who can negotiate most woods roads with an unwieldy load of logs.

Many of the truckers I know have put at least one over on its side with little damage to vehicle or driver. When you're navigating narrow, unimproved, ice snow-covered woods roads with grades that would make a skier shudder, stuff happens! I was quick to point out that Walt had never qualified in that category, so it was obvious he could not really call himself a log truck driver.

I was talking with Phil Delong at Gil Martin's daughter's wedding about the subject just last week. I asked Phil if he remembered the time his lunch box fell off the seat and he reached for it, ran in the ditch and flopped it. He told me that was nothing; he has flipped the one he is driving now three times. Phil is what I call a real driver.

Driver error! Courtesy Howard Wieman

I was driving into a job one day and came upon Dennis Thibado calmly greasing his truck. The road had given way on one side and his tractor trailer with a full load of hemlock was on its side. I mentioned it to a driver at Brandreth the other day and he told me he had the same experience. They both said it's an easy way to grease the truck but a hard way to get it there.

It's easy to see just from what I have said up to this point that it is one of the most expensive trucking operations in the world. It's a hard way to make a living.

Jack Foster Sr. once asked me if I knew why they had the two big mirrors on each side of the cab on the log trucks. He said it was so you could watch yourself starve to death.

Adirondack TIM-Berrr!

Chapter 19 | Mart Allen

Speak About Characters and Log Buyers Come Up

Adirondack Express, March 26, 1996

During my career in the woods and hinterlands, I have run across some diverse and colorful characters. The log buyers and my interaction with them provided me with some of my most enjoyable and memorable experiences.

Rod Carlson of Gutchess International was the gentleman of the group. Low-key and knowledgeable, it was easy to do business with him. I learned some of the vagaries inherent in the log business from him.

Rod being the first to buy seven-foot, six-inch birch veneer, I was curious as to the use and destination of the logs. They were to be loaded into containers and trucked to Baltimore where the containers were placed on rail cars, which then delivered them to the Port of Los Angeles. The containers were then stacked three high on the decks of ships and transported to Taiwan, where they were made into door skins. The door skins then were sent back to Blount Lumber in Laconia, N.Y., for the manufacture of the completed product. Laconia is roughly 100 miles from where the trees were harvested in the Town of Webb.

George Ramsey was a crusty old veteran who ran a yard in Inlet for Weyerhaeuser and Commonwealth Plywood. He was perhaps the most experienced veneer buyer of the lot, but faced increasing pressure from the export log market.

Bill Helmer [owner of Helmer's Fuel in Old Forge] stopped at the yard one day and asked a few questions about the log business. Not knowing who he was or what he was up to, George told him in short order where to go. Like many of us, George's bark was worse than his bite. He was a fair man and I liked doing business with him.

A forester demonstrates marking a pine tree with a paint gun as a landowner watches.
Courtesy *The Northeastern Logger*

Norm Wilday is an ex-logger turned log buyer who is as tough as he looks. Norm would scale logs all day in sub-zero weather in summer work clothes with light slippers on his feet. He and his partner, Bernie LaRocque, never had to look at a table to determine a log's volume. They had them memorized.

The first time we did business, I asked Norm how he paid. Norm produced an envelope with 50 grand in cash in it, and showing it to me replied, "Here's how I pay."

Norm worked fast and was not one to waste time. A young buyer was looking over his logs and taking an inordinate amount of time to grade them. When Norm could take it no longer he told him, "You better head for your car, I've got my foot raised."

A typical scene. Courtesy Mart Allen

Frank Taio was a young man from Taiwan, factory-trained and meticulous in the examination of each log. He also would have been a candidate for Norm's raised foot.

Sometime after our business dealings were long over, I discovered too late that we had taken advantage of Frank. We had used a set of log volume tables one of my foresters had made up and some of the odd-length logs had been given five more board feet than they should have been. A friend of mine was present some months later when Frank discovered the error, which at $1 a foot cost him $5 more per log than it should have.

Bucking logs with a chainsaw. Courtesy Mart Allen

Frank was philosophical about the whole matter. He looked at my friend and said, "Fred, I buy one whole load air."

Adirondack TIM-Berrr!

Chapter 20 | Mart Allen

Adirondack Woods Became Home to East European Lumberjacks

Adirondack Express, April 2, 1996

Most of the early lumberjacks were gone by the time I came to the Old Forge area. I did, however, come to know and admire two of them.

Both came here in the early 1900s from Eastern Europe. Both men were bachelors and had no family in this country. They were hard workers and hard drinkers, as well as men of their word.

George Goulish was from Russia and was working on Neil Barker's preserve crew for the Adirondack League Club when I first knew him.

A woodsman from the old school, he knew how to use and care for the crosscut saw and the double-bit axe. His axe was sharp and he guarded its use by other members of the trail crew. Finding it left unattended one day, the boys embedded it in a limb and left it buried in the trail where George was sure to find it. Although the axe wasn't dulled, George did not appreciate the joke.

Another winter day at a log landing. Courtesy Mart Allen

River drivers with pike poles. Courtesy *The Northeastern Logger*

George demonstrated that experience often times is better than technical training. He was cutting up a black cherry tree for firewood when the League Club forester happened by. George was being lectured about cutting valuable timber crop species for firewood when he pointed out that the tree was a cull. "Sure," the forester replied, "but you didn't know that before you cut it down." George tapped his head with a finger, looked the forester in the eye and said, "I know the tree."

The Adirondacks was host to WW II prisoners from Italy and Germany. Courtesy Lyons Falls History Association

He was a good worker and he knew it. Barker fired the whole crew for leaving a broken down dozer in the middle of the road, but George refused to be fired. "I no quit," he told Neil. He wasn't fired either.

The other logger was a native of Estonia named August Mayer, or Gus. I first met Gus at the Deerhead Tavern (now The Old Mill). He spoke with a heavy accent and although he was hard to understand, I loved to visit with him.

The Geneva Conventions established a clear set of rules to follow. Among them was that prisoners must receive adequate provisions and supplies (food, clothing, living quarters), and if put to work, they must be paid. Courtesy Lyons Falls History Association

A merchant seaman, he crossed the Atlantic eight times before settling here and working in the woods.

He told of the size and variety of fish in the Baltic Sea, emphasizing their size (like all good fishermen) with his out-stretched arms. I naturally queried him about the hunting in Estonia.

Nearly 1,000 WW II POWs were held at Pine Camp. "Prisoners lived in concrete compound, spending their 'hours of confinement' in cells similar to those...in a Western." —From "Whatever Their Experiences At War, POWs At Camp Drum Led A Tolerable Existence," June 28, 1973, *Cortland Standard.* Courtesy Lyons Falls History Association

Big game was plentiful, but regulations were strict and transgressors punished harshly. People in the village would conceal guns under their clothing and slip off to hunt on the way home from church.

Two famous poachers, according to Gus, were finally caught by the gamekeeper. Their weapons were confiscated on the spot. A straight strong stick was passed through both coat sleeves across their shoulders and tied to their wrists. Like scarecrows they were sent packing back to the village.

Not so bad really, until you learn that they were made to expose themselves before the sticks were put in place. The sentence was concluded with the further admonishment: "Next time I shoot you."

Both George and Gus are buried in the Woodsmen's Section of Riverview Cemetery in Old Forge. A collection was taken up at the Deerhead to put a headstone on Gus's grave.

CAMP NEAR HAWKINSVILLE HOUSED GERMAN POWs

Between Woodgate and Boonville, on the site where the NYS Dept. of Environmental Conservation now has a shop. The Civilian Conservation Corps. established a camp during the 1930s. In 1944, it was made over into a Prisoner-of-War camp for Germans. One building from this complex was moved; to Camp Russell in the late 1940s and now stands along Route 28. The following article is reprinted from a newspaper story of July 13, 1944.

Interest has been centered on a group of German prisoners who were brought into the old CCC camp on the Hawkinsville Road from Pine Camp (now Fort Drum) last Sunday by convoy The number of prisoners held within the stockade has not yet been released, but is in excess of 100.

For the last month or so considerable work on the old camp several miles from Boonville has been done. Barbed Wire stockade with guard towers has been erected and the whole enclosure well lighted with flood lights.It is understood that a great majority of the prisoners now in the Hawkinsville Camp were captured a month ago during the invasion operations at Normandy. After they are given the necessary instructions as to how the work should be done, they will be employed by government contract by the Johnston Pulp Company of Port Leyden and will work continuously under guard.

The camp on the Woodgate Road is one of seven established in Central New York. One story about the camp mentions a runaway prisoner who returned very hungry after a period of time of not being able to find any civilization.

The Hawkinsville POW article is from a 1996 Snowmobile Trail Guide. Additional information can be found in Marty Podskoch's Adirondack Civilian Conservation Corps Camps: History, Memories & Legacy of the CCC (Podskoch Press 2011). Courtesy Woodgate Free Library

"A number of the POWs at the camp and at 18 branch camps across New York state worked for private employers who paid the government for their labor. Work included weeding onions, harvesting the pea crop, cutting pulpwood for the St. Regis Paper Co., and clearing snow off the streets of Watertown." —From "Whatever Their Experiences At War, POWs At Camp Drum Led A Tolerable Existence," June 28, 1973, *Cortland Standard.* Courtesy Lyons Falls History Association

The East European lumberjacks worked hard, and their pleasures were few compared to many of us here today. The fact that they believed this was the greatest place on earth in spite of it serves to point out how very hard life must have been from whence they came.

"During WW II, the bus brought German POWs from the CCC camp in Harrisville to the Croghan area for logging work in the woods." Courtesy Lyons Falls History Association

Adirondack TIM-Berrr!

Chapter 21 | Mart Allen

Closing the Woods Creates an Enforcement Nightmare

Adirondack Express, August 20, 1996

It's been 32 years since we had a woods closure in the Old Forge area. A woods closure is an action taken by the Governor to close all of the forestlands of the state to public access. It is an emergency proclamation to protect open lands under extreme fire conditions.

The impact on local businesses is devastating, and the Governor is under great pressure from two sides on whether to act or not.

There were three such closures during my tenure as a Ranger in the area.

The first one that I had to deal with was in 1963, from October 13 to October 31. A rash of fires and the danger of more forced the action. The situation in this area was compounded when we began to suspect that someone was deliberately setting fires. An emergency meeting was held, and the community and local officials came up with a plan.

A road block was set up on the McKeever Bridge, and all vehicles not having business in the area were turned back. People with camps were not allowed to occupy them.

The area was divided into units, and two-man patrols were on the job 24 hours a day. Everyone was questioned and a log was kept of licenses and times anyone was in a particular area, in the event a fire should occur later. The whole community worked together and we had no more problems with our suspected arsonist.

It was, however, a trying time for Jim Axtell, resident game protector. The new road from McKeever to Old Forge had just been completed a short time before. The shoulders had been seeded and fertilized to the extent they drew the deer out of the woods and to the grazing bonanza.

Courtesy *The Northeastern Logger*

It was hard to imagine the number of large-racked bucks in the area. Add several two-man crews of dedicated deer hunters on 24-hour patrol and you come up with one big headache for the local warden.

I like to think a truce was declared for the duration of the emergency, but will bet someone out there will get a big laugh out of that statement. I am sure some could not pass up the opportunity to put prime venison in the freezer! To sum it all up, I know it was a nightmare for Jim Axtell.

One person in particular I know well remembers the period, and for good reason. Dick Cohen owned the property upon which one of the many fires occurred, but that is not the only reason.

On his way home one afternoon, Dick came upon a fire along the South Shore Road, which had evidently been set. Having no tools at hand to fight the fire, he did the next best thing. He whipped off a very expensive sport coat and waded into the fire using the coat as a flail, containing the flames as best he could until help arrived.

Hot Shots battling a forest fire. Courtesy *The Northeastern Logger*

There is nothing like an emergency situation to bring out the best in people, and that woods closure in 1963 proved it. The cooperation and camaraderie that emerged as a result will remain in my memory forever.

Adirondack TIM-Berrr!

Chapter 22 | Mart Allen

COMMUNITY RALLIED IN FIGHT TO QUELL 1964 FOREST FIRES

Adirondack Express, August 27, 1996

Fortunately, we do not suffer the same conditions that precipitate the violent firestorms so common to the western states. The potential exists, but we are seldom faced with the almost yearly dilemma they confront.

The last woods closure I remember was in 1964, from July 3 to July 14 and again from October 17 to November 20. The first period was punctuated with several small ground fires smoldering away in the duff and leaf litter. Three more dramatic fires preceded the closure on October 17.

A fire destroyed the Sam Hill Camp on Little Moose Lake on August 10. The following afternoon a forest fire was discovered on Rose Mountain overlooking First Bisby Lake. This proved to be the most challenging fire I have ever been involved in.

Prolonged dry weather, dense spruce fir cover and high winds all contributed to make the above statement a fact. Its location on the top of the mountain, on the far side of the lake, at the end of a steep foot trail helped clinch it.

Courtesy *The Northeastern Logger*

By the time men and tools were able to reach the fire, it was late in the day and it was growing by leaps and bounds. The dense cover made it almost impossible to cut a fire line. The one tool we desperately needed was late in arriving on the scene.

The tool was a chain saw, and they were nowhere near as prevalent or as dependable as they are today. The first two saws to arrive on the scene both met an ignominious fate. The chain came off of the first saw and no wrench was available to put it back on the bar. Saw number two was finished on the first pull when the rewind rope broke. In those days we had one saw in the district to be shared by seven Rangers. Needless to say, it was never where it was needed.

Battling a blaze with fire swatters. Courtesy *The Northeastern Logger*

The wind gusted and the fire crowned toward the line and everyone had to run for cover. We had holes burnt in our clothing and six of us were treated the following day for inflammation of the eyes. The first Indian backpack of water never reached the fire. We drank it.

A portable Indian water pump. Courtesy *The Northeastern Logger*

Eventually, we began to prevail when enough men and equipment joined the fray. The biggest help arrived along with a cold front that roared in close to 4 a.m. It was a thunderous downpour that drenched both men and flames.

A third woods fire near Carter on September 14 was the last fire of any significance. It was in spruce and balsam slash, but quick detection and response from the Old Forge Fire Department made short work of a serious situation.

Rene Heroux had three pieces of heavy equipment near the fire that sped up the fire line construction.

Outstanding cooperation between the fire services and the public all combined to effectively check any more outbreaks.

History repeats itself, so we are sure to face similar conditions, and just as surely the community will respond. The new technology and the same spirit will be there to counter it when it happens.

Adirondack TIM-Berrr!

Chapter 23 | Mart Allen

Marking Timber Takes One into the Old Adirondacks

Adirondack Express, June 17, 1997

Those of us who work far from the environs of man know an Adirondacks few visitors know exists.

Foresters, loggers and rangers all share to some degree that unpleasantness that comes with the beauty of our surroundings. I had two days of it last week [June 10, 1997] and now that I am hard on the heels of 70, it's more difficult to take.

Log skidder pulls a twitch of logs. Courtesy Mart Allen

I was marking timber a mile and a half east of the Lewis-Herkimer County line on property bordering the Independence River.

The area is far from any influence of the fly control that much of the traveled corridors of the Adirondacks enjoys. It harks back to the days when the black fly tempered all outdoor activities.

The hot weather and deer flies teamed up with the black flies to make the work twice as demanding. I dealt with the situation as I have for years.

A man believed to be Rick Hunkins of Hunkins Excavating of Old Forge, N.Y. bucks-up a log.
Courtesy Mart Allen

I cover as much of my body with clothing as possible and the rest with fly dope. The heat and exertion of the work causes perspiration to dilute the repellent and it has to be renewed periodically. The flies let you know when it's time.

They are relentless in their attacks, but with proper protection, their bites can be avoided; their harassment cannot. It's impossible to keep them out of your eyes, ears or mouth. They work their way up under your hat brim and crawl around on the back of your glasses—all hard to contend with when your hands are full of tools.

The terrain is never easy timber; there can be no detours. Every potential merchantable tree has to be inspected from all aspects. A diameter measurement is taken at four and a half feet from the base of the tree on the uphill side. No mean feat when it stands on a steep slope, surrounded by witch hobble, briars, blow-down or thick spruce.

The final step is completed and all of the above hardships. Field data is compiled and advertised in a sale proposal.

The sale is shown to prospective buyers and sold to the highest bidder. After it all comes together it leaves one with a sense of satisfaction that's hard to duplicate.

Skidders and trucks hauled logs out of the deep woods. Courtesy Lyons Falls History Association

James Dubuar, legendary Wanakena Ranger School director, placed foresters in two categories. You were either a "dirt forester" or an "armchair forester." Guess which one you are likely to find doing the work I have just described!

Adirondack TIM-Berrr!

Chapter 24 | Mart Allen

TIMBER THIEVES BEWARE: YOUR BOOTY LIKELY TO QUALIFY AS GRAND LARCENY

Adirondack Express, June 22, 1997

This is a sad tale of woe and one all too familiar to me in my roles of forest ranger and forester. It is about possible timber theft and trespass and one of many I have witnessed in over 45 years of stump jumping.

It began last week (June 16, 1997) with an e-mail from a lady in Florida. She contacted my partner for some advice on her woodlot near Parish.

A logger had contracted her to inquire about a right-of-way across her property to another person's woodlot. At the same time he offered her a large sum of money for her timber. His entreaties ended with the line, "You may as well sell it to me because someone will steal it anyway."

A typical log landing of Rick Hunkins. Courtesy Mart Allen

Her father had left the property to her. She knew little about it and was only familiar with the narrow portion along a county road. She faxed us a map and asked us to check the site and give her our recommendations on a timber sale. We promised to check it out within the next two weeks.

Two days later, an unexpected rain and wet conditions moved our inspection up much sooner. It turned out to be a lucky break for the landowner.

Typical load of logs believed to be spruce fiddle-butts. Fiddle butt timber has a fine strain grain, free from knots. It is used in the manufacture of sounding boards for pianos. Courtesy Mart Allen

Entering the property from the roadfront and armed with her map, we started our inspection. What we found was shocking, but not totally unexpected. Many of the prime high-value trees had been cut.

Luckily for the owner, the job was still in progress. The trees were being skidded out to another lot on the highway. After checking out where the landing and logs were located, we went to the phone and notified the landowner.

She assured us that no one had been given her permission to enter the property or remove the trees.

The state police were contacted at her insistence and a trooper went to the scene and inspected the site with us. A state police investigator was waiting for us when we came back out to the road. He took a statement from my partner and they left to confront the perpetrator. The state police contacted us later that evening and reported their actions.

Landing with scaled yellow birch veneer logs. Courtesy Mart Allen

The logger was told to stay off the property and not to remove the logs from the landing. We were asked to take control of the logs and do an inventory of the total volume of timber removed. Returning to the scene the next morning, we were just in time to see the last four logs being loaded on a truck. We insisted they not leave until the state police arrived.

We ended up with three sheriff's deputies and a state trooper ordering the unloading of the logs. The following day we had them removed to a secure location. We are free to sell them for our client.

Where this will all end up is anyone's guess. The value of the logs is well over the amount to qualify the possible offense in the grand larceny category.

Norm Wilday scaling hard maple veneer on the Adirondack League Club. "This sale went to Gutchess from the Club." —Mart Allen. Courtesy Mart Allen

I have witnessed many such incidents of timber trespass over the years, but never any so open or blatant. Usually, the loss is not discovered until months or years later and the culprits are never found. This is particularly true in the case of nonresident owners.

There are several things one can do to prevent this from happening. The first is to have your property surveyed and painted. [Trees marked]. It should be posted in accordance with conservation laws and inspected at least twice a year.

In addition to Article 155 of the State Penal Law, which classifies the theft of property with a value exceeding $1,000 as grand larceny, the state now has a new law. It requires Department of Environmental Conservation environmental conservation officers to enforce trespass laws against timber thieves.

Editor's Note: *Mart Allen reports, "the state laws are much more inclusive and to the point than they used to be. At one point if the boundaries were not well-marked the trespasser only had to pay current timber stumpage prices. Today (2019) it is your responsibility to know whose land you are on.*

Part Three

TIM-BERRRR!

What started as the White Sewing Machine Company grew to manufacture crawler-type tractors. Cletrac, Inc. produced tractors for military and civilian use. Renamed Cleveland Tractor Co. in 1917. In the early 1930s, the needs of the Civilian Conservation Corps. and public works projects kept the plant operating through the Great Depression. Courtesy Lewis County Historical Society

Adirondack TIM-Berrr!

Chapter 25 | William J. O'Hern

THE AUTHOR'S INTRODUCTION INTO LOGGING

The question of what brings both younger and older men —and yes women—to work in the timberlands usually has a simple and practical answer: The need to earn a wage.

My own background helps me answer the question. I began working at Crockett's sawmill in Red Creek, N.Y., when I was 20. Why? It offered me a steady job. Unlike some young men who took to the forest because they were edgy or looking for adventure, I simply needed money. In 1967, loggers who supplied the mill with saw logs were bringing home $130.00 a week. I made far less. I hired on as a laborer and slowly worked my way up the ladder. I started as a yardman, then worked as a tail-sawyer, or someone who is responsible for piling timbers off of outfeed of the sawmill until the boss spotted my potential to learn how to grade lumber.

I was like the thousands before me over the decades who had taken a job in the lumber industry to earn a weekly paycheck to meet the needs of my young family.

Most of my co-workers were as fine as any men you would meet anywhere; intelligent, I thought, far above the level of the average white-collar worker, but simply restless. Some of the older men had been lumberjacks, had slept in lumber camp bunkhouses, and talked of older 'jacks who knew of the old days. There was talk of wood and iron bunks with mattresses filled with cornhusks and lice and sheets composed of a blue material similar to denim. Ambrose talked about a swamper—that was a man who went ahead of the gang and cleared out the underbrush. It was the hardest kind of work.

I ranked the work of a logger and sawyer in importance with that of a miner, a farmer, or a munitions-maker. The work was hard, demanding, and often dangerous, yet it was necessary.

I was raised by parents and grandparents who had lived through America's Great Depression. I'd been taught the value of working hard and being thrifty. I enjoyed my work and connection with the old-timers, some of whom had worked in the lumber camps for many years, and others whose experience was brief. I also came to admire how truly hard they worked for the pay they earned.

My fellow workers were people with pride. I liken them to modern farmers who are true heirs of their farming ancestors, for it was their pioneering work which developed the self-reliance, sturdiness, individuality and progressiveness that made the American farmer (and logger) what he is. Like farming, old-time logging embodied this indomitable American spirit.

I remember one of my favorite co-workers as "Harry Hornet" because he saved me from what could have been a worst-case scenario involving a nest of bald-faced hornets that always buzzed around the mill's freshly cut boards each summer. He shared tales of his grandfather, who was a lumberman.

Typical log yard at Gould Lumber Camp 9, ca. 1950s. Courtesy Bob Failing

Harry recalled how in his grandfather's day the lumbermen's winter home was a huge log shanty. A great wood-burning stove in the middle provided both light and heat. The smoke went up through a big chimney in the roof. There were cracks in the walls and roof. Snow and rain came in. He described the wooden bunks, three in a tier around the walls. The food consisted of salt pork, potatoes and bread, and molasses for their pancakes, with tea and coffee and a few vegetables. He claimed the men were "a healthy, robust, brave group, with axes, cant hooks and crosscut saws" for their main tools. They used horses, mules and maybe oxen to draw logs on bobsleds to the skidways every winter.

The sawyer, loaders and operators of trucks on the landing were some of the many positions important in paper production. Courtesy Lewis County Historical Society

The generation that followed Harry's grandfather went into the lumber camp by railroad, truck or automobile, depending upon the region. The "new-age" camps were much more like large, electrically-lit boarding houses, well-supplied with running water. There were cottages scattered about for the families of the superintendents and others in authority, and the camp complexes were larger than earlier ones. There was a store where the workers could be supplied not merely with necessities, but also in many cases with comparative luxuries.

Camp food was more varied and good, with unlimited quantities of cooked cereals, bacon, ham, chops or steaks, eggs, biscuits, doughnuts, griddlecakes, milk or cream and coffee, as well as all kinds of vegetables.

Top-loading by hand was physical work. Most often pulpwood was loaded onto a conveyor.
Courtesy Lewis County Historical Society

By the late 1920s–early '30s, the trees were still cut down and trimmed in much the old way with axes, but there was more mechanical hauling over the main haul roads. Some outfits even used gas-powered local engines with ropes that could snake the logs along for distances of a half mile through the woods over paths cut by swampers for that purpose. Logs were loaded on trucks and rail cars, often by powered machinery, and sent off to a distant sawmill.

In the sawmill itself, logs—instead of being sawed with a single upright or circular saw—were handled almost entirely by machinery with gang-saws, and there was a provision for handling what was formerly waste material so that it was cut into laths and shingles and often manufactured into various-sized wooden boxes and other smaller lumber products.

Moreover, those modern lumber camps had a trained forester, whose business it was to see that the waste, instead of being left in the woods to catch fire during the coming summer and destroy the forest, was properly stacked and burned. In many instances also, it was part of the forester's job to see to it that the cut-over land was properly reforested, so that in 30 or 40 years the land would produce as much as had been taken away.

Even in the distant camps, one found the newspaper and the radio, so that the men were kept up to date with the current events of the world.

You might say the industry could claim wonderful progress, and the changes had made the work much less hazardous and risky.

Positive changes continued for the industry. In December 1947, United States Secretary of Labor Schwellenbach raised the minimum age for most jobs in pulpwood logging. The order followed a study by the child labor branch of the Wage and Hour Division. Previously some jobs could have been fulfilled by 16-and 17-year-olds; the order, effective in February 1948, raised the limit to 18 for logging of pulpwood, excelsior wood (softwood shavings used for packing fragile goods or stuffing furniture), cordwood, fence posts and similar lumber. Exempted were office jobs and those away from the sawmill and the sites of felling, skidding, yarding and loading operations. It did not apply to jobs in repair or maintenance shops, living quarters, tallying and forest fire prevention positions.

"Harry Hornet" liked to recall tales of early lumbermen he'd known. Courtesy Lewis County Historical Society

I had learned a lot about safety by the time I began work at Crockett's mill. I had seen plenty of hazards when I worked at another mill and at the Hammermill Paper Mill in Oswego, N.Y. That job was an eye-opener for me. I was hired to be part of a quick-response repair crew. Our job was to resolve the problem when a large semi-liquid sheet of paper broke overhead while in transit over the array of rollers that squeezed and dried. Between learning how easily a person could get ground up in the huge vats with spinning beaters down into which we had to frantically force the massive sheets of liquefied paper, and worrying about the constant danger of negotiating through the narrow passageways inside the massive paper-making machine of rollers, pulleys and moving parts and the daily fear of hearing a crack much like the report from a .45 pistol that meant a gigantic v-belt had broken and was sailing helter-skelter at high speed with enough force to kill a person, on-the-job injury or death were pretty much constant risks.

"Harry Hornet" claimed the old-timers were a robust group of 'jacks. Courtesy Lewis County Historical Society

I had come to Crockett's with two missing toes and a missing finger. At Hammermill, it seemed every third worker had lost an eye, or appendage, or had been otherwise injured. My body part losses had made me gun-shy and had taught me a valuable lesson about job safety. So why take a job at another mill? To repeat, much like earlier folks who came into the lumber camps looking for work, I needed a job.

Harry, John and Ambrose are three older sawmill yard laborers I have long lost contact with but still often think about when I pass a dingy tavern similar to the one we used to gather at in Hannibal on Saturday nights to socialize and to listen to local country music bands. They enjoyed their work and were proud of their families' connection to logging, but in their own ways each steered me to think about an array of other career paths I might consider that were much less risky. By 1968 I had explored the opportunities available to me, and ultimately went on to greener fields. But I never lost my interest in the history of logging.

The use of cranes was a labor-saving (and safety) mechanical improvement to load logs.
Courtesy Lewis County Historical Society

I've always found people who take on risky jobs or attempt seemingly impossible feats, activities that could easily kill them, to be interesting characters.

I like gritty legendary Ogdensburg character Mary Jane Bushel's response when on July 21, 1936, at the age of 106, she was being praised for her recent accomplishment of completing a 200-mile motor trip from Ogdensburg to Rochester, N.Y.

Bushel explained that her dogged determination was learned from a lifetime of hard work. Not only was she driving long after others had stopped; she had assisted in delivering 500 babies (at an average of $2.00 apiece) by age 82, and at age 99 she rescued a man from the river behind her home.

"In my day I was a fine swimmer," she explained to a reporter from *The Morning Herald* newspaper. "I used to work as a logger on the river when

Surveys of forest resources made years before the 1960s indicated that there was hardwood in abundance in grades somewhat below that needed for veneer, sawlogs, dimensions and tool handles stock. Courtesy Lewis County Historical Society

The interior of the original Gould pulp mill was more antiquated than the Hammermill Paper Company mill the author worked at. Courtesy Lewis County Historical Society

they were short of men." Although many of her French-Canadian counterparts could not swim, she felt knowing how to swim offered her an extra ounce of protection when working on river drives.

By February 1948 new labor standards were established for the logging industry.
Courtesy Lewis County Historical Society

Gould Paper Company acquaintance Pat O'Brien was like Mary Jane Bushel and the men at Crockett's mill in many ways. He loved his work, loved logging, did what he had to survive and kept the old stories alive while insisting logging was still, and always would be, a hard, dangerous, magnificent job.

He also surprised me when I asked what he thought was the worst thing about being a logger. His response: "I recall my son once telling me that he wanted to grow up and be a lumber jack just like me. I didn't cotton to his admiration of my timber industry profession because of the long hours, hard, dangerous work, and long periods away from home and family. I could have killed him!"

Loaded and ready to roll. Author's Collection

Hammermill Paper Company in Oswego, N.Y. was acquired by the Marathon Paper Company in 1951. This photo shows the main plant entrance during the legendary and infamous snowstorm of 1958.
Courtesy Justin White and Mark Slosek

Interior view of the McKeever, N.Y. veneer mill. Courtesy Lewis County Historical Society

Adirondack
TIM-Berrr!

Chapter 26 | William J. O'Hern

AGED IN WOOD

In 1906 it was eleven hours from the time a dirty log was hauled out of a river until a paper mill's shipping department received and wrapped up a thousand-pound roll of newsprint and sent it off to a far-off city's big printing plant.

I found that to be a significant statistic, but I didn't give one iota about papermaking facts when I worked at the Hammermill Paper Company in Oswego, N.Y. My interest came long after I had left the company for greener and safer pastures.

We all handle paper and yet I suspect most of us give little thought to the process of turning wood into paper.

The workers the author met in the woods and in mills filled his head with stories of the old days as well as encouraged him to find a different, safer way to earn a living. Courtesy Lyons Falls History Association

The work of papermaking is at once intricate and yet simple. It is easily understood if one has an informative guide to show him though the big plant and explain the use of its many machines and utilities.

Before I decided to accept a job at Hammermill, I was given a tour of the plant's operation. I wish I had paid closer attention, but at that time my focus was more on the apparent plant dangers than on being enlightened.

Basically a log is hauled out of the river; it is cut up and ground into pulp and the pulp is carried by conveyors or by gravity into various machines and arrangements for papermaking, and after being subjected to many processes that eliminate the dirt and waste, it comes out at the end of a monster machine in the form of giant rolls of paper.

Calked shoes are various types of footwear with metal spikes worn by woodsmen to give them sure-footing on logs that rolled or moved without warning. Courtesy Lyons Falls History Association

I remember best the logs coming into the plant where they were cut and "barked" to a point where they shot down an incline into the grinding room. I believe all the other transfers of the materials in the course of paper manufacture were made by gravity.

I can still remember logs being carried up to the big circular saw that cut them into two-foot lengths.

The success of early paper mills depended a great deal on their location, both regarding access to the timber belts and the general formation of the land, which had much to do with convenience in handling the product from which paper is made.

Water power was not necessary, but it was desirable. There is a heavy and never-ending demand for water in a paper mill, and those that were operated by water had an advantage. The Gould Paper Company plant at Lyons Falls was one successful example of North Country industries.

By the first decade of the 20th century, the Gould company operated three plants in addition to the one at Lyons Falls. One was located at Port Leyden. It made manila and express papers. Another was located at Gouldtown on the Moose River and produced manila paper exclusively. There was also another mill on the Moose that produced pulp.

Dangerous work. Courtesy Lyons Falls History Association

The mill at Lyons Falls was admirably located. Nature provided an immense dam across the Black River, and behind the falls was a great water power which the Gould company utilized. The buildings that comprised the plant had been located with studied accuracy on the bank that sloped sharply toward the river.

A great many photos labeled "sulfite mill" surfaced when I searched North Country historical archives. I never gave a thought to what part their production had to do with papermaking until I Googled "sulfite."

How many times we absent-mindedly chewed the margin of a newspaper we have been reading, or in my case chewed paper to a wet mass to form little round spitballs I then projected through a straw, little knowing that a part of paper's composition is sulphuric acid!

One Gould paper-making report I read told that pulp that is made by the mechanical process alone contains no sulphuric acid, but in order to give it strength it must be mixed with pulp that has been cooked with the acid in great digesters that hold thousands of gallons. Sulphuric acid will not eat lead, and these digesters, which somewhat resemble immense upright boilers, are lined with lead and brick. The percentage of sulphite used in the manufacture of newsprint is about one-fifth according to a Gould document.

This Beaver River paper mill machine, once a modern piece of equipment, looks like a dinosaur compared to the paper-making machine the author worked on. Courtesy Lyons Falls History Association

The sulfite mill of the Gould plant at Lyons Falls was one of their largest buildings. All the acid that was used was manufactured and stored there and in its manufacture four tons of sulphur were burned every day in 1906, according to a Gould paper-making paper I used in research.

An informational article explained:

> The manner of treating the log for the sulfite mill is also different than it is for the manufacture of pulp by mechanical process. For the sulfite mill the logs are chipped, and the chips are cooked. For the other mill the logs are ground.
>
> After a log has been cut up into two-foot lengths the pieces are thrown into the endless chain conveyor and carried a short distance to the "barkers….."

From the grinders the pulp is carried by the water to the screens. These resemble a cheesemaker's vat in outline, but in the bottom is a fine screen which is constantly agitated, and when the pulp is washed over it the part that is of use in paper-making drops through the openings while the small pieces of knots and chips and other impurities are eliminated. The pulp passes through several of these screens before it reaches its state of purification....

Following the author's departure at Crockett's saw mill, the plant burned. Fires are common at mills. This Basselin sawmill burned in 1892. Courtesy Lyons Falls History Association

Sulfite was treated on what were called "wet machines." It was rolled out into a thick coarse mass and folded like a blanket. It then went to beating engines to be mixed with the other pulp.

A later Gould report gave the following step-by-step description.

"The process used at the Gould Paper Company plant [in 1957] originated and developed in the laboratory of the Bauer Brothers Company....

Here the hardwood logs, which are the "weed" type of logs unusable for hardwood lumber, are shredded into chips by powerful knives before the pulp-making process begins. This method greatly simplifies the pulp manufacture and enables technicians to keep better control over the process.

Whereas only spruce wood is used in the manufacture of softwood pulp, the hardwood process utilizes birch, beech and maple woods.

The Chip method results in a better product at lower cost.

Jack Swancott, grand marshal of the 72nd annual New York State Woodsmen's Field Days. Each August a notable woodsman is chosen to head the annual N.Y.S. Field Days Parade in Boonville, N.Y. 2019's theme was "Managed Forests Provide." This is the largest industry parade in the Northeast featuring equipment, log truck competitions, bands, floats, VIPs, queens and wood nymphs and the coronation of the yearly Miss Forest Queen and Miss Jr. Forest Queen and plague presentation to the honorary Grand Parade Marshall. Author's Photo

The hardwood pulp is mixed with bleached Kraft, a trade-named pulp from the South to produce the final Gould product, a high-seen paper used for publishing books, magazines and for converting purposes....

The first step is the depositing of the chips in a chip metering bin where they are automatically weighed and the correct amount is dumped into a rapid cycle "digester" with 175 cubic foot capacity.

A valve in the digester mouth then closes automatically and the pump delivers a pre-determined volume of 2.5 per cent caustic solution to the digester. In this solution, the chips are impregnated for only 20 minutes under a pressure…. This impregnation is a highly important step in the process as it breaks down the fiber structure of the wood.

Before trailers, horses and wagons hauled rolls of finished paper from mills. This load was on the way from Beaver Falls to Castorland. Courtesy Lyons Falls History Association

The chips, with the caustic solution drained away, are then blown into a bin from which conveyors take them to a machine known as a "Pressafnder" according to a Gould manual. Here they are crushed between revolving plates of heavy stainless steel for the first fiberizing operation.

A conveyor then takes the chips to a refiner which further processes these. Then they go to another refiner for more "brushing."

Now approaching the consistency of pulp, the stock is diluted so that it can be pumped to a screen which sorts the unusable fibers out of the mixture. The stock accepted by the screen is then pumped to cleaners for washing.

Thickened again after this washing, the stock is carried, again automatically, to a tile-lined acid tower where it is mixed with sodium hypochlorite for bleaching.

From the bleach tower it is pumped to another refiner where it is processed once more through a long pipe to the paper mill.

> There, mixed with the softwood stock in varying proportions, it passes over screens and rolls to come out as the finished paper….

Just why the apparatuses were called "engines" was never clear to me. They looked like large vats, which, when in operation, were nearly full of pulp. Concealed paddles or "beaters" agitated the mass until the acidic solution was thoroughly mixed with the other material.

I was told the beating engines the pulp went into were Jordan engines, which were merely refiners. Then it was screened again before it went into the paper-making machines.

I assume the Gould making paper at Lyons Falls was similar to the process I saw at Hammermill.

It was all immense paper-making machinery. The novice would only see the big and complicated framework, supporting a dozen or so rolls that were intensely heated with steam.

This was a large sawmill crew compared to the crew the author worked with at Crockett's sawmill.
Courtesy Lyons Falls History Association

I was aware of the pulp when it came in upon an endless wire, soft, slimy and full of water. It was spread out the entire width of the machine and was carried along rapidly until it reached the dryer—a hot roll—about ten feet beyond. Here you began to see a semblance of an eight to eleven-foot web of paper. It was still too wet to bear its own weight, so it was carried swiftly along on blanket belts. More water was squeezed out, and then the web ran through the calendars, a set of rolls that give the paper equal surface on both sides, and then on and over many heated rolls and reels. I was not interested in learning all the mechanical functions.

It was during this process of papermaking that I remember reaching the decision I would not make a long-standing career at Hammermill. I had earlier worked at Solvay Process flaking caustic soda. It was hot, dangerous work. The paper mill was as dangerous. I worked around enormous vats and beaters with a so-called safety rail around them to help prevent a worker from falling in that intimidated me. It became very clear on my first workday that the safety rails would not completely protect me.

There was sometimes a break in the line of the papermaking process, when huge, wide hot sheets of semi-liquid paper tumbled down, filling the narrow walkways within what seemed to be a city-block-size piece of machinery, and engulfing my troubleshooting crew at great speed and volume.

In order to clear the area of broken paper, it was necessary to pull and kick the colossal, heavy, hot sheets down into vats. Only by clutching on to the safety rail with one hand and climbing over the side to kick the paper down into the vats, while in fear of falling into and being chewed up by those spinning beaters, could we usually accomplish the work.

From the point where the pulp entered onto the seemingly endless wire to the reel was a great distance. My job didn't require that I understood just how it was done. I just knew how a soft, watery, slightly-clinging mass could be changed within seconds to an eleven-foot roll of crisp, tough newspaper stock.

However, I saw the process at the plant. Earlier work experience had exposed me to the felling of logs, and at the paper-making factory I learned how those logs— wet, dirty and bark-covered hours earlier—became a giant web of paper that comes out after going through a calendaring machine that gave the paper a glossy finish to then be wound upon a reel at the rate of feet per second.

The experience educated a young man to be "aged in wood."

Pat O'Brien enjoyed talking about his connection with jobbers, lumber camps and old-time 'jacks. He grew up in the Adirondack North Country when lumbering was still big business. The ring of the axe and the thundering crash of the giant trees that punctuated the otherwise silent atmosphere in the virgin forest were strong in his memory.

He fielded many lumbering questions, including who those men were, how they existed, what they did, their philosophy of life and details of the lumbering firms that hired them.

Pat made it very clear that while the old days might seem exciting and colorful, I should have no illusion about the forestry industry. The work was hard, the hours were long and there was constant danger. In his later years, he worked for the Gould Paper Company and later as a scaler for the Georgia Pacific at Lyons Falls, N.Y.

"I recall my son once telling me that he wanted to grow up and be a lumberjack just like me," O'Brien told me. "I didn't cotton to his admiration of my timber industry profession because of the long hours, hard dangerous work, and long periods away from home. I could have killed him!"

Pat didn't pull any punches with me either.

He was a gifted story teller right up to his death. Pat's the only person I know who insisted on two grave plots and stones. One stone has the typical inscription. In another burial plot his headstone reads: "See, I told you I was sick."

On my last visit with Pat he handed me a copy of this poem, "Log Drive: You or the Devil or God," which he wrote on September 10, 1980. Pat had a "feeling" for the logger of earlier days. His poem captures the risk and hard life involved in what he called "following the wood by water." Each time I pass by the Constableville cemetery my thoughts drift back to him. Courtesy Lyons Falls History Association

Adirondack TIM-Berrr!

Chapter 27 | William J. O'Hern

Growth and Reproduction of the Forest

The Adirondack Forest Preserve is state land. The part of New York State's constitution that has to do with conservation is Article XIV, which says that all state-owned Forest Preserve Lands "shall be forever kept as wild forest lands. They shall not be leased, sold or exchanged, or be taken by any corporation, public or private, nor shall the timber thereon be sold, removed or destroyed."

Article XIV guarantees the preservation of the Forest Preserve. I believe Gifford Pinchot's quote speaks to Article XIV: "The purpose of conservation (is): the greatest good to the greatest number of people for the longest time."

Over the decades many have questioned if the Forest Preserve is best served by prohibiting cutting of trees. I don't believe the question is even debatable.

My comments on growth and reproduction of the forest focus on private land—small and large parcels.

I look on logging my small wood lots as a natural thing. I see my own forest management practices as a way to derive an economic benefit and at the same time promote recreational opportunities, create a home for wildlife, and protect my woods—making them healthier and allowing them a more pleasing appearance.

Logging can be a means to those ends.

To learn the best way to go about achieving those goals, I'd suggest finding a trusted forester.

Back in the early 1980s I sat with Donald "Red" Perkins. He was born in the first frame house constructed in Old Forge in 1896.

He told me about how he became a lumber jack in 1909. His father lumbered at Third Lake where the family owned a sawmill. At 13, he said, "I was skidding logs with a team of horses."

Loggers engaged in forest management practices. Courtesy Lewis County Historical Society

I gathered a lot of local logging history from him about saloon fights, the rough and tumble nature of 'jacks, the "bawdy houses" in Utica that lumberjacks loved, how demanding the work was in the old-style logging days. What I wasn't prepared to hear was descriptions of the careless lumbering operations that he emphasized "made thousands of dollars at the expense of the environment."

Donald Perkins started out relying on logging to make a living but he cared about the forest.

Old-style logging method. Logs were stacked in great piles on the frozen surface of a river called a "landing" to await spring break-up. Courtesy Lewis County Historical Society

Retired forester Mart Allen thinks in a similar vein. On a late winter day in 2019, 91-year-old Mart and I talked—well really, he talked while I listened.

Mart began by pointing to a favorite lithograph that hung on his wall. It was of a German forester, one of the legions of Europeans who influenced Gifford Pinchot in his battle to establish American forestry.

In reflection, Pinchot said of his profession: "I had no more conception of what it meant to be a forester than the man in the moon.... But at least a forester worked in the woods and with the woods—and I loved the woods and everything about them…."

Mart Allen feels similarly. Proudly lined up on a shelf next to the lithograph sit his prized American Forestry Series textbooks: *An Introduction to American Forestry; The Theory and Practice of Silviculture; Commercial Timbers of the United States; Forest Mensuration; Forest Insects; The Management of Farm Woodlands; Economics of Private Forestry; Cost Control in the Logging Industry;* and *Range Management.*

During our chat about woodlot management, I heard a lot of technical lingo I didn't understand and practical information I understood. A forester knows a lot about the growth of trees.

Silviculture was not something my co-workers talked about at Crockett's Sawmill. It deals with the life cycle of trees—growth and reproduction. Frederick S. Baker, F.E., author of *The Theory and Practice of Silviculture*, writes: "The forester usually aims to grow the maximum amount of bole wood, which is the equivalent of lumber, in the shortest amount of time. To accomplish this, he has to understand the growth habits of the forest in general and how they may be bent to his purpose."

Addressing that goal, Mart first broke into the life cycle of the tree after the seed has germinated and the seedling has sent down its radicle, spread its first leaves to the light, and is no longer supported by stored food materials.

He then moved on to when the forest is mature and ready for the logger's saw. It is then that the forester's attention turns from the problems of forest growth to the question of securing reproduction of the stand of timber, involving seed production, dissemination, germination, and establishment.

To me this is pure science, so I was surprised when Mart told me forestry is an "inexact science."

Only then did I learn how greed and dishonest practices come into play. "I could go on all day," Mart said, "citing examples of foresters I'd never trust." It was here that Mart's wife, Nancy, broke into the conversation, proudly saying, "Mart Allen is the most trusted forester in Old Forge." To that I'll add that he is one of the good guys who care about the forest throughout the Adirondack Park and beyond. I say that because I have heard so many people heap praise on him, his honesty, and his commitment to the well-being of the forest for generations to come.

So what's the best solution for private forest land as opposed to the Adirondack Forest Preserve, which contributes very little, compared to what it might contribute, toward a stable economy?

A forester's function includes problems of forest growth to forest regrowth.
Courtesy Lewis County Historical Society

I've learned from Mart that small and large land owners need to measure the health of their own forest. With the help of a trained forester, they will need to look at every element in the system. That may sound like a lot, but all that's needed is a checklist and some time to look around in the woods to determine what nurturing the ecosystem needs

Many people believe that woodlands should be left alone—that it is almost sinful to cut down any tree. The truth is that woods sometimes need a little help from us to keep them healthy. Trees face threats from natural disasters and invasive species. A good woods steward deals with these with advice from a good forester. People who trespass on your land can threaten the health of your forest too, running over seedlings with ATVs and snowmobiles or cutting trees that don't belong to them. If your trees are damaged or in a state of decline, they'll need your help to regain their vigor. However large or small your woodland is, by keeping it healthy you also contribute to the broader ecosystem and to the natural resources of your community. And it doesn't stop there. Everything is interconnected, so you will be bolstering the ecosystem of your state, your country, and even the entire earth.

Before I left Mart's house that afternoon he handed me a paper he had prepared titled "How to Judge a Woodlot."

The long-time forester notes that, stimulated by technological advances, modern thinking in which lower-value trees are left standing close to higher-value trees to encourage them to grow up instead of out has changed the appearance of harvested timber stands to make them look denser.

Since that's really what he was saying I suggested some edits and a title change. I have included Mart's handout he so generously wrote for me below. A foresters' educational background is far different from that of a novice like me, but I include his information so readers can grasp a sense of how forester language while coming across as a forward-looking common sense in silvicultural matters.

Loaded trucks headed to Gould's mill was once a common sight in Lyons Falls, N.Y., 1949.
Courtesy Lewis County Historical Society

Adirondack TIM-Berrr!

Chapter 28 | Mart Allen

Why Woodlots Look Different from Each Other: How to Judge a Woodlot

"Without natural resources life itself is impossible. From birth to death, natural resources, transformed for human use, feed, clothe, shelter, and transport us. Upon them we depend for every material necessity, comfort, convenience, and protection in our lives. Without abundant resources prosperity is out of reach." —*Gifford Pinchot*

A layman once asked me about differences in the appearance of harvested timber stands. He was a very mature woodsman and outdoor enthusiast who had noticed a marked distinction among various timber tracts over long periods of time.

Time has brought about stark differences in the appearance of timber stands as it has in all things in nature. Various technologies have been incorporated into operations, which has expanded the size, scope and appearance of job sites and overall complexion of residual stands, which are less visually satisfying now than they once were because of the changes in the various uses of wood and in their value to industry. Trees that once were considered for limited use had their value enhanced by technology. Others trees achieved value that previously were thought to have none whatsoever. This became particularly noticeable in the Adirondack region of New York State.

Changes in technology made it possible to open up mixed hardwood stands to abruptly and convert trees into various grades of pulp unlike previous grades. These were trees that were left standing because their removal was too costly, trees that consumed space and nutrients that could have been better and more economically used for producing timber. This had a markedly huge impact on the appearance and value of Adirondack timber stands.

Prior to this period the only species that were routinely cultivated by clearcutting were the coniferous species, primarily red spruce and eastern hemlock. This practice was carried out mainly because the shallow root systems of both species made them very susceptible to windfall and because of the nature of their regeneration and tolerance to other species during their growth. As a rule of thumb, hardwood species normally are cultivated by other methods and thus their growth results in more or less uneven age classes that produce an entirely more dense appearance.

My forestry training taught me that the best use of lower-value species was in their "training" of certain other more valuable hardwoods. In other words, many of the lower-value trees that would qualify only for pulp or pallet timber should be left standing to coax the higher-value trees to grow up and not out. The reasoning behind this premise is greater today thanks to modern technology.

Healthy woodlot. Courtesy Lyons Fall History Association

Looking east from Otter Brook bridge in the Moose River Plains, circa 1950s. Forest regrowth has dramatically changed this scene. Courtesy Lewis County Historical Society

There is a perception in some quarters that this has caused some to believe that what once was saw logs and veneer is now pulpwood. This stems from the drumbeat of the paper companies' alleging that leaving any of the lower-value species behind was detrimental and financially inadvisable during timber harvests. This is hard to defend when comparing the relative value of the two products. A certain percentage of those lower-value trees are still more valuable, in my experience, in training other hardwoods than in their value for pulp.

Regardless, much of the above I believe is the true nature of, and reason for, the difference in the way recent timber stands appear in contrast to times past. Think. Appearances have great value.

The old-time logging camp is a part of history. Courtesy Lewis County Historical Society

Chipping debarked waste slabs was an important changes in technology as well as providing sawmills some additional income form otherwise waste material. The International Paper Company was one of the pioneers in the use of chips from mill residues in the paper mill at Ticonderoga, New York. The chief supply was made possible, at first, largely through the efforts of John Eaton in establishing central chipping plants at Rochester, Vermont, and Chestertown, New York.
Courtesy Lewis County Historical Society

Successful maple sugar woodlots rely on proper woodlot management. It is estimated that America's northeast small woodland properties total something around 11 million acres of forest land. Some foresters have referred to that commercial forest land as a "problem in American forestry"—meaning in most cases land owners would benefit from talking to a forester who could develop a woodlot primer to show the essentials of woodlot management. Courtesy Lyons Falls Historical Association

ADIRONDACK

TIM-BERRR!

Part Four

End of an Era

Early bark lumber camp shack. This vintage photo was found in Cora and Ted Luther's house on Goose Pond Road in Harrisville, N.Y. Courtesy Ross Young

Adirondack TIM-Berrr!

Chapter 29 | William J. O'Hern with Mart Allen

END OF AN ERA

The days of the old-style methods of logging that Barbara Bird had experienced were over by the time Mart Allen began his career as a New York state forest ranger in 1958. Six years earlier Bird had published *Calked Shoes, Life in Adirondack Lumber Camps.*

Three decades had passed since she had begun to experience life in various Gould Paper Company lumber camps. Bird's narrative revealed details of lumbering life and tales of wildlife to thousands of visitors who knew the Adirondacks only as a recreational destination. She devoted one chapter to experiences with camp cookhouses and her short involvement as a substitute cook during the absence of Billy Williams, Camp 7's cook.

Linn tractors relieved much of the brute suffering and made it possible to haul logs long distances. A tractor could make a twelve-mile round trip twice in a day. When Barbara Bird visited the Moose River landing, below Camp 9, she said, "I marveled at the mechanical ingeniousness of man."
Courtesy Lyons Falls History Association

Bird recalled, "Cooking became my chief occupation, and it took time and ingenuity to produce adequate variety in our meals. The supply of fresh foods was short, although there was no lack of other provisions."

Ginger cookies, pies, and cakes comprised her first day of cooking in a wood-fired kitchen range she dubbed the "Iron Elephant." In reality, the baking in the cookhouse was done in a Blodgett bake oven she described as, "capable of baking twenty loaves of bread at a time."

Moose River, spring 1896. With the first call of the robin, Adirondack log drivers start to move their "sticks" downstream. Barbara Bird experienced similar log driving scenes on the same river throughout the 1920s. Courtesy Lyons Falls History Association

In seemingly no time at all she baked, "four pies, a mammoth loaf cake" and a batch of ginger cookies followed by extra-large baking powder biscuits that met the approval of the 'jacks.

"The fuel for all cooking was wood, of course," Bird pointed out. That for immediate use was piled with great care near the stoves. There was never any chance that green or wet fuel would be found in that lumber camp kitchen.

"My success with baking made me attempt a full menu. I experimented with a tender beaver, which I cleaned and trimmed carefully and placed between two loins of pork in a big roasting pan. This was kept in the oven for many hours at a moderate temperature. The result was not half bad, if you could forget what it was you were eating. It was not as good as venison, but tasted much better than bear meat."

There were no further culinary trials with wild meat. Instead she became more skilled baking practical hot breads: Johnnycake, biscuits, muffins, gingerbread and rolls. Flapjacks and coffeecake replaced morning toast.

And there was a wide choice of main dishes such as a salt pork and vegetable concoction named Jagasee, Spanish Rice, Sauerbraten, steaks and other savory foods.

Log drivers Willie Snyder and Charles Austin did not do their job with ballyhoo. They needed to ride logs and handle pike poles and peaveys skillfully—or quit. There was no in-between. White water men couldn't wise-crack themselves out of a jam and no alibi would save their life if they had to "ride her out." Courtesy Lyons Falls History Association

Tons of food supplies came into camp on tote sleighs. She explained, "The idea was to transport supplies for the summer operations while the good ice roads made travel easy. It was an ordeal to tote over corduroy in summer, when coffee in the bean, fresh meat and other perishables were carried. "

Barbara's husband, Roy, enlightened her on proper food storage. "Dry groceries such as barrels of flour, sugar, canned goods and cases of tea can be safely stored in one end of the cookhouse. But the storage of fresh vegetables poses another problem." They needed to be "kept cool in summer and kept from freezing in winter, when the temperature" might drop to thirty to forty degrees below zero, Fahrenheit. That is why cookhouses were located near a spring or year-round brook and why there was always a "hillock or step bank close by where a root cellar was dug out."

A properly constructed earth shelter insulated with straw and a ventilator would safely hold a variety of root crops, barrels of vinegar, salt pork and other meats.

Forestport saw mills were once the heart of business in the Birds' hometown.
Courtesy Lyons Falls History Association

This was not the type of cookhouse Mart Allen visited near Balsam Lake in the Moose River country. Wilfred Dechene's camp had electricity, freezers, and gas cooking stoves.

By the 1950s technology had changed, and mechanized harvesting methods pushed out the horses, bobsleds, axes, two-man saws, pike poles and need for deep-woods lumber camps. Later, even more efficient tools and modern equipment have made the memories of the oldsters who remember those first improvements as prized as those of the older generations had become.

Mart Allen, who at this writing [2019] is 91-years-old, is an example of the men and women I have had the privilege of knowing who, while recognizing that computers and sophisticated machinery have taken over the logging industry in the 21st century, fall back on memories of an earlier time. Change is inevitable. Transformation from "old" to new will always occur, and with change comes the recognition that memories become more important to preserve as a historic record of the past.

Learning a cook's little girl was sick with quite a fever, Barbara Bird put fresh oranges, aspirin, Vicks™ Vaporub and an enema bag into a small pack basket and walked from Camp 7 to Camp 5.

She recalled, "We found the distracted mother and father trying to persuade the little patient to eat. They were offering her roast pork. The suggestion of orange juice instead of the meat won approval. Roy and I offered to wash dishes. Sick child or not, the lumberjacks would expect supper to be ready on time.

"Half an aspirin tablet in addition to the other treatment must have produced a cure for we saw the child playing contentedly when we stopped to see her a few days later. She had given us quite a scare. A sick child in a lumber camp thirty miles from a doctor is no joke."

Courtesy Lyons Falls History Association

Mart Allen closes this chapter with his memories of the food in a typical Adirondack logging camp.

> I have thought about it many times, how to describe the experience of eating in an authentic old-time lumber camp. It is something that will not ever be duplicated again, at least in my neck-of-the-woods.
>
> When I first began my working career in the great north woods, there were still several working lumber camps scattered

about in the remote parts of the Adirondacks. I had the privilege of being a table guest in two of the camps and count them as among my most enduring and memorable experiences.

I had a camp on my beat as a New York State Conservation Department forest ranger in the Moose River Plains area near Balsam Lake. I used every excuse I could to stop by around mealtime or for coffee break with the cook. His doughnuts were the old-fashioned fried cakes my mother made.

The first Adirondack camp I had the pleasure of eating in was near Conifer, N.Y. where my best friend Morgan Roderick and I were visiting to apply for a job. Thankfully, we did not get the job, but were invited for supper. Being new to the routine but fortified by the knowledge of the protocol and etiquette associated with camp dining, we hung back and felt our way into the process.

Mart Allen enjoyed his time talking with old-time bushworkers who recalled life in early logging camps. Photographer Dante O. Tranquille. Courtesy Town of Webb Historical Association

The table was all set and the food was placed in bowls and on platters; the men then took their places and began to eat. The cook and the assistant cook stood guard, surveying the entire scene, alert to replenish any dish that started to get the least bit empty. Dead silence reigned over the entire scene, with signs and gestures the only means of communicating that one of the diners was requesting some item be passed their way.

I knew from stories I had been told that the food was great, but I was bowled over by the amount and variety of the dishes. There were at least four kinds of meat, each prepared a different way, the same for potatoes and gravies. The amounts and varieties applied to the vegetables and desserts as well. Every meal was a smorgasbord of solid wholesome food sans any frills one might find at a conventional smorgasbord.

A typical-looking lumber camp kitchen. Photographer Dante O. Tranquille. Courtesy Town of Webb Historical Association

Both breakfast and supper were table-busting extravaganzas laid out before the men who soon absorbed the vitamin and calorie overload wrestling the timber from hill and swamp out to the various mills. Most carried their lunches unless their work brought them back in the vicinity of camp at noon. The

A modern wood-burning stove made a warm, inviting spot to gather around.
Photographer Dante O. Tranquille. Courtesy Town of Webb Historical Association

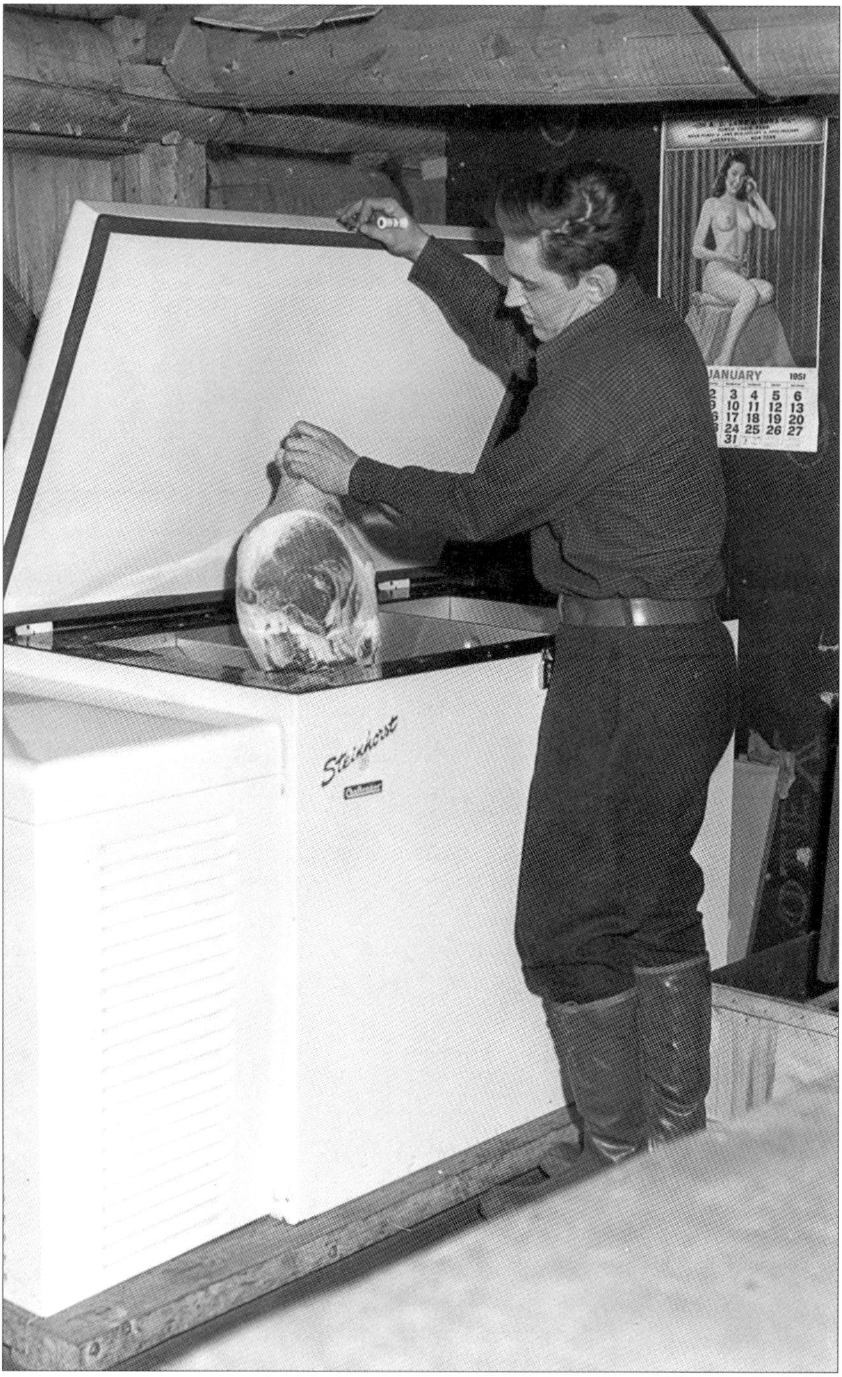

1950s food storage included large chest freezers.

Photographer Dante O. Tranquille. Courtesy Town of Webb Historical Association

work was grueling and the men needed all the energy they could get to keep going.

Traditionally, Adirondack lumberjacks in large part were bound to camp for extended stays simply because of logistics, and the time constraints that daily travel would entail. The food was a big incentive for recruiting workers, much in the same way submarine sailor chow reportedly does for the Navy. Now I will have to see if my best friend Roderick backs up my analogy from his personal experience with sub fare.

Peeling mounds of potatoes the old way. Photographer Dante O. Tranquille. Courtesy Town of Webb Historical Association

The Rev. Frank Reed, in his book *Lumber Camp Sky Pilot* [1965, second edition], writes in great detail about lumber camps in general throughout the Northeast. He indicates that at their peak during World War I, there were 150, but that the number declined to only twenty in 1933, during the Great Depression. They began to increase in 1938 to sixty camps, and by 1940 employed 3,000 men. By the 1960s, the camps as everyone knew them became pretty much a memory.

Rev. Reed's book (and movies, now digitized) are the most insightful look at the history of logging in the northeast, with many photographs depicting life in a logging world that was dangerous, exciting, and productive.

Power machinery and equipment had replaced much of the more physical work in the timber camps of 30 to 40 years ago when Mart dropped in. Photographer Dante O. Tranquille. Courtesy Town of Webb Historical Association

Adirondack TIM-Berrr!

Chapter 30 | William J. O'Hern

DECHENE'S LUMBER CAMP THROUGH TRANQUILLE'S CAMERA

Dante Tranquille (December 19, 1905–April 9, 1981) of Utica, N.Y., was a well-known and award-winning central New York photographer. Tranquille worked for many years as staff photographer at the Utica *Observer-Dispatch*.

He received many awards during his career and was honored when two of his photos were selected for "The Exact Instant," a show of 100 of the best news photographs of the century at The Museum of Modern Art in New York. The Town of Webb Historical Association photographic collection contains many of his Adirondack Park photographs taken in the 1940s and '50s.

Dechene's Camp bunkhouse, Moose River Plains, 1959. Wilfred Dechene was a logger who resided in Tupper Lake. He had an extensive program for Donald Rice on the south branch of the Moose River in cooperation with Clarence Strife. Wilfred's father Auguste lumbered in the Adirondacks for many years. His first job was as a jobber for the Newton Falls Paper Company in 1898. Photographer Dante O. Tranquille. Courtesy Town of Webb Historical Association

Wilfred Dechene. Photographer Dante O. Tranquille. Courtesy Town of Webb Historical Association

OPPOSITE TOP: **Chain saws, chipper chains, crawler cranes, log and trailer trucks, bulldozer blades, hydraulic connections—the list of tools and equipment could easily go on. While a well-manned and managed cook house is of the utmost importance in a lumber camp, so too is the need for a skilled mechanic and a well-equipped shop. Dechene's Balsam Lake camp, while far off the beaten path, had facilities manned by experienced technicians who were ready to adjust, repair or completely rebuild just about any piece of equipment.** Photographer Dante O. Tranquille. Courtesy Town of Webb Historical Association

This 'jack is sharpening his chainsaw. Modern cutters were just as skillful as the old-timers but out-paced their former counterparts who could have turned out only four or five cords daily around the turn of the 20th century. Photographer Dante O. Tranquille. Courtesy Town of Webb Historical Association

P&H

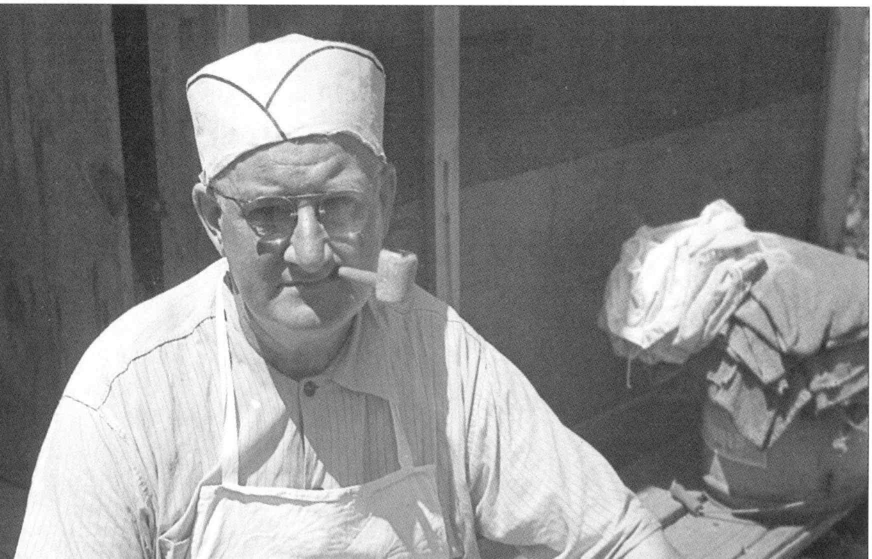

OPPOSITE TOP: **Mechanized equipment like this loader made much easier work of uploading single 16-foot logs at Wilfred Dechene's landing in the Moose River Plains near Inlet, New York.** Photographer Dante O. Tranquille. Courtesy Town of Webb Historical Association

OPPOSITE BOTTOM: **A cookee (a cook's assistant) takes a smoke break. Cookees typically learned the trade on the job. Knowledge of a variety of tasks was needed to keep the vital kitchen procedures flowing flawlessly.** Photographer Dante O. Tranquille. Courtesy Town of Webb Historical Association

Machines eventually replaced horses, and men worked an eight-hour day. Dechene's International caterpillar winches hardwood logs to a landing. Photographer Dante O. Tranquille. Courtesy Town of Webb Historical Association

Slow-moving black bears were not uncommon camp visitors. Photographer Dante O. Tranquille. Courtesy Town of Webb Historical Association

OPPOSITE TOP: **The kitchen was the absolute domain of the cook. Here the cook prepares a roast. By 1959 menus and food choices were wide-ranging. No longer were cooks limited to old-time staples like pork, molasses, beans and bread prepared in a variety of ways.** Photographer Dante O. Tranquille. Courtesy Town of Webb Historical Association

OPPOSITE BOTTOM: **Cookhouse dining manners greatly changed over time. The old rule of no talking at the table was rigidly enforced and a man was given his walking ticket if he abused it. In Dechene's era they talked quite a bit—but the gabbers were seldom the lumbermen. They were usually some visiting big-shots.** Photographer Dante O. Tranquille. Courtesy Town of Webb Historical Association

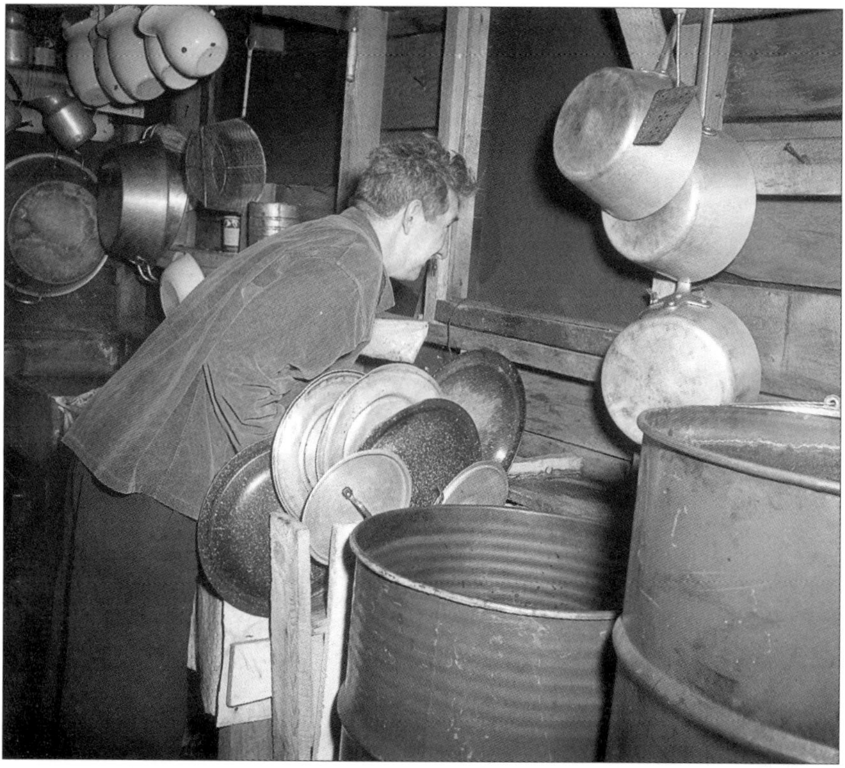

OPPOSITE TOP: **The photographer caught this cookee peering at the bears from inside the kitchen. They were undoubtedly attracted to the delicious smells emanating from the building.** Photographer Dante O. Tranquille. Courtesy Town of Webb Historical Association

OPPOSITE BOTTOM: **Watching the lumbering bears from a safe perch.** Photographer Dante O. Tranquille. Courtesy Town of Webb Historical Association

Camp bears provided abundant material for Tranquille to capture with his camera. While the bears hoped for leftovers, camp residents and visitors alike alternated between fascination, fear and frustration. Photographer Dante O. Tranquille. Courtesy Town of Webb Historical Association

The lens of Dante O. Tranquille's camera captured high-quality photographic images of logging-camp life and of the men who would be the first to admit they got pretty good meals—a fact Mart Allen would corroborate to this day. Photographer Dante O. Tranquille. Courtesy Town of Webb Historical Association

This snapshot might tell the story of two not-so-trusting loggers when bears came into camp.
Photographer Dante O. Tranquille. Courtesy Town of Webb Historical Association

ADIRONDACK TIM-BERRR!

Part Five

EYEWITNESS TO LOGGING

Eleanor Shue was pretty near like every wife at Lyons Falls whose husband worked in the paper mill or out in the woods. She knew all about logging and paper marking and that Karl's routine was like the other Gould employees—to get up early and start work and work they all would.
Courtesy Lyons Falls History Association

Adirondack TIM-Berrr!

Chapter 31 | William J. O'Hern

EYEWITNESS TO LOGGING

From *Adirondack Logging* by William J. O'Hern

The desire to tell what we have seen is as old as humanity. Silas Conrad Kimm recounts how the drop in lumber profits finished off numerous North Country logging towns that had come into being only because of logging operations, and how hard times led to the theft of fiddle butts.

Fiddle butts are the finest clear butt logs of Adirondack black spruce and were once the principal supply for the manufacture of boards for pianos. Kimm told, "When a man could get as much or more for a single log than for a team load of ordinary lumber, the temptation to hunt for such logs was great, and he hunted for them without regard to ownership."

"Experience alone did not make a good log rider. After years of trial a man may be able to stick on a log after a fashion, but he must have a certain native aptitude if he is to become an expert. The grace of an expert log driver is like that of a bird in flight, and his quickness, precise judgment and superb poise mean life or death." —Barbara Bird. Courtesy Lyons Falls History Association

A January 10, 1889, Rome *Daily Sentinel* article, "Thieves Cut Down Forest Trees," tells that the state's forest commission received almost daily reports that the best spruce trees were being cut down. In 1889 butts were "worth $25 a thousand feet in the log." Fiddle butt timber has a fine straight grain, free from knots. "They are sawed into boards five-eighths of an inch thick. This is planed down to half an inch and made into sounding boards for pianos. Samuel F. Garmon, the chief forest warden, has been actively engaged in endeavoring to catch these depredators...."

Forests have long supplied wood for a myriad of products. Courtesy John Fram

The Rev. Frank A. Reed explained that on December 7, 1941, when the United States was faced with the challenging demands of an overwhelming increase in wood production, "the Northeast, though no longer in the forefront as a lumber producing region, nevertheless expanded its capacity and miraculously supplied 12 billion board feet for the needs of war."

Forests have long supplied wood for a myriad of products. Wood has played an important role in the history of civilization. Humans have used it for fuel, building materials, furniture, paper, tools, weapons, and more. Demand for wood has not diminished, and if anything people have grown more appreciative of fine wood. Our relationship to this natural resource has remained comparatively unchanged over time, and methods of developing and managing woodlands have evolved into some of the best management practices to naturally renew and replenish millions of acres, while ensuring that future generations will have the wood they need for products and the forests they need for recreation.

Life in the Adirondack forests has never been limited to recreation. While countless vacationers to the mountains derive pleasure from sporting activities, logging operations have long been carried on along numerous lakes, rivers, and in the far-off backcountry. Photographer Dante O. Tranquille. Courtesy Town of Webb Historical Association

Look around you. You'll see wood everywhere. So perhaps this is why we take it for granted. Wood will always be a part of our lives despite the prevalence of plastic (which, unlike wood and wood products, takes forever to break down). We are dependent on forest products in so many ways, and we probably can't imagine our lives without them.

Sustainable forestry initiative programs are the best management practices to protect water quality and wildlife. "Sustainable forestry means," according to the American Forest & Paper Association, "managing all our forests to meet the needs of the present without compromising the ability of future generations to meet their own needs. It means practicing a land stewardship ethic that integrates the growing, nurturing, and harvesting of trees for useful products with the conservation of soil, air and water quality, and wildlife and fish habitat."

Even though we can do so many things "paperlessly" now, most people probably don't give much thought to the fact that their electronically-ordered stuff comes in cardboard boxes and is often packed in paper. Of course, these can and should be recycled.

Loggers aren't all cut out of the same bolt of cloth. There was no monotonous menu by 1958. Old-timers often saw no coffee, fresh fruit, milk or vegetables to speak of. Mart experienced just the opposite. Photographer Dante O. Tranquille. Courtesy Town of Webb Historical Association

We owe a continuing debt of gratitude to the forests and the people who work in forest industries. Loggers aren't all cut out of the same bolt of cloth, but some sweeping statements do pigeonhole many loggers. They start early and often work late into the night repairing equipment. They work erratic hours and days. They tend to be independent (some people claim stubborn) individuals who believe in free enterprise, hard work, and the freedom of the out-of-doors.

Lumbermen—part of America's vital workforce. A sawyer and tail sawyer talk in a mill.
Photographer Dante O. Tranquille. Courtesy Town of Webb Historical Association

"Eyewitness to Logging" is an assemblage of vintage logging images that capture the scenes once common around lumber camps, centers of the logging industry built exclusively for the famed lumberjacks. Here you will find photos of early mechanical logging equipment, old-time logging scenes, and personal recollections of life in the lumber shanties.

"Logging with cat at Page." N.Y. Courtesy Lewis County Historical Society

Logging, of course, is still going on. The differences are in the extent of the cutting, the modern techniques and equipment used, and the total disappearance of the old-time techniques and company-owned lumber camps in the Adirondacks and the North Country.

ADIRONDACK LUMBERING WORKFORCE

By 1948, personnel in lumber camps had changed with the passing years. Thirty years earlier, Adirondack woodsmen could have been divided into three major groups: (1) The American woodsmen who came from Adirondack villages or from the lumbering areas of Pennsylvania, West Virginia or New England; (2) French Canadians who came to the states previous to World War I in the early days of the war; and (3) Central Europeans who had come over previous to World War I. These included a large number of Poles and Russians with some Swedes and Lithuanians. There were also a few Irish and Scotch. Courtesy Lyons Falls History Association

OPPOSITE: **Most of the French Canadians settled in northern New York and continued their lumbering activities, while some became operators. Many of their children did not follow a woods-related program but went on to earn advanced degrees, own businesses and follow professional careers. A large percentage of Central Europeans continued in the lumber camps, but most of those did not marry. Thus, American woodsmen decreased in number.** Courtesy Bob Failing

Bob Failing on June 21,1950, three days before his engagement to Cheri L. Houghton.

The Revered Frank A. Reed predicted that by the close of the 1940s, woodsmen of the future would undoubtedly be recruited, as previously, from three possible sources: (1) American young men who attracted by opportunities to lumber jobs where there was more mechanized equipment, better living conditions and the chance for advancement; (2) French Canadians who might or might not be bonded; and (3) some displaced persons from lumbering areas of Europe. Courtesy Bob Failing

The men from all three groups had grown older by 1948 and averaged around fifty years of age. By the latter 1960s they had disappeared from the active scene of Adirondack lumbering. Bonded French Canadians came to the Adirondacks early in World War II to supplement the work of American woodsmen. The average age among them was much younger than that of American woodsmen. These men rendered a real service in a time of scarcity. Courtesy Jim Fram

That a greater appreciation of the forest has developed has been evident, since about 1919. In earlier times when lumber and pulpwood were abundant, few thought about the future supply. As forest resources became somewhat exhausted, men began to think in these terms, and to plan perpetual lumbering programs. By using selective cutting methods, better fire protection, better pest control, and a more effective program of reforestation, foresters sought to provide for an inexhaustible supply of lumber—a renewable resource adequate to supply the needs of coming generations. Courtesy John Fram

SAFETY AND THE USE OF TOOLS, A SAMPLER

Clear all obstructions to get a secure footing before starting a saw. Always inspect trees carefully for loose limbs and rot. Photographer Dante O. Tranquille. Courtesy Town of Webb Historical Association

OPPOSITE: **Safety manuals of the 1950s such as the Woods Safety Handbook by Leland W. Hooker reported nearly 20 percent of all accidents in felling and bucking involved the chainsaw. In almost every case, cuts were sustained because the saw moved suddenly and unexpectedly out of its normal path. It told operators could be trained to recognize the conditions under which a saw would buckle or be deflected, and thus avoid dangerous situations. "A saw has teeth but no brains; the man has to supply those," it counseled.** From the American Pulpwood Association safety poster No. 5

Beaver Falls Loggers. An engine must be shut off except when the saw is actually in use.
Courtesy Lyons Falls Historical Association

Boots with non-skid soles should be worn at all times. Olney Failing's Otter Lake log landing, 1948.
Courtesy Bob Failing

'ATCH OUT FOR FALLING LIMBS

HREE MEN HAVE BEEN KILLED RECENTLY

YOU COULD BE NEXT

Keeping tools sharp is of the utmost importance.
Photographer Dante O. Tranquille. Courtesy Town of Webb Historical Association

Always make undercuts first if it's necessary, top cuts second when bucking.
Photographer Dante O. Tranquille. Courtesy Town of Webb Historical Association

Trousers should be cut off (staged) at a height of eight to ten inches. Heels catch in cuffs and long trousers catch on snags and brush. Cheri Failing adhered to this principle which her husband taught her. Courtesy Bob Failing

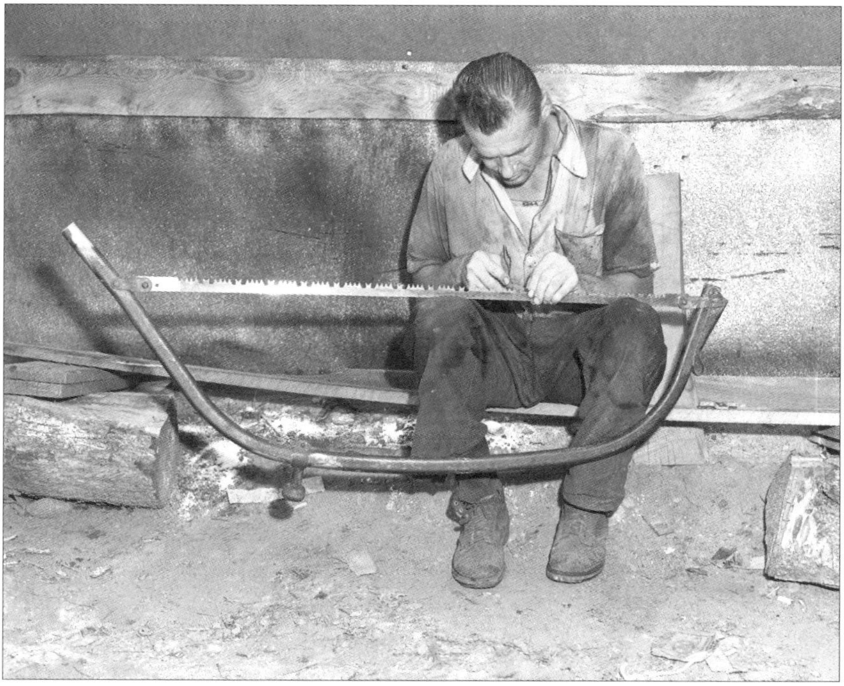

A well-filed saw will cut easily and discourage pushing or riding, which leads to buckling and possible injury. Photographer Dante O. Tranquille. Courtesy Town of Webb Historical Association

Suspenders should be worn instead of belts. Trousers supported by suspenders do not bind at the knee and seat readily as do those supported by a belt. This is an important factor in the woods, where failure to step high enough over a log or pile of brush can cause a serious fall.
Courtesy Town of Webb Historical Association

Camp 2 landing, Osceola, New York. Keep metal wedges in good condition. As soon as the head of a wedge begins to get burred or mushroomed, grind it off. A mushroomed wedge is apt to turn the sledge or axe when it is struck, and particles are easily broken from it and can fly into the eyes.
Courtesy Bob Failing

The Rev. Reed conducting an outdoor service for lumberjacks at a camp at Little Moose Lake. Lumber camp ministers earned the respect of even the most hardened 'jack. One reason was their engaging manner of speaking; another was the level of their-thought-provoking sermons.
Photographer Dante O. Tranquille. Courtesy Town of Webb Historical Association

Rev. Reed talks with lumber camp cooks. It has been said The Reverend spoke to his congregation on "a person-to-person" level. He understood the lumbering life. A logger's life was not an easy one. They faced accidental death, complications from injuries, sickness, disease, and in extreme cases, death from alcoholism and suicide. These were some of the realities of life, and The Rev. Reed worked them into his lumber camp services. The Reverend's 1949 "Hoeing One's Garden" is an example of how, in his Gospel stories, he illustrated real life values to which the lumberjacks could relate. Photographer Dante O. Tranquille. Courtesy Town of Webb Historical Association

O.F. Failing's trucks parked on Sunday, Talcottville, New York, 1953. Courtesy Bob Failing

A Rev. Reed Gospel story

St. Francis of Assisi, hoeing his garden, was asked what he would do if he were suddenly to learn that he was to die at sunset that day. He said: "I would finish hoeing my garden."

This seems to me an answer to all the troubled young people these days who are beginning life in a world that appears to hold no security for them or for anyone, young or old.

Why should they bother to go to college when the atomic war is just around the corner? Why should a young wife have a baby when the ceiling may collapse on its crib? Why should one paint a picture or write a song or begin a novel?

We can't be sure of anything, these young people say, not now, or next year or the year after that. "Why should we try to make a life for ourselves?" they ask. "Why should we go to classes or take examinations or get married or look for an apartment or try for a job? Next spring, or some spring too frighteningly near, it may all go, the life we have begun. Our world is in deadly peril, we have lost the promise of tomorrow."

St. Francis put the answer in a simple metaphor: Go on hoeing your garden. The task is still here—the house to build, the book to write, the examination to prepare for. If the future looks dark, so did it on the morning before the first Christmas—and in the year 5000 B.C. And however dark it is, we shall meet life better if we have fulfilled the present to the best of our ability. Today is still ours, along with the obligations to live it to the full. As St. Francis said, we must go on hoeing our garden.

In Rev. Reed's service as a lumberjack sky pilot, he helped to connect the loggers with the outside world through his paper, *The Lumber Camp News*. The Reverend is about to deliver a bundle of newspapers. In this snapshot he is removing bundles of the *News* that will be left in lumber camps.
Photographer Dante O. Tranquille. Courtesy Town of Webb Historical Association

Rev. Reed logged hundreds of miles during his ministry walking from camp to camp.
Photographer Dante O. Tranquille. Courtesy Town of Webb Historical Association

Two integral parts of Rev. Reed's missionary work were to advocate for safety and to be an understanding friend. Photographer Dante O. Tranquille. Courtesy Town of Webb Historical Association

RICH MEMORIES

Linn tractor on Sand Hill at Camp 9 returning with a string of empty sleighs, having deposited logs at the Moose River landing. Courtesy Lyons Falls History Association

Perfect teamwork. There was no bungling, no hesitant decisions among these men.
Photographer Dante O. Tranquille. Courtesy Town of Webb Historical Association

"Those caterpillar diesel engines [that supplied power to the camp] were designed to burn low-cost, non-premium fuel—single orifice fuel injection valves gave users thousands of trouble-free service hours," shared one former mechanic. Courtesy Bob Failing

A Former Logger Recited a Prayer Long Memorized

"God, our Father, we ask for guidance
and strength during the day of the hauling season.
Give us, we pray, suitable conditions to haul
the wood, strength for our daily toil, and grace
sufficient for each emergency.

"Enable us to see our task as an opportunity for
service to Thee and to our fellowmen, and
to work with a will for the achievement of great goals.

"We ask this in Jesus' name. Amen"

Kelsey Lord skidding logs, Otter Lake 1948. Still, those mechanical and power tool sounds remain rich memories more than decades after they routinely echoed through the Adirondack woods.
Courtesy Bob Failing

At Alder Creek, N.Y. gas station, 1950. Swancott and Failing pointed to youthful images of themselves. They had been close friends with Harold. All three often worked together. It's never possible to find a way to tell all the remembering.

Shirley Linck recently gave Harold's (her deceased husband) album filled with snapshots from years of logging jobs to the Black River Canal Museum in Boonville, N.Y. Nary a picture had been labeled. Logger Leigh Portner recognized scenes of one log job "over at Copper Creek," he claimed. Portner made the judgement based on his knowledge of a particular Linn tractor shown.

This past Fall I revisited a group of long-retired loggers well into their eighties and early nineties—men who had a hand helping Adirondack Logging become a reality. With the exception of one semi-active eighty-five-year-old logger, they no longer work in the forest today. But it's not surprising they claim to still hear the grinding of truck and tractor gears, the whump of tall spruce collide in to a thick blanket of powder snow, and the roar of whining chainsaws and say they can still smell the thick odor of gasoline and diesel suspended in cold, dense air. Photographer Harold Linck. Courtesy Bob Failing

Harrisville, New York, 1959. Courtesy Bob Failing

I Miss You Most

"Funny how winter brings back a memory," a logger told me. "Late snow and colder weather always gave a boost to the hauling program after a late start and a mild January." Courtesy Bob Failing

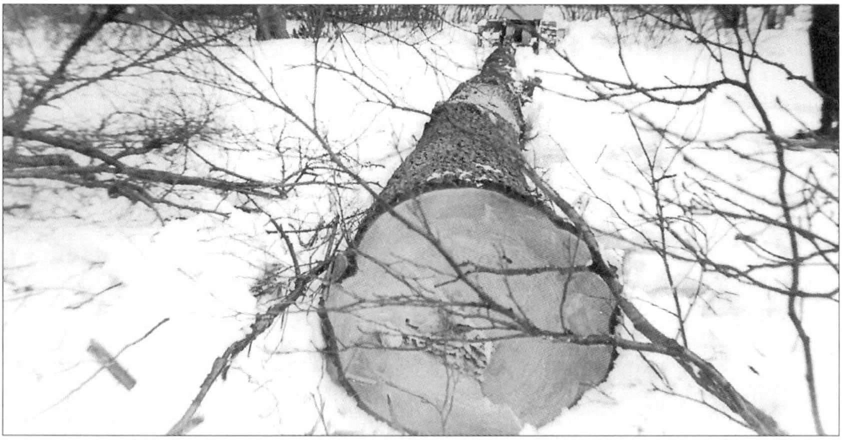

The man was nostalgic as he talked about a winter's night. He said, "The world was colder than any other time of year," but that was when he felt closer to those old logging memories than any other time of year. For a long moment he grew silent before ending his thought, "Yes, don't God know I miss you most in the wintertime." Courtesy Bob Failing

The logger continued his memory. "And it's funny how summer still found you always on my mind. In the loneliness of fall, I can almost hear you call. But it seems I miss you most in the wintertime."
Courtesy Bob Failing

LUMBERING MEMORIES NEVER FORGOTTEN

Lumbering was once big business in the Adirondacks. The forest resounded with the ring of the axe and the ear-piercing whine of a chainsaw. Teamsters listened to their horses' "language"— neighs, whinnies, nickers and snorts. And all heard the thundering crash of the giant trees, and the pulsing roar of diesel-powered motors that punctuated the otherwise silent atmosphere. These sounds—combined with the smells of fresh-cut timber, cookhouse meals, horses, and diesel—are not easily forgotten.

Adirondack Logging[4] has answered many questions about those men and women who worked in the lumber woods—how they existed, what they did, and why they chose a lumbering way of life. I've also included many details about the logging firms that hired them.

And yet, there exist so many undocumented tales of events that have passed into history with no explanation.

That is exactly what I feel has happened to a series of snapshots taken by photographer Dante O. Tranquille. Throughout the late 1940s and early 1950s he visited Gould Paper Company operations—he stayed in their logging camps, he followed river drivers, and he went into the timber woods, snapping images that interested him.

It has been over sixty years since he took his last logging picture. One website tells he was a well-known Utica, New York photographer and worked for many years as staff photographer at the Utica *Observer-Dispatch*. He received many awards during his career. Tranquille was 76 when he passed in 1981.

The following gathering of photographs is in the collection of the Town of Webb Historical Association and appears here with their permission.

Past memories are often triggered by activating the unconscious through the power of a picture. Wouldn't it be wonderful if some old-timers spotted themselves and remembered the event?

For the sake of history, these select Tranquille pictures exist as a kind of scrapbook, snapshots of life in the lumber camps, and of lives and events and occasions that have blurred over time—and yet will never completely fade thanks to the efforts of a caring photographer who captured poignant moments that are now frozen in time.

We all have distinctly special memories that we cherish and continue to create all through our lives—for ourselves and for others. Tranquille's work highlights the importance of recording those moments that will later spark memories. Otherwise they can easily be washed away as the years pass.

Enjoy a journey back in time.

Gould Landing, North Lake. Horses enjoyed a bath as much as the men. Photographer Dante O. Tranquille. Courtesy Town of Webb Historical Association

Wash day. Hygienic conditions improved over the years. Washing and shaving, mending of clothes and hair-cutting went on when weather was bad or logs weren't moving. Photographer Dante O. Tranquille. Courtesy Town of Webb Historical Association

Lumberjacks thrived under tough conditions but that didn't mean they didn't take time on Sunday to be a bit of a softie. Photographer Dante O. Tranquille. Courtesy Town of Webb Historical Association

Making pies. A cook in a logging camp was an important personage. Photographer Dante O. Tranquille. Courtesy Town of Webb Historical Association

No longer can hunters hop a ride on the Glenfield-Western "Gee-wiz" railroad on its way to Page and Michigan Mills. Waiting are Shawn John Alger, Henry Gremo and Henry Sattler near Glenfield, N.Y.
Courtesy Joanne Sattler

Measuring logs. Photographer Dante O. Tranquille. Courtesy Town of Webb Historical Association

A horse patiently stands by on a warm sunny day awaiting instructions.
Photographer Dante O. Tranquille. Courtesy Town of Webb Historical Association

There was work to be done. No time today to be spinning yarns.
Photographer Dante O. Tranquille. Courtesy Town of Webb Historical Association

Jump starting, was a technique used to get a big sleigh loads of logs moving. The method relied on a luff team that was attached to a block and tackle attached to the side of a sleigh.
Photographer Dante O. Tranquille. Courtesy Town of Webb Historical Association

Break time. A crew of subdued river drivers. They'd be on the job for the rest of the day.
Photographer Dante O. Tranquille. Courtesy Town of Webb Historical Association

A driver sits atop a pile of logs. Photographer Dante O. Tranquille. Courtesy Town of Webb Historical Association

Men strained and pulled at resistant logs. Onlookers marveled at their knowledge of just which logs to attack in order to keep the log mass moving.
Photographer Dante O. Tranquille. Courtesy Town of Webb Historical Association

The foreman tirelessly traveled up and down the river to make sure there were always the right number of men in the right places. Photographer Dante O. Tranquille. Courtesy Town of Webb Historical Association

BOOM! A small charge of dynamite in ice two-feet thick, would theoretically produce a slow explosion.
Photographer Dante O. Tranquille. Courtesy Town of Webb Historical Association

BANG! A dynamite charge needed to be prepared by a river boss and helper to blast a trouble-some rock in the river that caused a log jam. Photographer Dante O. Tranquille. Courtesy Town of Webb Historical Association

Men would ride logs as if they were glued to them.
Photographer Dante O. Tranquille. Courtesy Town of Webb Historical Association

Not all logs rode free downstream. Some formed "centers" on the heads of islands or boulders.
Photographer Jim Fynmore. Courtesy Lyons Falls History Association

A force of water and logs. These grim battles relied on the ingeniousness and courage of white water men. Driving logs was no child's game. Photographer Jim Fynmore. Courtesy Lyons Falls History Association

Etched in retired white water men's memories were the marvelous spring river drive days.
Photographer Dante O. Tranquille. Courtesy Town of Webb Historical Association

A big truck next to an ever bigger wood pile.
Photographer Dante O. Tranquille. Courtesy Town of Webb Historical Association

Conveyors moved pulpwood between the river to the paper plant in Lyons Falls, N.Y.
Photographer Dante O. Tranquille. Courtesy Town of Webb Historical Association

The former Woodmen's Clubhouse in Thendara, New York once served as the community's four-room schoolhouse. In addition to serving a meeting room and affordable dormitory for loggers and place for banquets, the clubhouse was also used for *The Northeastern Logger* office for three summers.
Photographer Dante O. Tranquille. Courtesy Town of Webb Historical Association

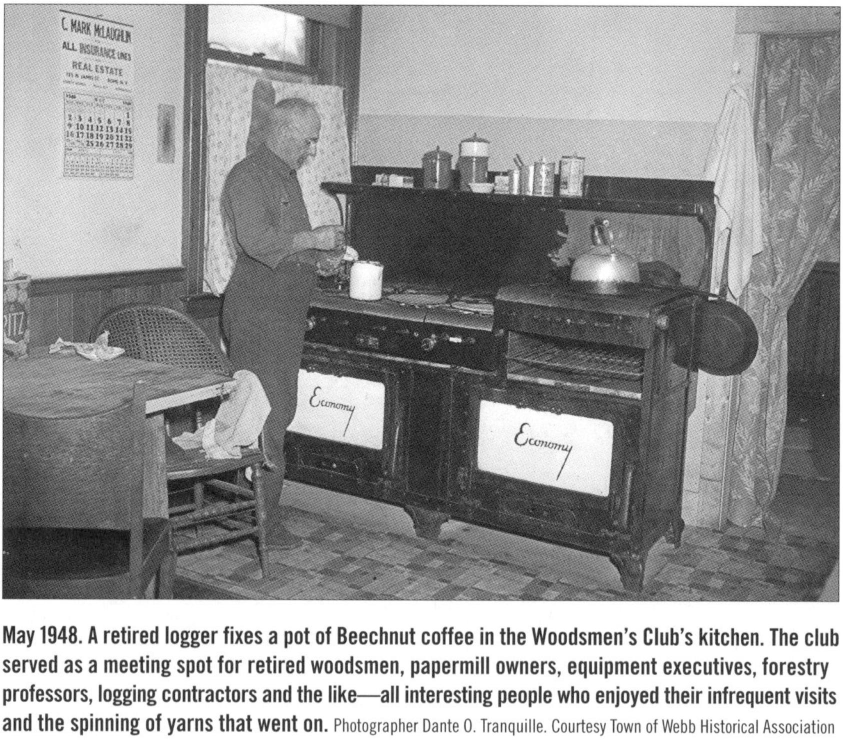

May 1948. A retired logger fixes a pot of Beechnut coffee in the Woodsmen's Club's kitchen. The club served as a meeting spot for retired woodsmen, papermill owners, equipment executives, forestry professors, logging contractors and the like—all interesting people who enjoyed their infrequent visits and the spinning of yarns that went on. Photographer Dante O. Tranquille. Courtesy Town of Webb Historical Association

ADIRONDACK TIM-BERRR!

Part Six

Woodsmen's Heritage

Portable logger's shack on display at the Woodsmen Field Days in Boonville, N.Y. in 2018. Photo by author

Adirondack TIM-Berrr!

Chapter 32 | Mart Allen and William J. O'Hern

WOODSMEN STILL CELEBRATE THEIR HERITAGE

In 1997 Mart Allen attended two of the three-days of annual events at the 50th anniversary of the New York State Woodsmen's Field Days held each year in Boonville, New York. His column "50 Years Later Woodsmen Still Celebrate Heritage" appeared in the August 26, 1997 *Adirondack Express*.

Mart was captivated with the idea of a Woodsmen's Field Days. The concept originated in 1942 with the formation of the Woodsmen's Club in Old Forge and by 1997 had continued for half a century. He wrote, "The first field day was held in Tupper Lake, New York in 1948 to preserve the heritage of logging, lumbering and wood-using industries as exemplified through woodsmen's competitions."

Lumber and paper are tree farm crops. Courtesy The Northeastern Loggers Association archives

"Professional woods workers compete with each other for the title of New York State Woodsmen's Champion and Lumberjack Champion," he wrote. "The latest in industry tools, technology and equipment are displayed, with many finished wood-based products. Nearly every countenance of the forest industry is represented.

One Cut Ahead. Jim Fynmore and his camera was a familiar sight throughout the Central Adirondacks for over fifteen years. Photo Jim Fynmore. Courtesy Ed Fynmore

"The technical and educational viewpoint was represented by three of New York's professional and technical schools. The College of Environmental Science and Forestry and its affiliate, the New York State Ranger School at Wanakena, were joined by Paul Smith's College and SUNY Morrisville with displays. (The) New York State Department of Environmental Conservation added its expertise to the above organizations to collectively educate and to disseminate knowledge and advice to technicians, forest landowners and the public at large.

Jim Fynmore (Rt.) stands outside his Boonville, N.Y. studio with an unknown man. Fynmore's logging photos appeared in numerous magazines. Courtesy Black River Canal Museum

"The Northeastern Loggers Association ably represents the logging industry. Located in Old Forge, it publishes a monthly magazine dedicated to advance progressive, environmentally sound and safe timber harvesting practices to its many members through the 22 Northeastern states it covers. The entire industry is predicated on one general theme 'Managed Forests Provide Forever.'

"The latest figures available to me [1997]...show some encouraging statistics. Over 60 percent of New York's 30.2 million acres is forested, more than any other Northeastern state. Forest land increased by 1.2 million acres between 1968 and 1980, a century-old trend that continues today.

"Eighty-three percent of the 18.5+ million acres of forest land is classed as commercial forest land. State-owned Forest Preserve portions of the Adirondack and Catskill Parks account for most of the noncommercial forest land. Ninety-four percent of New York's commercial forest land is privately owned, with non-farming citizens owning the largest amount.

"Timber growth and removals increased between surveys with 2.8 cubic feet of timber being grown for every cubic foot of timber being cut.

"Thirty-year projections show a slight decline in forest land, but increasing timber volumes. With forest conditions improving, numerous forest management opportunities exist to further improve the conditions and substantiate the validity of the theme, 'Managed Forests Provide Forever.'

"Timber production is only a small part of the value received from New York's sustainable forestry initiative. Improved air and water quality, benefits to wildlife and recreation are only a few of the many other advantages also derived."

Allen "highly recommended that "people attend future field days. He predicted even "the most uninterested will find solace in the many and varied food offerings. At the very least you will leave with an overwhelming desire to operate heavy equipment."

In 2019 the annual August event continues, made even more popular by the varied Lumber Jack and Jill events and multiple other wood-related spectator happenings that appeal to men, women and children alike. Up-to-date information as well its history are available on the New York State Woodsmen's Field Day website and on Facebook. A history of the event also appears in *Adirondack Logging: Stories, Memories, Cookhouse Chronicles, Linn Tractors and Gould Paper Company History from Adirondack and Tug Hill Lumber Camps* by William J. O'Hern (In the Adirondacks, 2016).

Come and Eat It. Fynmore's photographs captured every day scenes to the natural beauty of the mountains, lakes, forests and streams. Photo Jim Fynmore. Courtesy Ed Fynmore

Men at Work in the Woods. Photo Jim Fynmore. Courtesy Ed Fynmore

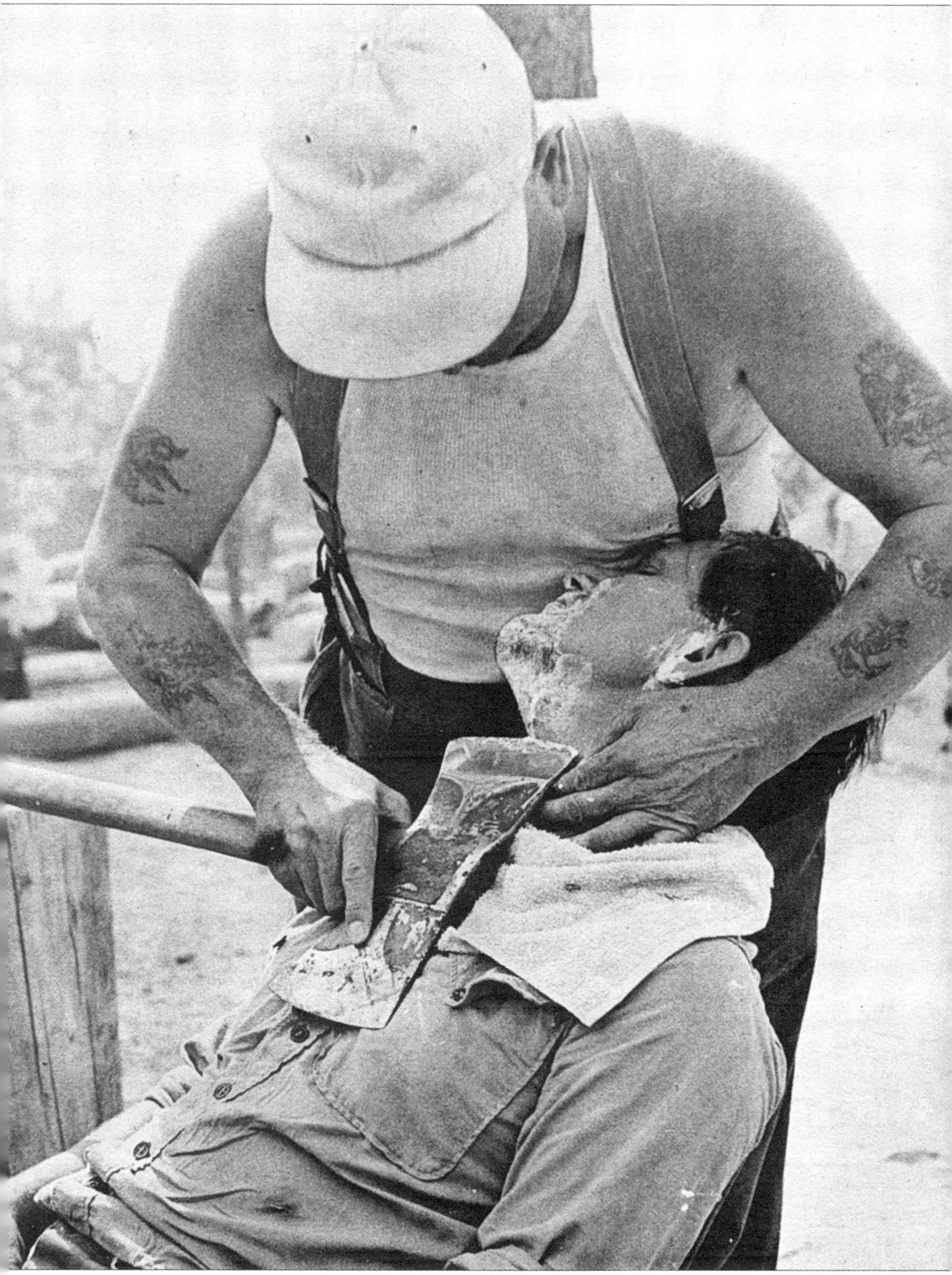

Close Shave. Photo Jim Fynmore. Courtesy Ed Fynmore

Woodchopper. Photo Jim Fynmore. Courtesy Ed Fynmore

Shades of Paul Bunyan! Oil Heat in the Bunkhouse. Photo Jim Fynmore. Courtesy Ed Fynmore

The Big Day at Tupper Lake. Photo Jim Fynmore. Courtesy Ed Fynmore

The Drive. This once typical scene has given way to top-heavy log trucks.
Photo Jim Fynmore. Courtesy Ed Fynmore

Wilderness Log Road. Photo Jim Fynmore. Courtesy Ed Fynmore

Sky Pilot, Rev. Frank A. Reed. Photo Jim Fynmore. Courtesy Ed Fynmore

Box Seat. Photo Jim Fynmore. Courtesy Ed Fynmore

A typical Lumber Camp Root Cellar with Deep Freeze. Photo Jim Fynmore. Courtesy Ed Fynmore

A snowbound Lumber Camp. Photo Jim Fynmore. Courtesy Ed Fynmore

Bucksaw. A lumberjack of old. Photo Jim Fynmore. Courtesy Ed Fynmore

BOOM! Dynamiting a Log Jam. Photo Jim Fynmore. Courtesy Ed Fynmore

A Few Minutes' Work. More spectators attended the annual Woodsmen's Field Days as the years went by. Photo Jim Fynmore. Courtesy Ed Fynmore

This Gould Paper Company camp looked like a ghost town during the day when all the 'jacks' were at work in the woods. Photo Jim Fynmore. Courtesy Ed Fynmore

Adirondack TIM-Berrr!

Chapter 33 | Jim Fynmore and William J. O'Hern

THE ANNUAL NEW YORK STATE WOODSMEN'S FIELD DAYS

"Lumberjacks liked to test their strength," Jim Fynmore wrote in his 1955 *The Central Adirondacks* picture-storybook. Fynmore was a noted Boonville photographer who provided dozens upon dozens of high-quality photos for the Rev. Frank Reed's *The Northeastern Logger* magazine. He also covered the early Woodsmen's Field Days begun by Reed.

"In the early days," continued Fynmore, the 'jacks "carried chips on their shoulders and would fight at the drop of a peavey. Central Adirondack lumber camps witnessed many spur-of-the-moment contests between Tupper Lake and Utica that served as airings for bare-fisted Jack Dempsey types.

"The lumberjack of the old school is fading from the picture. Mechanization has brought into the woods younger men who adapt themselves more easily to mechanized methods, men who are proud of their athletic ability.

A late 1940s NYS Woodsmen's Parade in Tupper Lake, New York. Fourth from left, The Rev. Frank Reed.

Courtesy Goff-Nelson Memorial Tupper Lake Library

The LUMBER CAMP NEWS

VOLUME 10; NUMBER 3 | PUBLISHED MONTHLY AT OLD FORGE, NEW YORK | JULY, 1948

Field Day Planned-Old Forge July 17

PROGRAM

Parade 12:30 P. M.—

Participating units: Town of Webb School Band, New York State Music School Band, Old Forge Fire Department, Covey-Pashley Legion Post 893, The Boy Scouts, The Girl Scouts.

Cross-Cut Saw Contest—

Each two-man team will roll logs onto the skids, saw them into short lengths and pile them between stakes. Contestants will be judged by the quantity sawed and piled in ten minutes. Prizes: 1st team, $50.00; 2nd team, $20.00.

Axe Chopping Contest—

Contestants will be judged by the quantity of blocks chopped and piled in fifteen minutes. Prizes: 1st place, $40.00; 2nd place, $15.00.

Bucksaw Contest—

Contestants will be judged by the quantity of blocks rolled onto skids, sawed and piled in fifteen minutes. Prizes: 1st place, $40.00; 2nd place, $15.00.

Tree Felling Contest—

Contestants will each chop down a tree and attempt to drive a stake by felling the tree onto it. Prizes: 1st place, $40.00; 2nd place, $15.00.

Chain Saw Contest

Two-man teams will roll logs onto skids, saw them into blocks and pile them. Contestants will be judged by the quantity piled in ten minutes. Prizes: 1st team, $50.00; 2nd team, $20.00.

Forest Fire Fighting Demonstration—

This demonstration is put on by the New York State Conservation Department.

Log Rolling Contest in Lake—

This will be an elimination contest with two river drivers to a log, each trying to roll the other off. The winners on each log will compete with each other until first, second and third place winners have been determined. Prizes: 1st place, $40.00; 2nd place, $15.00.

Awarding of Prizes—

Awarding the Grand Prize—

The Grand Prize will be a Mall Chain Saw furnished by the Slade Tractor Company of Albany, N. Y.

A BUCKSAW CONTEST

CONSERVATION PLEDGE

I

Pledge as an American
To save and faithfully to
Defend from waste the
Natural resources of
My country—its soil
And minerals, its
Forests, waters,
And Wildlife

Truth

"Truth is within ourselves; it takes
no rise
From outward things, whate'er you
may believe.
There is an inmost center in us all,
Where truth abides in fullness.
—Browning.

Frank McCormack Dies at Bangor, Maine

Frank McCormack passed away suddenly at the E.M.G. Hospital, Bangor, Maine, Saturday, May 22, 1948.

Frank was formerly employed by the Parker Young Co., Lincoln, N. H., and the Houlton Plywood, Houlton, Maine. For the past two years he worked for the Atlas Plywood Corp., Howland, Maine.

He is survived by his wife, Mrs. Jennie (Boucher) McCormack, and two daughters and one son.

Frank was a splendid workman, an efficient superintendent, a courteous host, a real friend and a Christian gentleman. He will be greatly missed by a host of friends in the woods.

Committee Planning Interesting Variety of Contests, Prizes

A Woodsmen's Field Day will be staged near the beach on Old Forge Lake on Saturday, July 17. On this occasion many woodsmen will match their skill and strength in a variety of events in which the axe and saw play a prominent role

The program will include contests with the bucksaw and the cross-cut as well as chopping contests and log rolling. The New York State Conservation Department will give a demonstration of forest fire fighting, and several distributors of woods tools and machinery will exhibit and demonstrate their latest equipment.

The list of judges includes John Curry of the U. S. Forest Service, H. V. Hart of the St. Regis Paper Company, Sid Lawson of the Atkins Saw Company, Mr. E. Blue of the New York State Conservation Dept., Prof. Edward F. McCarthy of the New York State College of Forestry and Perry Leary, State Forester of Vermont.

The Committee

The Field Day is being promoted by the Woodsmen's Club. It has been planned by a committee consisting of Louis Seheult of the Finch Pruyn Company as chairman, James E. Davis of the Gould Paper Company, Clarence Strife, Joseph Lindsay and Don Kiefer of the C. J. Strife Lumber Company, Roy Lavoy of the Oval Wood Dish Company and Philip W. Burdick, Supervisor of the Town of Webb.

Kinne Williams, Al Woodford and Ernest Blue of the New York State Conservation Department are the committee in charge of the Forest Fighting Demonstration.

A local committee composed of Leo Burke and Floyd Farmer of the Old Forge Fire Department, Jake Berkowitz of the Covey-Pashley Post of the American Legion, and Leslie Wilcox of the Lions Club are in charge of local arrangements including the parade.

Substantial prizes will be given for each of the events. The Grand Prize of the day will be a Mall Chain Saw provided by the Slade Tractor Company of Albany, N. Y.

July 1946 announcement in *The Lumber Camp News.* Courtesy The Northeastern Loggers Association

"Organizing the talents of these new citizens of the forest was introduced 17 years ago [1938] by the Rev. Frank A. Reed of Old Forge, the respected 'sky pilot' of the lumberjacks. A Woodsmen's Club became the starting point for what is now the Woodsmen's Field Day."

Fynmore found the event "picturesque" and said it was "worth traveling miles to see."

July 1954 Woodsmen's Field Days. The Northeastern Loggers Association's archives

The annual three-day event highlights the old and the new.
Photographers George Capron and Betty Hoag. Courtesy *Boonville Herald.*

Lumber Jill and Lumber Jack competitors come from all over the United States.
Photographers George Capron and Betty Hoag. Courtesy *Boonville Herald.*

2018 NYS Woodsmen's Field Days official guide booklet.

The Woodsmen's Field Days continues today. Due to the event's size and the planning work involved, the non-profit organization the NYS Woodsmen's Field Days, Inc. employs two full-timers and one part-timer throughout the year and relies on hundreds of dedicated volunteers.

Held annually the third weekend in August, the three-day action-packed event now attracts over 45,000 spectators to the village of Boonville; it is billed as one of the top three lumberjack (and lumber Jill) shows in the United States by professional lumberjacks who engage in fierce competition throughout the weekend.

A mixture of Jim Fynmore's early scenes and images of recent events grace this chapter.

67th N.Y.S. Woodsmen's Field Days parade on August 15, 2015.
Photographers George Capron and Betty Hoag. Courtesy *Boonville Herald.*

Adirondack TIM-Berrr!

Chapter 34 | William J. O'Hern and Mart Allen

MART'S BARK

Listen to the voice of a mixed woodland forest. Not to the raucous duet of crows, or the buzz of swarming deer flies, or even the love-struck chorus of peeping tree frogs emerging from a warming vernal pool.

Listen to the voice of a mixed woodland forest. Not to the raucous duet of crows, or the buzz of swarming deer flies, or even the love-struck chorus of peeping tree frogs emerging from a warming vernal pool. Listen instead to the harmony of the falling leaves, the soft plunk of beechnuts, acorns and hazelnuts, the snap of twigs, the faint gurgle of spring water emerging from deep inside a rocky ledge, the scamper of furry critters in their search for nuts and berries, and the periodic crash of a large widow-maker's limb. Some of what falls nature has intentionally shed in its continuing renewal cycle. Some has been dropped and been redistributed by animals feeding in the canopy; some is the result of a natural catastrophe—a tree so overpowered by the muscle of a hurricane-force wind that its anchoring roots are ripped from the earth and it collapses under the power of a horrific storm.

All these sounds in the Adirondack forest are indicators that the ground beneath it is building deep with debris. Over time a spongy layer of humus-rich topsoil cushions the forest floor. To a traveler whose footstep is familiar with the northern woodlands, with its hemlock, spruce, pines, and tamaracks and stands of beech, maple, cherry and oak, the soil underfoot is justifiably rich.

What happens to all the litter? It gets recycled. Fallen organic matter slowly breaks down and decomposes thanks to a partnership that includes snails and earthworms, ants, fungi, roots of living trees, bacteria, and other non-visible agents that continuously dismantle vegetation into essential nutrients for a new generation of plant life.

Foresters who work in the woods are more familiar with this renewal. Making their living in a forest setting, they also know the fine art of conservation.

Mart Allen has been plowing through the legacy of the Adirondacks since he arrived after getting out of the Army in 1947.

Allen has lived in Thendara, New York, with his wife and family since 1958. He is a retired forest ranger and private preserve manager. It was Allen's weekly column for the *Adirondack Express* that first got my attention. He wrote about Adirondack folks—the young and the old-timers and events, times, and incidents that portrayed the Adirondack land.

Mart relishes history. He also never backs away from controversy, often punctuating his point with stinging remarks. I call that Mart's Bark. It's part of what makes him such an interesting person.

I remember in February 2006 there were newspaper articles telling about the impending plans to close down the existing boat launch site on Seventh Lake and automobile access to the Moose River Plains Recreation Area. From many people's point of view, these plans represented two more steps in limiting public access to public land. They were followed by announcements that the Adirondack Council testified on the Adirondack portion of the state budget that the state was in need of more funding to address "key Adirondack programs." Mart wrote: "What programs have they ever proposed other than limiting use of state lands to exclusive special interest groups?"

"I graduated from the New York State Ranger School at Wanakena in 1951, and in the fall of 1952, I took a job as a field engineer building a General Motors plant in Syracuse, New York. In late winter the work slowed and the boss asked for a volunteer to take a leave of absence. I decided it was time to test the trapping waters."—Mart Allen. Courtesy Mart Allen

That got under Mart's skin. He shouted loud and clear in his February 21, 2016, column, "To Make a Long Story Short" in *Adirondack Express.*

> If you have followed the pages of the *Hamilton County News*... you have seen the writings of Jack Leadley Sr. Jack is a native Adirondacker who has remained true to his roots, not one of the backsliders who have sold out to the "Protectors." The Protectors are the plethora of so-called environmental groups who are hell bent on "Saving" the Adirondacks. Their idea of saving it is regulating and restricting any activity on private and public land that does not meet the criteria they deem acceptable to their way of thinking.

Columnist Allen went on attack, referring to what the Adirondack Park has become since the Adirondack Park Agency (APA) "was imposed on the region in 1972. It opened the flood gates for the Protectors, a pretentious bunch of elitists that have imposed their ideas on everyone else as to how all real property in the Adirondacks is to be used, under the guise of protecting it from harmful environmental activities."

In 1952 there was no limit on beaver in Adirondack Park wilderness areas, and I decided to set up a camp and stay through the end of beaver season in April. This was long before the advent of snowmobiles, and all travel would be by foot, mostly on snowshoes. Courtesy Mart Allen

"Beavers were stretched on yellow birch hoops, skins sewed to the frames with chalk line and a needle made from a key used to open sardine cans. I did a lot of improvising at the camp." —Mart Allen.
Courtesy Mart Allen

Leadley and Allen shared a common opinion. Both felt that much of what they enjoyed about the Adirondack Park was being taken away from them for what they saw as "shallow and phony reasons." Allen said, "I use the word phony instead of disingenuous because it describes the situation much more accurately and succinctly."

Allen continued:

> The original Protectors were all wealthy and many were owners of large tracts of land. Nearly all obtained their wealth through extraction of the earth's natural resources and my guess is in this age of enlightened awareness they wanted to salvage some semblance of decency plus retain the sanctity of their playgrounds. They found an able ally in Governor Nelson Rockefeller, who after smarting from brother Lawrence's [sic: Laurance's] failed attempt to make a National Park of the region found a way to stick it to the opponents and help his rich friends enhance their holdings by ramming through the Park Agency.

Allen and Leadley both penned a number of columns that lamented the changes in the management of state land since the inception of the APA. Allen roared about "…the radical views imposed on it and the D.E.C. [Department of Environmental Conservation] by the Protectors. I say imposed because every unit management plan instituted by the D.E.C. was dictated by representatives of the Protectors and the D.E.C. were willing and complacent co-conspirators in any action that gave them more power and extended their empire."

"There weren't many dehydrated foods back in 1952, but I utilized what was available. Potatoes, slab bacon, salt port, oatmeal, rice and canned milk rounded out my stores. Fresh beaver provided most of the meat, and I learned several ways to cook it." —Mart Allen. Courtesy Mart Allen

You can bet this was only the tip of Mart Allen's sting at what rubbed his bark. In another 2006 *Adirondack Express* article that piqued his interest, he voiced concern:

> The Association for the Protection of the Adirondacks is outraged by the removal of trees along Route 3 between Tupper Lake and Saranac Lake. How about the three acres of Forest Preserve land that was cleared on Route 28 north of the Rondaxe road this

past summer? I only wish the Protectors would be as assiduous in their tracking of the Park Agency and D.E.C. in their monitoring of the regulations in place for activities on the large private land holdings, but then of course they are not going to step on the toes of their biggest financial backers. The real suckers are the people like myself who once believed they were really serious about protecting the Adirondacks and not genuflecting to the "Iron law of oligarchy," which is to survive at any cost.

In the final analysis all we little folks can do is bitch the way Jack, Stan Ernst and me [sic: I] do while trying to keep our sense of humor and make damned sure as I now do to not support such a complete bunch of phonies.

The Credul Equipment Co. gave Mart Allen a 1959 Polaris snowmobile to test over his beaver trap line. Marty reported the early model did meet his needs in the in the rugged Adirondack League Club backcountry surrounding Gould's former Camp 9 near the south branch of the Moose River.
Courtesy Mart Allen

Allen is also an interesting man to listen to in person. Sitting around a warming tent stove with Allen's good friend, Jack Plumley, at Jack's deer hunting camp at Chubb Pond, the friends would talk politics, reminisce and share personal experiences in the company of Jack's sons.

Jim Plumley remembers that his father told his boys not to push Mart's buttons. "We knew the subjects that could ignite Marty's anger," he told me.

Camp 9 was Gould Paper Company's main headquarters from 1930 to 1947. It was located a short distance from the expansive Canachagala Stillwater, the place known as Moose River Landing where logs were stacked in preparation for the annual spring log drive. Courtesy Lawton Williams

It was better to learn from Mart what hunting and fishing used to be like and learn about some wild foods he knew were available throughout the year just waiting for some young entrepreneur to come along and harvest them.

By wild I mean the gathering of wild fish, game and plants from the fields, woods and waters. The variety of the different wild foods one can find is surprising. Mart likes them best when fresh.

He'd say, "Maybe it is still some small part of the old hunter-gatherer in the far reaches of my psyche, but I seem to derive some inner pleasure in being able to provide for my family as my early ancestors once did."

Mart believes the extra effort to hunt, fish and gather wild food is well worth the extra cost.

Wild leeks are a favorite food of the Allen family. He finds them in most hardwood stands on the periphery of the Adirondacks. They are easily gathered in large quantities. Mart shares:

> Their flavor is much stronger than the domestic varieties found in the produce section in food stores and tends to go a lot further. A small handful makes a delicious potato leek soup. I freeze them in the vacuum seal pouches and they keep perfectly. They are best gathered in the spring and enjoyed by many raw the same way green onions are. Be warned they are not for the faint of heart and garlic pales in strength when they are eaten raw.
>
> Mushrooms are another wild food I enjoy and any excess are frozen and keep very well for later use. Wild mushrooms can be poisonous, and unless one knows what they're gathering they should avoid them. I find the best way to freeze them is lightly sautéing before freezing. They were the first food I tried canning and I ended up spoiling a big batch of pasture mushrooms, the most eminently edible of all the wild varieties.

September 20, 1946. Young Mart Allen is heading off to the Army and his siblings stop to pose for a picture with their brother. Lt. to Rt. Clifford, Andrew holding Joe the dog, Adelia and Mart.
Courtesy *Adirondack Express*

Wild game constitutes the largest segment of wild foods we preserve. The key to all wild meat is meticulous cleaning and freezing as quickly as possible; the same goes for fish. Deer are probably the most-utilized wild game, and proper handling before preserving or even eating fresh for that matter is important to flavor, while improper handling is the direct cause of many people not caring for venison. The age and condition of the animal is of course a factor as it is in domestic meats as well. Cooking and seasoning depending on the various cuts is the final factor determining the quality of the end result and determines whether or not the diner enjoys the meal.

Warden Camp, Moose River. Courtesy Mart Allen

Mart admits he can honestly say he had eaten venison for years but never thoroughly enjoyed it until he discovered the truth of the above statements. For years, everything but the choicest cuts was boned and ground into hamburger.

Mart had never had a roast that he could honestly say he truly enjoyed. It all changed when he discovered a marinade for all furred wild game:

Recipe **Roast Venison**

1 Quart Water
1½ Cups Vinegar
2 Chopped Onions
1 Carrot, Chopped
1 Clove of Garlic
1 Teaspoon of dried Thyme
4 Sprigs of Parsley
12 Whole Black Pepper Corns
1 Tablespoon Salt

Simmer 1 hour, cool, and place meat in marinade in refrigerator for 24 hours. This is enough for a 6 or 7-pound venison roast.

For years Mart said he was fooled into thinking wild food was free food, but that is very seldom the truth with gasoline and auto expenses being what they are today. It does give me a certain sense of satisfaction to know that if I had to I could put together some semblance of a meal without going to the grocery store for the ingredients. Wild foods are no different than many domestic foods; handling, preparation and method of cooking determine how they will taste."

Jack Plumley's permitted Chubb Pond deer camp. Courtesy Jim Plumley

Acquiring and eating wild foods is about as close as Mart will ever get to knowing what has been carried down through the centuries from his earliest ancestors, who gathered and hunted for every bit of their sustenance. He likens it to "the male human in all his glory."

Mart Allen and Jack Plumley share past deer hunting tales. Courtesy Jim Plumley

Mart will tell you straight out what he misses. He wrote about it in his September 13, 2005, *Adirondack Express* column, "The Adirondacks I Once Knew."

> I miss the Adirondacks I once knew, the days of plaid shirts, wool pants and Bean boots, the days when the Adirondacks was noted for trophy deer and wild brook trout. A time before state and private land were restricted in their use to preclude any activities special interest groups deem inappropriate.
>
> More than anything else I miss the people who wrested the improvements we see today from the rugged wilderness, the people who created the nucleus around which what we see today was built. I miss the culture and philosophy that went with it.
>
> Many of my favorite people are what I call woods people.

> Their livelihood, if not principally derived from the vast tracts of uninhabited forestland, was tied to same. Early on, recreation in the form of hunting, fishing and timber harvesting were the backbone of the Adirondack economy. Many people were engaged in a combination of both.
>
> They were proprietors of hostels catering to early recreationists. Many were guides showing sportsmen where and how to harvest the area's vast resources of fish and game. Great numbers harvested the unbroken tracts of prime timber. Some furnished the various goods and services to all segments of the communities. They were all rugged individualists noted for their trust and honesty.
>
> I came to the Adirondacks in the beginning of a once-typical hard winter, one of the eight newly-appointed forest rangers under the first open competitive civil service examination for the position. We were not paid much by today's standards, with the exception that we had secure year-round work. We were welcomed into the community and quick to recognize and appreciate the warmth and generosity unique to early Adirondackers.
>
> The year was 1958 and somewhat at the start of a change in a culture that was waning.

Mart feels 1970 was a watershed year for change. From then to the present time he sees "forestry, hunting and fishing are in their death throes. An area that once drew much of its wealth from extraction of natural resources does so in ever-declining degrees.

> "It does not mean that it's not a positive trend but merely it's hard for me to accept. It's difficult to see a way of life you embraced and saw so many positive aspects of denigrated and discarded. Trashed and replaced with what in my humble opinion is a shallow and disingenuous façade of pretentiousness. Worse yet is to see the people who represented the old ways gone forever, a once homogeneous population reduced to an insignificant handful. The history and character of the region are preserved and lauded by the nouveau Adirondack elitist; the people's culture and way of life, however, are not."

In 2013 Mart made up his mind to add a good book that portrayed the common people of the early Adirondacks. His *Adirondack Character Builds a Community* (MHA Press) shares selections from his long-running column in the *Adirondack Express*. Those essays tell a true picture of the people he was writing about very effectively—Adirondackers he is proud to have known who have been a part of the culture and spirit Allen holds dear.

Sit with Mart at his kitchen table that offers a panoramic view of the middle branch of the Moose River that flows past just feet away, and the forest backdrop beyond, and you can imagine how sensitive Mart probably grew as he penned his Adirondack community columns.

Ask him about his Adirondacks and he will tell you "The hearth makes the home and people make the community."

> Sure I was particularly drawn to the area by the beauty, remoteness, waters and wildlife, but without ever really being aware of it realized people truly are the reason we grow to love where we live. At least that is the way it was with me when we settled here years ago. Sadly, I see much of that changing as our population changes.

End of another day of Adirondack logging. Courtesy Mart Allen

Mart Allen (foreground), dressed in a Conservation Department's ranger uniform early in his career. Allen remembers: "I don't recall who the two men or the location. I do remember we were surveying the boundary lines on private property that was under consideration for purchase by the state."
Courtesy Mart Allen

When I came here I assimilated into the community, adapted to its ways and respected its traditions, became part of the culture. I did not radically try to bend everyone to my way of living or impose my lifestyle or views on everyone else. The last thing I wanted to be was a social engineer. I came not as an invader but to assimilate. I see that all changing today.

The Adirondacks have always been unique in their ruggedness, the terrain, weather and remote areas which have been the last to be settled. The people who settled it and opened it up were unique as well. They paid their dues in blood, sweat and tears as the saying goes. The new pioneers buy their way into the community, and that's all well and good as long as they do not come as invaders.

> Our region is also unique in that it is the only region in the entire United States that is zoned by others from outside of the region. It has caused much angst and consternation for many who see long-established traditions altered or eliminated altogether by those who paid little or no dues in its initial development. It is a story that is played out in nearly every region of the world when people become a minority and subject to outside interests who covet what they have developed. The sad part is few if any outside of the region are even aware that it is happening. Textbooks used to teach real estate professionals here in New York state that it has no zoning laws. The instructor in Utica, N.Y., where I took a course was not aware of the fact that it was false. I would not be surprised if this was the only state in the nation that has zoning laws pertaining to a particular region.
>
> It has instilled a feeling of frustration and hopelessness in many of the older residents who see their sovereignty usurped. I feel more of an affinity toward the old-timers who represented the early spirit of the area than I do the invaders. They are slowly disappearing and their memory and culture is fading from the local scene. They have tried to understand and welcome those who have discovered the riches of the area. The invaders tend to try to make it in an image that is diametrically opposed to the concepts and culture of the old timers. In large part many newcomers have been attracted to the area because of the openness the early residents showed to them. It unwittingly helped to bring about the conditions early residents no longer understand and now resent. They see their mores and traditions being supplanted by those they, in many instances, came here to escape.

Mart takes his commitment to his Adirondack community seriously by driving to visit with old-timers at the Sunset Nursing Home in Boonville, New York, where residents recuperate or spend their final days. He encourages everyone who knows of a friend or neighbor who has to spend some time there to stop in and say hello. "And while there," he adds inspirationally, "give a smile and a friendly greeting to anyone else you may see who looks like they need some encouragement. There are many."

It's Mart's appreciation for the natural world and people that I find inspiring. He shares with you his feelings about a vanishing way of life. There are stories about children and grandchildren you would otherwise never know. He is resigned to the fact that the clock cannot be turned back, and without speaking about it he is thankful he and others he once knew had the chance to enjoy what time they did have.

Paper mill workers, 1889. Mart empathized with long-retired, proud and rugged North Country individualists who were neighbors, many the children of pioneers. During visits with old-timers conversation centered on former days of farming, mill, the wild beauty of the Adirondack North Country—even the old days of rumrunning. Courtesy Lyons Falls History Association

Of old-timers Mart has known he has said much that others can learn from:

> I knew, admired and respected many older people when I was growing up. I learned a great deal about life from them, from some on how to conduct my life and from a few how not to. I never realized it until I became much older, however.
>
> I was reminded of one of them the other day when my truck began to skip and buck, or at least I thought it did. For some reason I thought of Horace Turner, an old mechanic in my hometown of Phoenix, N.Y. He had a reputation for being the best, and if you had a problem with your vehicle he could fix it when no one else could.

I had just such a problem with my old '32 Ford with the '36 rebuilt V-8 engine. My problem was that it would lose power when I pulled out to pass, which happened to be everything ahead of me on the road.

Horace worked out of his garage in back of his house in a residential section of our village, which was unusual for even that day and age. He worked strictly on a reservation basis and you were lucky if he found time to favor you. I got lucky, and when my appointed time arrived and I explained my problem he solved it without ever lifting the hood. "I will fix it," he said, "and it will cost you just two dollars. He then lifted the hood, removed the air filter cap, removed the loose felt lining in it and threw it in the trash can. It was being sucked down over the intake on the carburetor when the car reached a certain speed.

The point I am trying to make is not about cars but about people, local characters every community has. Many were indispensable members of the area, and if they were not, at least they were unforgettable people who left a lifetime impression on you.

Bill Willis was one of those people and one of the most irascible people you would ever hope not to meet, but I admired him in spite of it. He delivered freight from the train station to the surrounding areas in his neat and clean small pickup truck, ever-present cigar clenched in his teeth.

Every Halloween we would sucker some new kid to trick or treat old Bill's house while we watched back in the shadows to see the results. Bill would calmly open the door and step out on the porch without ever saying a word, take the poor sucker by the collar, march him over to the edge of the porch and help him off with the side of his foot.

I did learn he had a soft spot for kids who were industrious, enterprising and knew how to respect their elders. I was his paperboy and he always bought a favor from me, a Syracuse Post Standard calendar, for a quarter while telling me I was the best paperboy he ever had. It was a real compliment coming from a guy who insisted on the penny change from the weekly thirty-four cent cost of the paper. I really knew I was doing the right thing when he hired me to help him with freight deliveries in his advanced years when the boxes became too heavy for him.

Bob Woods owned the local meat market and was the friendliest man one would ever meet. He was good to the kids and gave them a free slice of smoked bologna, which the market was famous for, every Thursday when it was made. A practical joker, he sent a friend and me way out on the edge of our town to a farm with a huge package of what turned out to be cow leg bones. He told us the farmer, Gerald Gregg, who was also the Justice of the Peace, would pay us for the delivery. He laughed and gave us ten cents apiece.

Years later a friend and I were ticketed for killing a muskrat that was crossing the road. It looked like $3.75 to us, but turned out to be against the law to take any bird, animal or quadruped on or from a public highway. Another old-timer who I forgave years ago turned us in and we came up in front of Judge Gregg. He fined us $12.50 apiece and offered to cut the cards with us double-or-nothing, showing that he still had his sense of humor.

The list is endless of people none of us will ever forget for one reason or another, and whether we know it or not we all take away something from them one way or another.

I tip my hat to Mart Allen for his thoughts and barbed opinions, his collection of essays, his work as a forest ranger, and his care as a forester, and for his philosophical attitude toward conservation and his tribute toward certain people who in their different ways have contributed to the variety and the improvement of the Adirondack environment. You don't have to share all his opinions to like Mart.

I share with Mart an interest in the Adirondack Forest Preserve and its citizens. Because of that, and also because of Mart's humor, his humanity and his ability to write, I find him an intelligent nature lover, a professional forester and conservationist, and a thinking citizen.

His voice at times might feel as prickly as a porcupine's quills, but it's that delightfully tell-it-like-it-is persuasive style that makes him the lightning rod he can be.

"The Forester at Home" is an essay Mart wrote on January 10, 2006. I think it's a fitting closure, for in 2019 93-year old Mart Allen is at home in his peaceful Moose River setting.

Many of our greatest writers and artists have drawn their inspiration from the environment as Mart has.

> When I supposedly retired in 1992, a good friend gave me a picture that I cherish and it is prominently displayed on our living room wall. It was painted by Ludwig Knaus in 1886, depicting an old German forester at rest in his home. I look at it frequently and picture in my mind's eye what kind of day he is reposing from. From his looks I expect he is not far removed from my own age. I recently returned from an afternoon of marking timber for harvesting on snowshoes, and after settling back in my easy chair in my stocking feet I gazed over at the scene and imagined that we had a lot in common in spite of the time difference.

It is done in dark somber tones with the wall in the background in even darker tones, making one look closely at the objects hanging thereon to discern what they are. In the center of the picture a tall lanky old man sits in a large armchair with one leg draped over an arm. He is dressed in worn, loose-fitting clothing, holding a three-foot-long stemmed porcelain pipe in his mouth, gazing off in the distance with a pensive look. He has slippers on his feet and under a nearby chair with a jacket draped over the back, on the wide rough plank floor, lies a pair of high leather boots. It is evident that he has had a hard day, and one could presuppose he is contemplating the results or outcome of his work.

On the walls in back of him are various trophies of hunts gone by, mounted owls, hawks and an assortment of antlers from members of the deer family. A double-barreled shotgun hangs by a sling on a peg along with a game bag and powder horn. You have to look closely to see an otter skin hanging there as well. A small bird similar to our common flicker or woodpecker is mounted on a tree branch protruding from the wall.

On a small stand to the forester's right, on a crumpled white tablecloth, the only bright color by far in the whole painting, sits the remnants of his lunch. A cup and saucer with a spoon standing in the cup are the only utensils visible.

Mart Allen at his home, March 19, 2019. Mart stands in front of his bookcase of eleven American Forestry Series books. His prized Ludwig Knaus lithograph hangs to the left and out of the picture.
Photo by the author

Above the table is a series of open shelves with some dog-eared papers stacked haphazardly on them. Immediately below them is what appears to be a calendar with the date 1842 on it.

In the far right of the scene is a huge cast-iron stove or furnace that goes all the way to the ceiling. Kneeling in front of the open door facing a glowing fire is a chore girl stoking a roaring fire.

I sat watching a glowing fire burning away in the Earth Stove fireplace insert with the glass door and the electric blower pushing the warm waves of wood-fired heat out into the room, contemplating my day's work much like the old forester in the painting, and weighing the similarities. The fireplace unit sits on a raised stone hearth above two trophy deer heads our son took many years ago. My Bean boots hang on the mantle drying along with my heavy wool socks and grandchildren's snow clothes. Three shelves set to the left are crammed with all sorts of books, many unread by me. A stack of firewood sits to one side on the hearth.

The scene of the old forester captures his way of life and the things that are important to him in much the same way that what I like to have around me say to those who know what they are looking at who I am and what I enjoy. I could never hope to paint a scene the way the artist Knaus did, portraying his character, so I have tried taking a photograph that portrays at least part of mine.

The "Forester at Home" used to be sold by the Society of American Foresters to raise funds for their projects. It is no longer done because the image of the chore girl upset the female members of the society as being too sexist. Some people never will get it, and it's a waste of time trying.

Mart Allen's association with the Adirondack country has been pleasurable and memorable as well as both insightful and incite-ful. It provided him a good living as a forester and a way to vent his annoyances and celebrate his joys as a columnist. No, the land has not remained the way old-timers once knew it, and many may wish it had stayed unchanged. Virtually nothing in life is permanent, though, and I believe all of us have in common a desire for the Forest Preserve to be properly protected and wisely used, as does Mart Allen.

ADIRONDACK TIM-BERRR!

Part Seven

THE LUMBERJACK BUSINESS

"So then I says to him, I says, let's get into the Lumber business . . ."

Adirondack TIM-Berrr!

Chapter 35 | William J. O'Hern

WOOD-RELATED STORIES

I confess that throughout the years of my logging-related research, those evenings I stayed a bit longer at kitchen tables and in living rooms, looking at old snapshots and listening to the diverse aspects of scientific forestry, older methods of logging and logging life, of porcupines, coyotes, white-tailed deer, and the Forest Preserve, I thought how knowledgeable the old-timers were as they shared aspects of their woodland life.

In their own way, each revealed a fresh philosophical attitude toward conservation, and there were tributes to certain fellowmen and women who in their different ways have contributed to the variety and improvement of the Adirondack environment.

Smaller camps featured log bunkhouses with tarpaper covered roofs, and an outhouse out back. These simple structures were warm and comfortable enough for 'jacks' to sleep well after a good day of hard labor. Courtesy of Thomas and Doris Kilbourn. (The Rev. A.L. Byron-Curtiss Collection)

Linn tractor at Whitney Park. Very often today's loggers can be heard to wistfully say they are a bit nostalgic and have a sense of a "wandering, lonely woodsman feeling." It's a wish they could go back to a simpler time and place. It is a sentiment Dan Christmas says hangs in his mind.
Courtesy Patti Bateman Quinn

For instance, Byron Cool told it was not unusual for Gordias Henry "HP" Gould to be seen in the woods, supervising the logging in the headwaters of the Black River. He was a hands-on president, coming up the hard way. To Gould, efficiency and conservation were important.

Earl M. Kreuzer would wax over his time in the timber woods that spanned the era that began with old-style logging and ended with the age of mechanization. He said, "The river has been replaced by company roads and all sorts of mechanical equipment. Six days a week 16-foot-long logs were twitched to central loading areas; teams of horses pulled sleds [sleigh bunks] of logs to the river. This could only take place in winter when frozen earth and snow made a packed surface.

"At the banks the logs were unloaded and piled, readied for the spring river drive. Each crew could prepare tens of thousands of logs during a winter's work. To ensure a continuing supply of timber year after year, the companies used forest conservation practices such as selective cutting.

"The forester would come in and cruise the timberland with his compass, maps, notebooks and so forth. The trees were plucked like you would a garden crop. Coming into an area, they might take a third to a half of the existing volume. A typical operation today with mechanical equipment might take nearly everything."

A Santa Clara Lumber Company ambulance sleigh for transporting sick horses, 1922. Courtesy Mark Friden

In Earl's day, loggers would not have known the word "ecology," but according to J.C. Ryan, another old-time logger, the basic principles connected with that word were very much in the minds of all early loggers, because nothing meant so much to them as having good water to drink and good food to eat. They instinctively knew that keeping the forest healthy would also keep their families healthy, that everything was connected. Today, with our modern conveyances and all types of electrical devices, radio, television, telephone, running water and refrigeration, we take for granted the things that meant so much to the early logger.

While probably more credit goes to their lack of pollution than their prevention of pollution, the early loggers did carry out many preventive measures, and they used only biodegradable materials and rigidly policed their environment.

As I read the transcripts of my interviews, I realized Earl and others were examples of the originals of their days. They were a dying breed, even though that's an overused term—those self-reliant, hard, solitary men—perhaps a bit competitive, and fiercely proud of their skills. Yet their concern for the continuation of a healthy forest for future generations shows a kind of gentleness of spirit one might not expect to find.

Novices who go afield following a logging might have a fundamental misconception about timber harvesting. I did until I learned more about the discipline. Conservation and silviculture have made strides since the early foresters and loggers like Earl.

Simply stated, forests require disturbance to regenerate. Disturbance is a crucial component of forest diversity, and timber harvest provides a measure of control of where and how disturbance occurs.

Today, foresters talk about three main approaches of timber harvest practices: clearcutting, shelterwood and selection methods. While each are different and are applied to specific forest types, they have three commonalities:

- All provide wood fiber for thousands of every-day products.
- All create environmental conditions that encourage the natural regeneration of the forest.
- All improve the ecological, commercial and social values of the future forest.

During the winter, loggers banked logs on frozen flows and stacked logs in "rolling banks" along streams and rivers to wait for spring runoff. When high water conditions were right, blocks were knocked out and the logs went tumbling into the turbulent current. Courtesy Town of Webb Historical Association

Clearcutting can look unsettling to a neophyte's eyes. HP Gould knew it over a hundred years ago.

According to Bill Cook of the Michigan State University Extension's website https://www.canr.msu.edu/news/timber_harvest_methods, "Clearcutting is the solution to forest types whose seedlings or sprouts require full sunlight. Seeds and buds respond well to the warmed ground. The abundance of light produces excellent growth, some of the fastest we have.

"The 'catch' with clearcutting is appreciating how nature did clearcutting before there were people to wield chainsaws and harvest processors. Wildfire, wind, insect outbreaks and floods were common ways nature employed to level large tracts of…forest in order to allow sun-loving forests to regenerate.

"With our tremendous dependency upon forests, the losses from these natural events are typically regarded as negative and something to avoid, if possible. Clearcutting is an economical and ecologically viable way to reduce the negative effects of natural catastrophes, at the same time accommodating the ecological requirements of these kinds of forest types.

Mart Allen explains, "Clearcutting, generally speaking, only makes sense with coniferous species. It makes very little sense in our mixed hardwood stands."

Forestry is a very inexact science and opinions vary. One forester might declare that there are a great many foresters who they would not let mark trees for hardwood.

Cook continues to explain selection harvesting—perhaps the most misunderstood timber harvesting system and certainly the most complex.

"When stands of trees become overly dense, forest health risks increase. Removing the higher-risk trees and leaving the trees with higher potential improves the quality and character of the forest. The partially-opened canopy allows enough light to accelerate individual tree health and vigor, and allows seedlings to grow. The young trees eventually replace the older trees as the older trees either die or are harvested.

"The 'catch' with the selection system lies in the ability of tree seedlings to tolerate shade conditions on the forest floor. Given the diversity of [some forests], it should be no wonder that some tree species will grow in the shade and others will not. For those shade-tolerant tree species, forms of selection management work well.

"The 'dark side' of selection management is when the wrong trees are 'selected' for harvest. High-grading, diameter-limit cutting, and other unscrupulous practices can do serious damage to a forest. Secondly, selectively harvesting a forest type that cannot regenerate under the residual shady conditions can also inflict damage."

Bill Cook, forestry educator. Courtesy Bill Cook

The shelterwood harvesting system, according to Cook, is a forest management system that, “lies somewhere in between the visual extremes of clearcutting and selection management. The parent forest is removed in several stages, with each stage successively establishing optimum environmental conditions for tree regeneration and then nursing the regeneration along to a point where the remaining parent forest can be harvested. Red oaks and white pine stands will often benefit from shelterwood harvesting.

A Metavic log loader and Kubota tractor. Managed forests mean healthier forests. Courtesy Dan Christmas

“Forest management and timber harvest systems utilize a very deep reservoir of forest research and experience. Practices are well-grounded in the applied ecological sciences, despite how some might appear to the casual observer.

“The notion that tree cutting is ‘bad’ has become a culturally-ingrained misconception. Wood is a renewable natural resource, providing an edge over any other raw material. The harvesting and processing of wood products also incurs the least amount of negative environmental impact, by any measure."

From the earliest foresters on, all knew that all trees die. It made sense to use some of them to supply the country's needs. Cook explains: "In the USA, each person uses about 9–10 pounds of wood per day...Forest-based industries provide markets for wood products, which expand forest management opportunities. These industries have become especially important in our rural areas.

"Managed forests provide for healthier forests and produce more of all the values we want from forests. Many environmentally-conscious groups somehow twist forest harvest into a negative enterprise. There are many great environmental causes to choose from these days, but opposing tree cutting is just not one of them."

While some extreme protectionists harbor fear and trepidation against logging, the establishment of great blocks of the Adirondacks and Catskills Forest Preserve has ensured a large portion will be kept strictly "forever wild," where once it was ravaged by lumbermen and the fires that came after them.

Even though the restrictions of New York's constitution may seem a bit too rigid, because of them New York still has its woods, and that is the important thing—to leave the Forest Preserve alone.

While some people might argue for a program of timber cutting in the Forest Preserve similar to what New York used in the salvage operations conducted after the storm of 1950, that sort of forest management will not be permitted, no matter how many strongly-expressed opinions there are for cutting in the interests of both forest and wildlife management.

What I find most interesting is the view of Dan Christmas, a hometown lumberjack-forester.

Listening to him, one realizes that among his profession, a logging job is not just a logging job. Certainly however cutting is conducted in the woods, it doesn't look pretty while it's going on, and for years afterward.

Dan likes to see wood being used. He likes *good* logging jobs. He also likes to walk the abandoned log roads and look at the new plants and animals moving in as Nature reclaims its own, a reclamation accomplished with truly astonishing rapidity.

Dan shares a common bond with the past. He wants wisely-used and properly-protected forest land, but is truly astonished at the rapidity of change that continues in his profession.

Adirondack
TIM-Berrr!

Chapter 36 | Dan Christmas

REFLECTIONS OF A LUMBERJACK-FORESTER

So much has changed in "the woods" over the last 30-plus years. Many of those early years, the characters I've met and the experiences I've had are now, sadly, a bygone era. And the thing that makes it the hardest, along with seeing the modernization of "the woodsman," is that there is no one to talk to about those days in the woods. Most of the woodsmen I knew were older, and they're now gone—or close to it—so there is nobody to reminisce with.

Once in a while I'll have a sit-down with some old-timer who has worked in the woods. When that happens, I lose all track of time. We share remembrances, drop names of big men we knew, and tell stories only we can understand without explanation.

This is what it was like back then.

In the early 1980s I came to a small Adirondack town called Tupper Lake. Much like other remote towns in the northeast, Tupper was a woodsman's town—hard-working, hard-charging, risk-taking men who knew "the lady of the woods" was there to take you if things went wrong.

When I got to Tupper one of the first things I noticed was the size of every lumberjack's arms. Whether barrel-chested or skinny as a rail, everyone had big strong arms.

The second thing I found out was that each could sharpen a chainsaw freehand, so it would throw long ribbons of sawdust, while the saw literally pulled you into the log you were cutting. Those early days where intimidating... guys like Leon, Slim, Nutsy and Pisser started at 4:00 AM and usually hit the tavern by 4:00 PM.

Trees where all cut with chainsaws as big as a car motor, with razor sharp chains that cut through a tree like a hot knife through butter. You had to know

Daniel M. Christmas, president of Christmas & Associates. Courtesy Dan Christmas where that tree wanted to fall, because once you made your cut it was on its way. There were big trees to cut, forty or more inches on the stump, and when they came down, all hell would break loose.

That big timber took down or broke off anything in its path, and the good lumberjacks had one eye on the tree and one on the flying limbs, broken splinters and whipping tops overhead.

Tools of the trade. Courtesy Dan Christmas

Skidders in those days where manually-operated shifting levers, winch lever and clutch. There was no enclosed cab and rarely did they have doors.

In winter most operators put a grain bag full of hay on the steel floor to protect their feet from the cold iron, and if they could they reversed the exhaust toward the cab, which gave some warmth at thirty below. Skidders where loud and echoed off the mountains and valleys below. If you've ever heard the starting and revving of a Detroit diesel, you know it can carry for miles.

Dan and son Marc hold what he called his "chopper." Today, Marc uses his logging experience passed on from his dad. Courtesy Dan Christmas

Many of us cut limbed and skidded our own "hitches" or loads. The wood we cut was mostly pulpwood and some logs. A good lumberjack could bring out 70 or more trees per day. I was paid $1.25 per tree and could cut 75 per day, and if things were going well I'd try for 100 trees. That was big money, and if you did it you bought the first round at the bar.

I learned quickly that if things started badly on any day, they stayed bad, so it was best to either quit while you were ahead or be damn careful. I also learned that despite having an over-abundance of testosterone, when you're tired, wet or distracted, you'd better know when to stop, because that's when the lady of the woods is close by.

Pine logs went to Canada, cherry to Vermont and birch and maple went to the plywood and furniture companies throughout the northeast. Softwood pulp (spruce and fir) had to be cut into 4' bolts and went to paper mills that made fine writing paper. In order to load a tractor trailer for these mills, we had to "bunch pulp" with a hand-held pulp hook in piles stacked about 4'–6' wide so the loader could pick them up and load each of eight tiers on the truck.

Dan's Kubota tractor and Metavic log loader are specially built for low-impact logging.
Courtesy Dan Christmas

Kubota's mini-excavator is ideal for sorting logs in the woods. Courtesy Dan Christmas

This was very dangerous, because as you bent over bunching pulp the loader was working above your head, and it wasn't unusual to have a big piece of wood drop out of the bunch as it passed over. Loader operators had to be good and careful. If you could help it, you did not bunch pulp under a new loader man.

As I bunched pulp, I began to see my arms look like everyone else's. Now I got it! Hardwood pulp was cut in 8' lengths and did not need to be bunched. It was sent to a different mill to be made into low-grade paper, newsprint and cardboard. Too bad we didn't have Amazon back then, with all their need for boxes.

While recycling was good for the environment (so they said), it was bad for the paper business, and thus the mills rationed out weekly tickets for how many loads you could deliver. There was intense competition and finagling for those tickets. Some weeks our crew would open the envelope to find three tickets for the week, which we could easily put up in a day.

Some of the bigger logging contractors (called jobbers) would estimate additional loads and advance us money to get by. This always led to trouble, discrepancies and even fist fights on the landing.

The biggest wood was deep in the forest, miles off the main roads. Temporary haul roads, called winter roads, were cut out of the forest for winter access to the big wood. Beginning usually in late December, subzero temperatures would arrive and we'd begin the 24-hour-a-day task of "roughing out" and freezing winter haul roads. I've seen winter roads cut through the woods for 10-20 miles, and to this day I'm amazed how we did it.

Many roads went through swamps and marshes that had to be cleared of all snow so they would freeze down deep. Roads started with brush and mud packed down and frozen with skidders or bulldozers. This usually involved a lot of getting buried in mud and winching each other out. It also meant that each night we parked machinery on log piles and cleaned the mud out of the racks for hours into the night. Otherwise, come morning, the tracks would be frozen tight and stay that way for days.

To build a winter road, you had to depend on cold weather, which meant long, late nights keeping the snow off the road so it wouldn't insulate it, crushing trees and brush in the low spots and building frozen highways through the woods sometimes 40 feet wide.

As the roads got frozen enough to hold tractor trailers weighing over 100,000 pounds the roads were then dragged with homemade drags made from railroad rails cabled together to cut the roads smooth. Eventually, all that mud, brush and ice would become a smooth highway, with trucks bringing out the big loads of logs and pulp at 50 mph. It was amazing to see the road break up and go back to nature in the spring.

Sometimes I'll travel by snowmobile along an old winter haul road barely wide enough to pass through, and I'll tell my fellow riders "I remember when we used to haul tractor trailers over these trails." Of course they doubt it.

Harland "Woody" Wood hailed from Malone, N.Y. Woody was Dan's old friend and confidante. This photo was taken on Bay Pond Mountain, in 1982. Woody is an example of the many older generation who willingly shared their experiences and skills to a younger generation who wanted to follow a logging career.

Dan reports Woody's stories of life in the North Country included his youthful days of scraping to make a living during America's Great Depression and his hitch in the Civilian Conservation Corps camps at Meacham Lake north of Paul Smiths in Franklin County. Courtesy Dan Christmas

Stacks of rotting logs still remain in the deep woods after 30 years, reminders of places where some loggers cut more than they could get hauled before spring break-up.

Summers were much the same: hard work, sore hands, sweat and of course, bugs. The fresh smell of leaves, turned-over dirt and sweet maple and cherry sawdust from summer is a smell any woodsman will remember in every story...every conversation

There's much more to tell about: the injuries and deaths in the woods, and the super-human efforts made to rescue others.

Unfortunately, in one more generation even the stories and memories of a bygone era will fade like the day's last echo of the chainsaw as it's shut off.

Today men have been largely replaced by mechanized equipment, whole tree processors, GPS locators, computerized enclosed cab spaces and equipment with tires the size of your house. The equipment skids everything out or runs it over, leaving only a few pole-sized trees that will take 100 years to grow into the size of the trees I cut.

Today's logging is monstrous push-button machinery that can cut through 200 acres in a week...the same 200 acres that used to last us all summer.

We used to say, as long as the young trees grew, we'd never run out of timber. We also said that if you could work in the woods, you'd never go hungry.

The production of "biomass" with today's equipment, requiring payments in the millions, is not sustainable for the long-term growth of the forest, the health of its animals and human enjoyment of traveling an old winter road or a walking through the trees. It's the end for the lumberjack, the woods and an amazing era.

Despite this outlook, I continue at age 60 to work in the woods with my sons as I did back then...freezing roads, piling wood and watching out for the lady of the woods. Today I cut 25 trees, not 75, and on a good day 30, not 100, yet I can still smell the sweet fragrance of fresh dirt, summer leaves and sweet maple and cherry sawdust. My arms somehow got smaller than they were back then, but my saw is still sharp enough to cut ribbons out of wood.

We cut on our own land and occasionally get a well-paying job from a landowner looking for "low impact logging," but the pay isn't enough. I do it anyway, because the woods is in my heart and soul and my memories can live on through my boys.

Years ago I asked an old lumberjack friend, "Hey Bump, what would you do if you won the lottery?" Without hesitation he answered, "Well...that's easy...I'd log it till the money ran out."

—From the broken heart of a lumberjack...DMC.

Adirondack TIM-Berrr!

Chapter 37 | William J. O'Hern

RITA P. CHIASSON, LUMBER CAMP COOK

"All right. I'd get up at 4 o'clock in the morning. First thing you know, I'd have my bacon in the oven, ah, my, my fried potatoes, I'd put that in the oven. It was great big ovens, y'know, restaurant stuff. Then...then I'd mix my pancakes....not...mix 'em my own self.

> *"I always kept the leftover of my pannicakes that I didn't use because it would ferment, and it would make the best pannicake, the pancake would be that thick. And then, then I'd fry...."* —Rita Chiasson. Living Traditions Oral History Project (MS 18-007), Adirondack Experience Library, interview conducted by fieldworker Tom Carroll on June 19, 1996.

Rita Poirier Chiasson knew the meaning of the expression "rise and shine." For 24 years she worked as a cook for smaller logging jobbers because she chose a less challenging daily program. Rita said she "didn't want to cook for more than 35 men at a time

Rita remembered all this when Tom Carroll sat down with the 82-year old at Rita's Tupper Lake home.

Carroll had heard of Rita and was interested in learning about the life of a lumber camp cook.

He had learned from books about peppery French Canadians and wild, freewheeling 'jacks who would pack up their poke and move on to another camp when they tired of one cook's style or didn't like the cooking. Lumberjacks always wanted to work where the food was said to be the best. Their days consisted mostly of eat, work, sleep, repeat—meals being the most enjoyable part of the pattern.

Rita could well recall what it was like to work at a big baking board, making great loaves of bread. To Carroll, her memories might have seemed like part of a dream as she spoke about baking raisin pie and doughnuts and perking large pots of coffee on a wood-fired cookstove.

As I listened to Carroll's "Living Traditions in the Adirondacks" tape and read a transcript of their conversation, a picture of how Rita came to work in the camps emerged.

Rita P. Chiasson. Courtesy Dan Christmas

A common logging camp dining room scene. Rita Chiasson prided herself on her ability to gauge quantities so as to serve huge and tasty meals to the deserving lumberjacks. Courtesy Lyons Falls Historical Association

Her stories and experiences bring to mind a silent, self-sufficient, resilient type of Adirondack woman whose lifetime speaks of hardiness and courage. And, she was not alone. It's easy to assume her diligent code of resourcefulness and living independently mirrored other Adirondack folks of her era, the mid-twentieth century Adirondacks.

Rita was among the rugged natives who championed hard work and thrived in the mountains in spite of deprivation and hardship. Her story is not one bit brooding, and I believe Tom Carroll came away from the interview with the deepest respect and admiration for this dear mountain woman.

Rita was born in 1914 on Canada's Gaspé Peninsula. She recalled coming to the Adirondacks when she was 10-years old."

Rita's cooking was top-notch table fare. Courtesy Forestry History Society

In 1924, her father Paul Poirier a lumberjack, moved the family from their Canadian farm to the North Country of New York, where logging jobs were more abundant. Rita said, "Father worked all over Canada, wherever the logging was good. He was gone as much as eight months at a time." When her two oldest brothers were old enough to work in the woods they went with their father.

Rita recalled the move made 72 years before the interview as clearly as if it had been yesterday. "Someone told my father that logging was good in New York State; there was lots of work there. Father began working for different people, Canadian jobbers, in New York, worked about eight months, then went back to Canada, and told Mother they were moving [to Tupper Lake].. Mother didn't want to go; she said they just talked Indian over there. He said no, there are some French families there, and a church that has the same name, St. Alphonse as in Canada, and he worked for French people. Mother said she didn't know a word of English."

Rita felt differently than her mother. "I was glad when we left Canada. I thought we were moving to a big city," she said.

Knowing only French when she began school, Rita picked up English in no time, but was discontented with the country school. She spoke of her teacher as "...good. I learned everything from her... [but] I didn't fit in with the other students." This was most likely because she "was two years older than most of her classmates" and her French accent made integration difficult in a time that was less accepting than today of individual differences.

She continued school until her fourteenth birthday. "I wanted to work," she said. Rita listed "cleaning house, washing, cooking, helping with the children" as typical jobs for women at the time.

While some girls worked in hotels as waitresses, there wasn't much industry in Tupper Lake. The village had the Oval Dish Corporation, but "they only hired so many people," she said. "You were lucky if you got a job there."

Making the best of the work available for girls then, she found employment as a live-in maid, cooking and cleaning for local families for three dollars a week. She used her earnings to purchase clothes by mail-order for her sisters, her mother, and herself.

At 16, she picked up work at a lumber camp. Rita said of that experience, "The man had a big job. And his wife was a cook. I was the chore 'boy'—did dishes, peeled potatoes and so forth." This ended when she had an appendectomy and lost her job.

Tom Carroll asked what Rita did socially as a teenager in Tupper Lake. He might have been surprised by her response, perhaps thinking she would have listed going to a favorite swimming hole, seeing a traveling circus, or attending a fiddle-playing concert or programs at the school. But Rita said she enjoyed dressing up. "I was young then, and Father was strict. I met my

Caption: Beans were a served daily in lumber camps. Bean-hole was an early brand used in household and in lumber camps. From a 1920s newspaper advertisement husband on a job, and Father never knew. And after a while I told Father that I wanted to get married."

At 17, Rita married a lumberjack with whom she had five children. The family moved to New Hampshire for a brief period, but Rita left "because they didn't like it." The marriage fell apart, and Rita raised her children in Tupper Lake as a single mother.

Rita wasn't worried about having to raise her kids alone. "No, I was young. I knew I could make it. I was 29 years old then. I moved into the house I live in now, rented it at first, then bought. Didn't own a car then, couldn't afford one. Didn't want something I couldn't afford. My father and family was still around then; they helped provide support." But Rita provided mightily for her own family.

Silence was observed as standard cook house etiquette. This hard-and-fast rule helped to maintain order and get the men off to work. Courtesy Lyons Falls History Association

Carroll said Rita worked in a few different places before she began cooking in the lumber woods. Rita knew people who had a lumber camp. She asked them if they needed a cook, because being from a farm family, she knew how to cook. She got the job. She was at the camp all week long, and had someone to take care of the kids. Wilson Dechene was the jobber, a big jobber. But the job wasn't a big job; they were clearing up for Paul Smith's College.

"After a while, word got out I was a good cook. After that I always had work," Rita explained.

Rita moved around from camp to camp. In summer, she cooked for men cutting softwood and at another camp in winter where the men harvested hardwood. Working May through February, she was forced to rely on unemployment benefits to get by in March and April. Her children stayed in town, cared for by friends and family, while she was in camp during the week. They spent summers in the woods with their mother and the lumberjacks.

"I would start in May, on the 15th, and get my last job in November, going into the woods in November and coming out in February. And I worked for a doctor in town, to supplement unemployment income, which was only $50 a week." At camp she earned $125 a week at first, but the pay went up after that.

Besides cooking for men who seemed to act "as if they were starving," she took care of the "van." The company van sold cigarettes, chainsaw files, provisions and supplies, clothing—a variety of things. Purchases were deducted from the lumberjacks' pay at the end of the week. Rita kept track of the transactions. She said it helped her hold onto her job. "I also had to keep track of how many meals the men ate, because they were charged $1 for each meal," she added.

Tom asked Rita to give some examples of lumber camp recipes. "There were home fries and hot dogs ground up together, fried in pure lard. Everything came in large quantities, pie fillings and so forth." Except for soft pies; she liked to make her own soft pies—lemon and butterscotch. "I made use of leftovers too, used leftover meat in soup and so forth. Didn't want to throw a thing out, maybe a few pancakes, but otherwise I used everything."

When Rita wasn't working at a lumber camp she often cooked for other people in Tupper Lake. She explains, "There's not much I can't do."

As the only woman for miles, Rita preferred working in camps with separate buildings for the kitchen and sleeping quarters. Although she always had her own room, if the men were in the same building, the odor of unwashed clothes and bodies permeated everything.

Some of the men chose not to walk to the outhouse when it was cold at night, instead using a designated spot at one end of their bunkhouse. Bad odors aside, Rita felt she was always on good terms with the men, and the jobber always made sure that she had no problems.

Rita Chiasson gave an account of her day at the camp as cook:

"Up at 4 AM, packed bacon and fried potatoes in the ovens—big ovens. Then I mixed pancakes. I always kept leftover batter, let it ferment, and used it as a starter. That made the best pancakes. I'd set the tables and ring the bell at 6 AM, everything on the table—fruit, doughnuts, toast, meat, etcetera. After breakfast I'd clean up. I had to keep the utensils, pots and pans clean. Inspectors came, and would close the camp if everything wasn't very clean.

"Every camp was against to have flies, y'know. There was screen door, screen this an' that'n, because that was against the law. They'd come and inspect, and see, they'd take the knife, and they'd take a sharp thing and go right at next to the blade like that, y'know, and see if there was any dirt in there."

Tom asked, "And if they found grease or dirt?"

"Camp closed. Closed," said Rita.

"Then I would start preparations for dinner, which was at 11:30 AM—it wasn't lunch, it was dinner. It was the same routine for dinner, then clean up, wash the tables and dishes, put the dishes on the table bottom side up [to keep flies and dirt off]. Then I got the potatoes ready for supper, and made seven pies, and two cakes, and two batches of cookies, every day—and doughnuts, 500 doughnuts every two days. I'd do that in the afternoon. Then supper would come along—steak, roast beef or roast pork, cabbage, potatoes, and so forth. I did everything by hand. Made eight loaves of bread every day, mixed and kneaded the dough by hand. There were no machines—wouldn't know how to operate a machine. And there wasn't a piece left for the next day.

"Talk about meals! Vegetables—I aways had vegetables [for] both meals. Corn y' know, then, my jobber would bring corn on the cob, y'know. He'd bring cauliflower. I'd fix that with a nice milk gravy. That was out of this world. Potatoes! It took a bushel. A bushel of potatoes. Supper was at 5:30 PM. No talking during meals. There was a sign at the door in French and English,

> which said no speaking at the table. The men ate in silence. An' so that was their supper. After supper I'd clean up 'n get to my breakfast again."

Tom asked Rita when she ate.

> "Ah? I hardly ate anything, and I was fat," she said. "It was just uh, the cookin' that kept me goin', y'know? I'd never sit down at the table. That's prob'ly why my poor feets are so tired today.
>
> "I did washing on Sundays—tablecloths, towels, wash cloths and so forth. The lumberjacks used a mixture of tar and grease and applied it to their skin to keep the flies away. It was dirty, soiled their clothes. Lumberjacks wore blue jeans, and the gum from the softwood got on them. The pants were so stiff that they could stand up on their own. But it washed out."

Rita described the layout of the tables, how she placed groups of condiments and salt and pepper, and serving bowls for each group of four men. She didn't want them passing platters and other serving dishes from one area of the table to another. She watched to make sure that each area had enough, and that one group didn't take from another. There was very little waste, and the men ate everything.

Tom Carroll explained, "Rita prepared food for the next meal while the men were eating, checking on them to make sure they had enough of everything, plenty of coffee and so forth.

"Rita told me she used to make bread at her house, and people would come by and she'd give the bread away. After her son fell ill, she stopped. She still has a coffeepot she bought from one of the camps.

"She was 35 miles back in the woods when she worked on (Gould Park in the area between Long Lake and Newcomb). When the camp first opened, she was all by herself. The jobber took her out there and dropped her off. The camp was a traveling camp. It came in on a trailer. They set that up, and the men started the next day. Rita said that the men were all gentlemen. No one ever insulted her. She said that one time she was cooking for another jobber, and there were lots of young loggers, and one said to her, 'Cook, you wanna go out tonight?' Rita said: 'Listen, if I'm gonna go out I'm gonna go out with a man, I'm not gonna go out with a kid.' Rita laughed at that and said she didn't take it wrong. So there was never a problem. And all her woodmen friends come every year to see her, and brought their wives. But if there had been any problems, she would only have had to say something to the jobber."

Rita said she didn't go home on weekends. "The job was a seven-day-a-week job. But I had people to talk to, the jobber and so forth. I never felt alone. And I had a little radio with me. I loved to listen to Western music—Hank Williams, Johnny Paycheck."

Tom says that even now Rita is not alone. Her son checks on her every day. And she takes ironing in and has plenty to do. And keeping busy stops her from crying (her other son is currently hospitalized after suffering a stroke during surgery). Her children visit her every Sunday, have a meal, and bring their friends. Rita will feed anybody. She always has lots of food on hand.

Tom explained that in Rita's day, she couldn't get on welfare because her husband was still living. She didn't know where he was—somewhere two states away. She didn't know until he remarried, although Rita said they were never divorced. "Somehow he got married, or shacked up with a woman who had been married before," she said. As far as Rita was concerned, she was still married and used her married name, mainly for her kids. Her husband (or ex-husband) came to Tupper Lake with his wife to see the kids. Rita said she never spoke against him to her children, and never let them speak against him, and the kids all loved their dad. When her husband died of Parkinson's Disease (his second wife had already died) Rita and her daughter went to the funeral home and Rita gave money for his burial.

Tom asked Rita about extra things she did, to hold her job. Rita said she did the bookkeeping, and was careful not to waste anything. She learned that on the farm, growing up. She also kept track of meals and purchases. She didn't have to do that; the boss should have done that, but he wasn't always there.

Rita told Tom they had lumber camps in those days in order to keep their men, because the bonded men had to have a place to live. "So that's the way they held their men. And good meals. And clean camps. Truck driver, bulldozer driver, loader man—they were all Americans. But the woodsmen were French. And they were workers. But toward the last, the Canadians were just like the American kids. They came here to see what was going on; they didn't want to work. Some jobbers were French, but not all of them. One was American—Linebecker."

Rita mainly stuck to the same camps all the time. She had her kitchens, with curtains in the windows. Rita said, "That was my home. I fixed the benches to make them look nice, and fixed my tablecloths, to prevent drips and facilitate cleanup. It was stiff tablecloth, nice oilcloth in them days. And the men liked that." Rita didn't see that elsewhere. One of her jobbers had two camps, and there was a man cooking in the other camp. She remembered, "The man cook gave the loggers instant potatoes. I didn't feed the men instant anything. They worked hard for it, they deserved it. And what went into their bodies was clean, too."

Tom Carroll was curious about where Rita got her recipes. Rita said she didn't really have any. "I cut some from raisin boxes and macaroni boxes. I made macaroni salad by mixing dry milk and evaporated milk and put it in the refrigerator. The men went wild with that. And it was because of my cooking, the jobber was happy; he had all the men he wanted" [The workers stayed on the job because they were satisfied with the quality of their meals.]

Tom asked if the men could choose what camp they went to. Rita answered, "If they weren't bound, there were no holds on them. But the men liked my camp. Usually the cook took a nap in the afternoon, but I didn't. That was my time to make doughnuts." Tom asked if any of the men around camp helped her, and she said she never asked for help.

Tom asked what it was like being in a wild area, in the woods. Rita talked about wild animals in the woods—coyotes, bobcats, bears. She remembered one time when she heard a coyote howl and the hair stood up on her head. But she wasn't afraid, because coyotes don't go into camps. "Only the bears go in, looking for food," she explained.

Tom said, "I asked Rita about a bear breaking into the kitchen. She said the chore boy hadn't emptied the garbage, though she had told him to. The bear got in through the window. Rita slept in the main camp; her bedroom was right next to the kitchen. She slept all by herself. The men's camp was in a separate building. Rita sometimes worked as far as 65 miles back in the woods, so of course there were bears, and coyotes. [Unfortunately Rita's bear story leaves us hanging. Her interviewer did not follow up.]

He asked if she liked the natural environment, saying a lumberjack he talked to mentioned that he enjoyed the woods. "Oh, the smell of the pine," she said, "and the air, was so fresh. You'd wake up in the morning, after the first week there, oh my God, you felt like a millionaire, you know? And you'd hear the birds." When she worked in a place that was "right up against a great big mountain, a German guy who worked there ran a hose" to a spring on the mountain, and Rita had running water right in the camp. She said that having a shower in the camp with warm water would have been nice, but she had warm water in a reservoir in the stove.

"If you like your work," Rita said, "it's not hard, and I was my own boss. The job boss always accommodated me. I'd make a list and he'd always bring extra."

Rita said when she was working near Utica, the men lived nearby, and they went home on Saturday afternoons and didn't come back until Monday morning. The jobber wanted to take Rita home with him, but she said no, she had to stay and make sure the heat was working, and wash her uniform, and do other chores, so she stayed in the camp. She always wore a white uniform, like a nurse, and a little hat "like they wear in the service" just to hold her hair. She wore an apron, and good, sturdy shoes, so her feet didn't bother her. And she wore a hairnet over her head, although it wasn't required by the jobber, to keep hair out of the food. Rita said, "There's nothing worse than finding a hair, in anything." She wanted the men to know that whatever went into their stomachs was clean. And she needed that job. It was good pay, more than other jobs. She had worked cleaning houses for a dollar a day, and that didn't amount to anything.

Tom asked Rita why she didn't cultivate friendships. Was it because she went her own way, and didn't want to bother with friendships? Rita said yes, she'd always been that way. Did that help her to do that kind of work, in the camps? Rita said yes, because if she had friends she'd want to be with them. When she was cooking, if you didn't have a job with a jobber, you couldn't just go into the camp. There was a gatekeeper [at Gould Park], and you had to sign in and sign out. She thought that would have made friendships difficult. She could have friends once she came to live permanently in Tupper Lake, but then "they'd be in my way when I have to make my earnings."

Tom asked what Rita and the loggers did for amusement in the camps. Rita said one jobber had television. "We were friends to start with. And they played cards. One played guitar. And some sang. Once when the state police were there a woodsman got up and started yodeling, and the policeman said that guy could go to Nashville and yodel like that. They sang, danced, played music. Fiddlers. And some of the guys cut hair, just like a barber, but never went to barber school."

Tom asked about Rita's children—what did they do when she was in camp? Rita said she boarded them out, one here, two there, and so on, and when she came home in the spring, she mended their clothes and listened to their stories. She took the kids with her when they were out of school, and the boss never charged her a cent for their board. Rita said that she did miss her kids when she was away from them, and worried about them. She wrote to them and they wrote back while she was in the woods. And her parents checked on the children, as did her sisters.

Rita's father helped Rita a lot, giving her wood, milk, potatoes, and whatever else he could. "God bless his heart, he's gone, but he's gone to heaven," she said. "He earned it. Mother and Father both died of cancer, Mother first, of uterine cancer. Father lived to be 84."

Tom asked if it was good to be free of her children while she worked in the camps, but Rita told him she often had them with her, the little ones. And in the summer she had them all. Rita said her kids used to love the camp. The boys would sleep in the men's camp, and how the men would spoil them. The boys drove the trucks, the pickups, and rode on the dump trucks. They helped Rita in the kitchen too, but they didn't become lumberjacks. Rita's daughter married a lumberjack, "...the nicest man in the world. Good to my daughter, good to me. He's a son. Levesque. He owns a garage in town now."

After she left the camps, Rita worked for the state for 15 years as a home health aide. She worked all the overtime she could. During one December, she worked 15 days overtime, a lot. But she retired because they changed the payroll rules, and made some overtime mandatory, so she would have lost money. She quit when she was 67.

So now she has a pension, and social security, and takes in washing and ironing. Tom noted that Rita had worked very hard all her life. Rita said she still does; she can't stop. At 82 she does ironing for 22 customers, plus three washings, every week. Plus her own. She is a fast ironer, having ironed all her life. She charges $5 an hour for ironing.

Adirondack TIM-Berrr!

Chapter 38 | William J. O'Hern

DEWITT WILEY SAW IT ALL

In 1981, Dewitt Wiley was chosen Grand Marshal of the 34th New York State Woodsmen's Field Days in Boonville, N.Y. For 42 years, Wiley was a logger for John E. Johnson. Wiley recalled that Johnson never once said that Wiley *worked for* him but always that he *worked with* him.

Wiley was born January 19, 1897. in Utica, N.Y.; his family moved to Port Leyden when he was "eight or nine years old," recalled Wiley. "I attended school there until 1913. Then at age sixteen I left to go to work in a bakery-grocery store." In 1915 he had the chance to earn more money in a paper mill. Wiley continued, "So I went to work for nine dollars a week. After a year at the mill, I started my logging career with [John E.] Johnson and Son, in a pulp mill. I earned two dollars a day loading logs." Wiley soon found out the wages paid in the woods were two dollars a day straight time plus board, so on November 21, 1916, he climbed aboard a buckboard alongside Mr. Johnson and went into the woods to work.

On several jobs, Wiley supervised the lumber camps. He remembered his grandfather, James Jordan, a blacksmith. "I spent a lot of my time around his shop," he said, "and I learned a lot about the trade. What I learned helped me out later when I was running lumber camps."

Dewitt Wiley was also an amateur photographer at the camps. Some of his logging pictures were published in early issues of *The Northeastern Logger* magazine. Unfortunately, most of the scenes he captured never included a courtesy by-line. As one illustration of the absence of Wiley's name, his granddaughter, Shelly Privett, pointed out, "My grandfather was not recognized in the magazine's May 1960 profile of Johnny E. Johnson." Interviewed in 1981, Wiley said he still had the camera he bought in 1918.

"It still takes good pictures," he claimed, "but the film is expensive."

Dewitt Wiley (Left) and Larry Muggins at Brandreth, 1926. Courtesy Leigh Portner

Wiley didn't mention his motivation for buying a camera to record lumber camp scenes. Perhaps the idea came to him after seeing Paramount Studio's "Big Timber" in 1917, or when he learned of the difficulties the film crew encountered filming the lumber camp scenes.

Throughout the early decades of the 20th century, motion picture themes often focused on lumbering, such as the popular 1932 story of love in a lumber camp, "Carnival Boat," starring Bill Boyd and Ginger Rogers. Audiences found the scenes connected with lumbering most interesting.

Everett-Dickerson and Gale Gydesen at Johnny Johnson's Pit Four. Photo by Dewitt Wiley. Courtesy Leigh Portner

Regardless of what might have been his inspiration, Wiley enjoyed documenting winter "Jack Frost scenes" in New York's Tug Hill country and in the Adirondack Mountains. A number of his original prints were part of the Rev. Reed's Memorial Woodsmen's Association's photographic archive until they were destroyed in a fire. Fortunately, his daughter Julie Hurley and his granddaughter Shelly have looked after three of his albums very well. The pictures Wiley took are mostly of early camp scenes, individuals he worked with, camp animals, deer—a favorite subject—and loading and hauling logs. The logs were cut, peeled, and piled in the woods in the summer. When the winter roads were frozen hard, the logs were drawn to landings by horses and tractors and driven by skilled "log rollers" on the river or hauled to the mill by trucks. Regrettably, Wiley never identified some personnel and locations in his collection.

Hardwood logs at Pit Four. Eva Bishop and Dewitt Wiley stand on a log boom in Pit 4. Dewitt was a tough, experienced, callused-handed "wood tick" who worked in the woods and enjoyed photographing his fellow workers in every-day situations. Self-portrait by Dewitt Wiley. Courtesy Leigh Portner

Had somebody had the presence of mind to record Dewitt Wiley talking about his logging pictures, many of his stories and his life's history could have been preserved. As it is, we can take what we do know and piece together how Wiley fit into the story when he worked at Johnson's camps and took his noteworthy photos.

Johnson's hardwood landing at Nickels Siding, 1916–1922. The railroad spur was a few miles south of White Lake station. Photo by Dewitt Wiley. Courtesy Leigh Portner

A Native American lumberjack poses with the camp's puppy for Wiley's camera.
Photo by Dewitt Wiley. Courtesy Leigh Portner

A log drive on Big Woodhull Stream near Forestport, N.Y. Photo by Dewitt Wiley. Courtesy Leigh Portner

Back in the spring of 1929, with the cooperation of Harry P. Gould, Johnny Johnson purchased the Everton and Meacham Tract at Meacham Lake, several miles north of Paul Smiths. The vast wooded tract consisted of 30,000 acres of virgin forest land. At that time, Wiley had been working for Johnson for 13 years.

Wiley remembered John Devignon became the pulpwood operator on this tract and made a cut of 125,000 cords, which was sold to the International Paper Company.

Horses and sleigh at an unidentified John E. Johnson lumber camp. Photo by Dewitt Wiley. Courtesy Leigh Portner

A significant development in pulpwood hauling took place on this job through the cooperation of Johnson, Devignon, and Wiley, as foreman. These men decided to try building the truck road up to the log pile in the woods. The stab was successful and led to the establishment of this method of trucking throughout the Adirondacks for both pulpwood and logs.

In 1981, the year Dewitt Wiley was interviewed for and became honored as the Woodsmen's Grand Marshall. He resided in Forestport, N.Y. Wiley had a daughter, Julie Hurley, and three grandchildren. He was a member of the Up and Go Senior Citizens, the AARP, and the Presbyterian Church and was a 36-year member and past president of the Masons. He was also president of Beechwood Cemetery Association.

From the start of his logging career in 1916 until his retirement in 1958, Wiley proudly boasted of the accomplishments of the loggers of Johnson's camps. He said, "We cut and transported about 900,000 cords of pulpwood and at least 60,000,000 feet of lumber products—largely hardwood. "The pulpwood alone would make a solid pile of four-foot blocks, four feet high, extending from New York to Kansas City."

Two unidentified lumber camp workers celebrate some time off. The extreme tipping angle of their beer and whiskey bottles is a sure indicator they were hamming it up as Wiley's snapped the couple.
Photo by Dewitt Wiley. Courtesy Leigh Portner

The contributions of men like Dewitt Wiley cannot be measured in the size of a wood pile but in how the wood they harvested was used to make products that improved people's lives and how the wood was transformed in various industries that employed thousands of people and supported the nation's progress by providing material for tools, furniture, cabinets, flooring, siding, and other building materials as well as newsprint and the many other kinds of paper we use. The list goes on and on, and there are jobs connected with every product. Jobs that all started in the woods with lumbermen.

Dewitt Wiley indeed saw it all from the days of old-style logging, when loggers felled trees with axes and crosscut saws and logs were skidded and hauled exclusively with strong draft horses though the early age of mechanization which introduced powerful Linn tractors, to the advent of logging trucks, which removed the need to move pulpwood from the forests to mills via water.

He saw tiny spruce seedlings grow into lofty trees, and during his retirement he passed along his wealth of knowledge about his active days of winding tote roads, the dazzling whiteness of the winter forest, Michigan plows, huge sprinkler boxes, The Cut, The Haul, and The Drive, men who would toss away their whole season's hard-earned wages in less than a week, and so much more.

Granddaughter Shelly says she's never forgotten Wiley's advice about chainsaw safety and how to properly fell a tree.

The wide assortment of Wiley's snapshot subjects preserves an eyewitness account of the old days of logging for future generations. And with a bit of imagination, today's viewers can imagine what he saw through his Kodak Brownie's lens—remote lumber camps, towering stands of evergreens, the primitive grandeur of virgin stands of wood, tote roads zig-zagging up and over mountains, and now-antiquated logging operations.

Dewitt captured these two unidentified camp workers soaking up rays of warm sunshine.
Photo by Dewitt Wiley. Courtesy Leigh Portner

Here his photos speak for themselves. More than mere images, they evoke honor and respect for this early logger who cared about his fellow workers and the world in which they lived, and thought enough of both to leave this legacy.

Dewitt labeled this scene "pulp skidway and bridge, Big Woodhull Creek, 1919."
Photo by Dewitt Wiley. Courtesy Leigh Portner

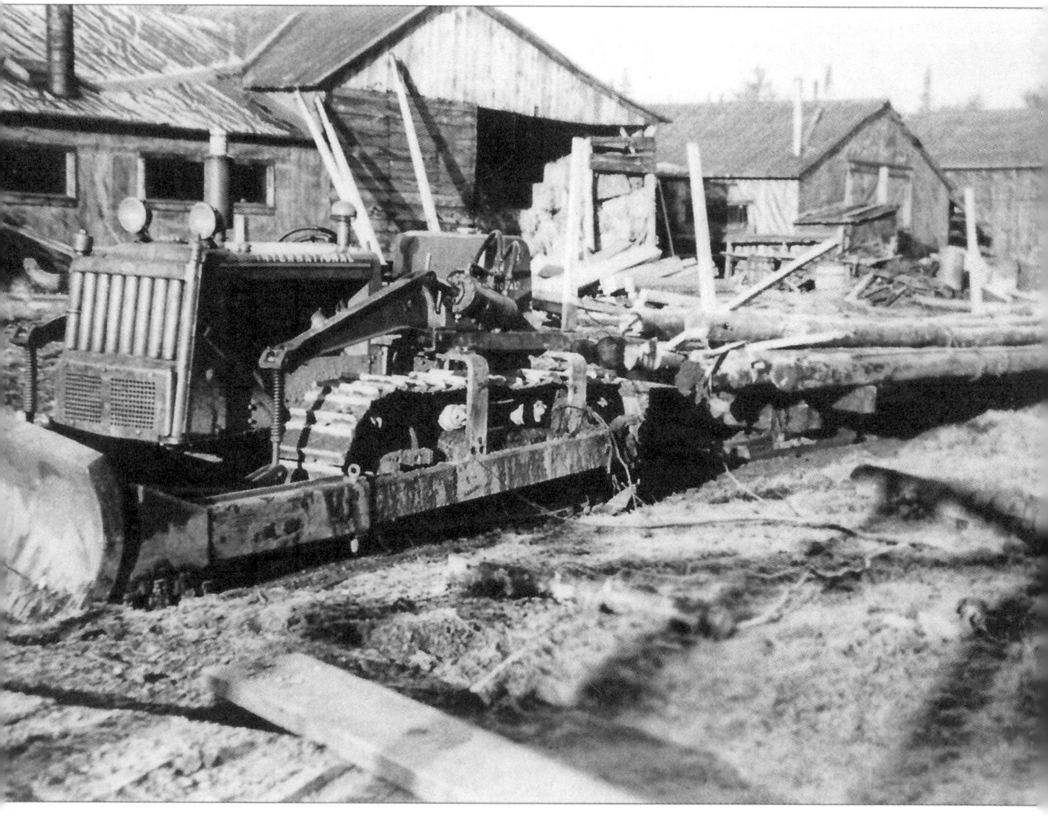

John E. Johnson's Perkins Clearing camp. Dewitt's experience spanned the era between old-style logging to the use of powered machinery. Courtesy Leigh Portner

Adirondack TIM-Berrr!

Chapter 39 | William J. O'Hern

Lyons Falls Women's Club Tours a Gould Logging Camp

I found a picture when sorting through the Lyons Falls History Association's collection of logging pictures. Club historian and president Shirley Van Nest pointed to the abandoned town railroad station from her back deck as she said the picture was snapped right there. The picture appeared in a very interesting newspaper article that was in the club's files.

The February 8, 1948, Sunday morning edition of the Utica *Observer-Dispatch* ran a photo feature essay about the Lyons Falls Women's Club field trip. The headline "WOMEN TOUR a Logging Camp" and 12 photos told the story. It's a shame that the actual glossy photos of Dante Tranquille, the *Observer-Dispatch's* chief photographer, have not survived. The photocopied newspaper pictures shows the women inspecting the lumbermen's sleeping quarters, heated by giant blocks of wood that were fed into an oil drum stove. (There was no fuel shortage.)

The club members ate with the loggers, and were pictured holding man-sized cups of coffee. They witnessed various logging operations, including a first-hand look at the transfer of logs from skidway to sled, the first stage of a journey to the paper mill. The images would have added to the immense Gould Paper Company historical collection that Van Nest oversees.

Gould's Twin Sister Camp, the chosen site for the expedition, was operated by foreman Hugh Dowling. It was located on Twin Sister Creek. James E. Davis, Woodlands Manager of Gould Paper Co., planned the excursion. Cars were provided. The group left the Hammicker Drug Store and proceeded to Fowlerville and then on to the woods camp, where they were met by Joseph McDermott, Woodlands Camp Superintendent, who conducted them on a tour to the log loader, where they saw logs being drawn by two-horse teams from the skidway to the loader, where they were hoisted onto trucks by a crane—each load carrying about seven cords.

From left, Miss Helen Schaefer (later Mrs. Roman Buckingham), Mrs. W. Sanders, Mrs. L. McAteer, and Mrs. John Todd, members of the Lyons Falls Women's Club stand beside the Lyons Falls railroad station before the 48 members leave to visit a Gould Paper Company woodlands operations in 1948.
Courtesy Lyons Falls History Association

The women were surprised to find how easy it was to walk over a hard-packed road of ice and snow. Later, they returned to camp, where they were served a delicious and appetizing lunch, "woodman's style." Camp cook George Hewitt, when asked how much bread the men consumed, answered "We bake 30 loaves of bread and 100 rolls three times a week." The meal featured standard camp menu food. No doubt some of the women thought the men had pretty healthy appetites, but according to all accounts people "out in the world" don't eat as much as people do in lumber camps. Although machinery was used in the woods as never before, some thousands of calories a day were required by each man to battle the cold and provide the physical energy needed for hard work. This became especially evident during World War II, when the federal government had to liberalize the meat and other rations copiously more than once before the logs began rolling in good shape up in the Adirondack Mountains.

To entertain the visiting ladies, typical lumber camp songs were sung, and the youngest lady present, Marie MacIntyre, was presented with a huge loaf of home-baked bread.

A typical men's barracks. Courtesy Lyons Falls History Association

Roy W. Shaver, Vice President and General Manager of Gould Paper Co., (then a subsidiary of Continental Can Company) and a Mr. Davis and Mr. McDermott spoke of the company operations. They shared some facts about the winter trucks and drivers. The operation relied on 12 to 15 log-loading

The women's club often took field trips to nearby lumber camps.
Courtesy New York State Archives #14297-87-4250

A Lyons Falls Woman's Club luncheon gathering at Hotel Parquet on June 25, 1948. The group includes Mrs. James Davis; Sally Trude; Helen Schaefer; Virginia Keleher; Mrs. Grace Durkee Jr.; Grace Hammerker; Rachel Fisher; Mrs. Ruth Brown, Sr.; Alta Potter; Marion Shaver; Kathleen Norton; Anita Dovnan (sic); and Margaret Hobat. Courtesy Lyons Falls History Association cranes. There were 50 hook men who loaded the trucks that would transport 43,000 cords in two and one half months, a total of 7,200 loads. McDermott said, "The owners and operators will be paid $180,000.00; 76,000 gallons of gasoline will be consumed by the trucks covering 533,000 miles. Another $50,000.00 will go to loaders and unloaders, tractor men and etc."

The Lyons Falls Women's Club often gathered in this historic tavern in Constableville, N.Y.
Courtesy Shirley Van Nest

All of the logs would be brought to the mill by truck during the two and one half months of frozen road season. The mileage would be equivalent to one truck making about 22 trips around the world. There were about 50 men employed at Twin Sister Camp.

Following a relaxing meal, the women visited the blacksmith's shop and camp store, then were taken by cars to the header, where they witnessed three trucks being loaded at one time.

The day's schedule included a stop at Camp 4 (the article didn't identify where) and then on to McKeever for a tour through the McKeever company store and back to Lyons Falls by way of Boonville.

The Women's Club greatly appreciated the generosity of the Gould Paper Co. in giving them this enjoyable trip, and as they departed learned that 1948 was a landmark year because Gould would no longer conduct spring log drives on the Moose River and the airport on the Black River above the mill would be used as a storage area.

The park below Lyons Falls has been a summer picnic destination for over a century.
Courtesy Lyons Falls History Association

The Gould Paper Company mill, Lyons Falls, N.Y. 1949. The plant was another field trip destination for the local women's club. Although the mill is now dismantled, the Lyons Falls History Association has preserved an extensive history of the operation in a museum that occupies several rooms in the local pharmacy. Courtesy Lyons Falls History Association

Four-foot pulpwood enters the mill on a conveyor from a huge woodpile located outside. The following scenes would have been what visitors would have seen. Courtesy Lyons Falls History Association

Massive vats of liquid pulp. Courtesy Lyons Falls History Association

A papermaking machine is a large, complex piece of machinery. Courtesy Lyons Falls History Association

Rolls of finished paper are being loaded into railroad box cars. Courtesy Lyons Falls History Association

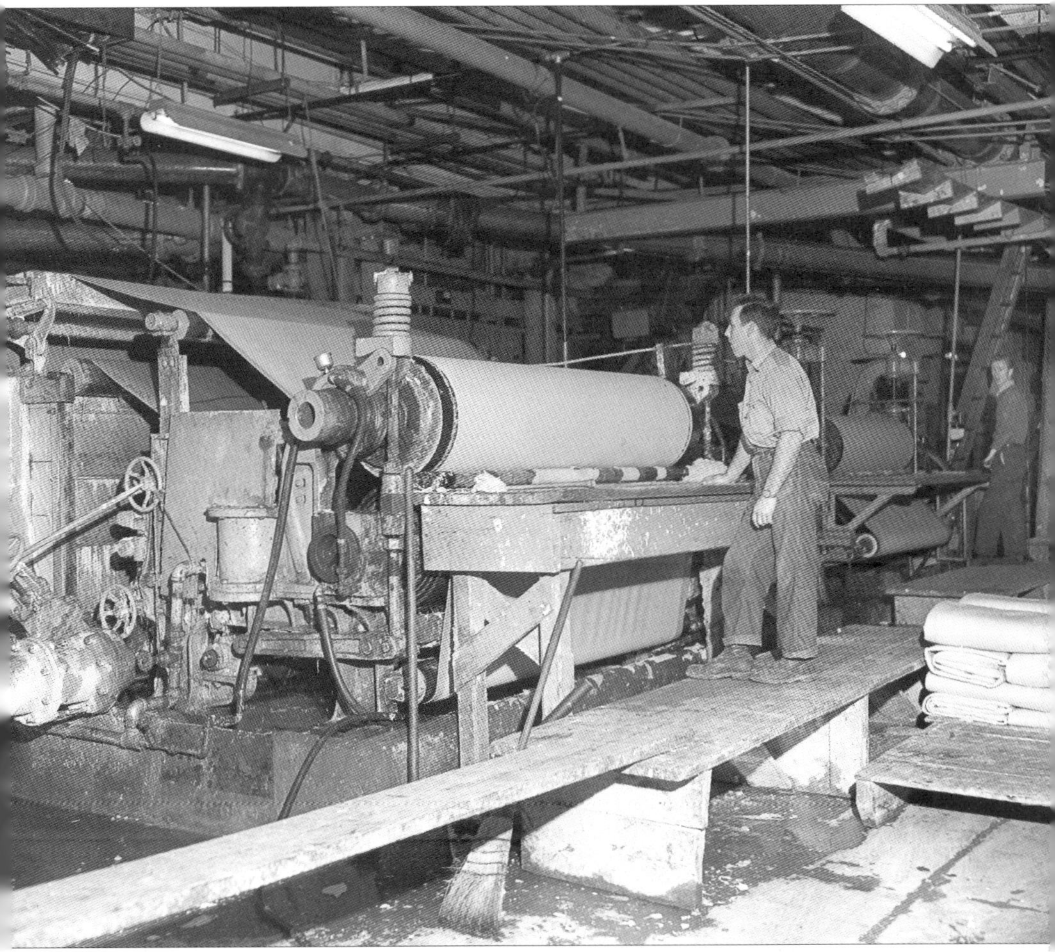

Finished paper begins to be rolled. Courtesy Lyons Falls History Association

Large rolls of paper being prepared for shipment. Courtesy Lyons Falls History Association

Finished cardboard tubes. Courtesy Lyons Falls History Association

Images of the former paper plant are only a memory imagined in mist in Lyons Falls.
Courtesy Lyons Falls History Association

Gould's ECHOES monthly magazine proved employees up-to-date information about the industry. The Lyons Falls History Association archives has almost a complete collection.

Courtesy Lyons Falls History Association

Adirondack TIM-Berrr!

Chapter 40 | William J. O'Hern

MARY TEALS' REMEMBRANCES OF TWO LOGGING ICONS

Around 1934 Teal's Express trucking company was awarded a major influx of new business. Their website reports "contract authority to haul paper from the Lyons Falls Paper Mills into the *Post-Standard* Newspaper in Syracuse, N.Y. This new contract became the basis for additional work in the Central New York Region and provided a base account for Teal's Express to grow on.

"By 1951 Teal's Express had expanded their authority into the Watertown and Dexter areas of New York. All family members, including Mrs. [Mary] Teal, were enlisted to help the business grow and prosper. Many local shop owners would give John Teal the keys to their stores so he could deliver food and produce at night, and, because of his reputation for honesty and integrity, they never had to worry about theft....

"In December of 1962 John Teal Sr. passed away, but the business continued on with his wife Mary and three sons, John, Robert, and Edward, as well as two daughters, Mary and Shirley...."

In addition to being involved with the family business, Mary Teal worked as the Lyons Falls town historian/ archivist. She enjoyed the human side of history.

When I talked with her in the 1980s, I was absorbed by tales of bygone days and at the same time eager to learn about current topics related to her town's paper mill, logging, and Northern New York. Older natives who knew family stories frequently shared snapshots and lovingly passed on their memories. These contributors supported the Lyons Falls History and their community because it was a good place to live. Many long-time families and their ancestors had been living all the while on the lid of one of the Tug Hill's richest treasure chests. While Lewis County residents might wish for a return to an earlier period in history when the local pulp and paper mill was a major employer, twenty-first century trends and lifestyles have changed the fate of many North Country communities. Because of the vast historical array of material Mary and her daughter Shirley Van Nest have preserved, a fascinating legacy to logging's rich past can be found stored in three places: the Lyons Falls History Association archives, the town's pharmacy former barbershop, and the Storms Bailey Home museum on Laura Street.

★★★

Old-time farm boys lived an active life outdoors, spending their days in fields and woods, either at work with axes, crosscut saws, draft horses, plows, and hoes, or on off days trapping, fishing, exploring, hunting, climbing trees and silos, swimming or playing in creeks and rafting on ponds. What might you guess they would do for a living as grownups?

Front row. Dorothy (with doll), John, Grandfather John B. Todd, Mrs. and Mr. Amsden, at Camp 7.
Courtesy Dorothy T. Payton

In the case of John B. Todd and Scudder B. Todd, their eventual professions were a continuation of their love of being in the great stands of Adirondack and North Country forests. J.B. Todd became a well-known Adirondack lumberman, woods superintendent for Gould Paper Company, and superintendent of highways in Lewis County. His son, Scudder B. Todd was the woods boss for Gould Paper Company's North Lake-Moose River operation. Scudder, and his wife, Hazel L. Todd, lived at Newport, N.Y.

Mary Teal found John B. and Scudder B. Todd's logging tales fascinating remembrances.
Courtesy Black River Canal Museum

These stalwart personnel were recognized natural woodsmen, trusted agents of the Lyon de Camp estate, and Gould Paper Company senior managers well-known to Mary Teal. Both were known for their interests in their community and attended to other business in Lewis and neighboring counties.

One enjoyment Teal engaged in was personal interviews. A number of her hand-written notes came my way when her daughter Shirley Van Nest handed me several pages of very roughly-scribed notes scrawled in a difficult, almost unrecognizable longhand. "That's typical of Mom's notes," said Van Nest. Yet, knowing Scudder Todd and the Rev. A.L. Byron-Curtiss were good friends of Mary's, and that at the time she was writing a biography about the Reverend, I accepted the challenge to decipher her notes.

Scudder Todd, woods boss of the Gould Paper Company's North Lake operations. Courtesy Fred Worden

They are representative of the kind of recordings many local historians take down that direct a ray of light on individual characters—a surviving record of someone long passed.

Teal's objective was to gather background on the career of Scudder Todd, the esteemed lumberman, but her meetings turned into something much more personal.

Mary's notes record the following.

> One day Marguerite Parrish, historian for the Town of West Turin, and I decided to go visit Scudder and find out more about the family, like great-grandparents and GGPs. We talked about family for a while and soon Scudder got talking about the woods and telling stories. Scudder tells the stories using everyday lumberman language.
>
> The Todds [Scudder and wife, Hazel L., who was born and raised in Fulton Chain–Thendara] made us feel so welcome. Mrs. Todd was a dear, lovely, sweet person. As we left we were invited to return soon.

About a week later I accepted their invitation and returned. Scudder told me that just back of the Buffalo Head in Forestport, there used to be a hotel. Later, the old building was used as John B. Todd's office [for Gould North Lake operations] and temporary living quarters. A lobby and rooms in the rear were used for woodsmen. Usually the 'jacks came there to sober up after the Big Spree and wait for the company truck to take them 18 miles to the foot of North Lake. The business office was a small room in the front of the building, the only furnishings being a huge safe, chairs and two desks.

JB [John B. Todd] would sit at the large desk taking an occasional puff on an old pipe. Bill, the bookkeeper, who wore thick horn-rimmed glasses, sat at a smaller desk. A wrought iron fence and gate separated their desks from the outer office. This divider was not really necessary to keep the tottering lumberjacks from leaning on the desks as they dickered for a higher wage until one upward thrust of JB's head was sufficient for them to stop their haggling and accept the company scale. His word was the law, yet behind the steel blue eyes was a compassionate understanding for these rough boisterous loggers.

Scudder remembered the B___[unrecognizable] were his neighbors when he lived on the farm in Remsen. Bill drove a team first and later one of Gould's early Linn tractors. His wife, Grace, cooked at the hotel. Scudder knew Fred Worden, who worked in the garage in Alder Creek and later worked at North Lake operations.

JB Todd was the woods superintendent for Gould Paper Company. The family used to live in Lyons Falls. Scudder Todd, his wife and son, John, eventually moved from Forestport to Newport, N.Y.

He told me on another occasion that Ed Wheeler stopped at the office to get a check. JB was sitting behind his desk smoking his old pipe and looking crosser than an old bear with cubs. Bill McCarthy, the bookkeeper, handed Ed Wheeler a check for $9.00. Then JB gets up slow like, opens the iron gate and says, "Ed, give me that check." JB didn't sound like he was fooling so

Ed said, "Sure JB, just put your little hand in mine." And, that was just what he did. He took Ed's check and tore it up. Wheeler winced and said to Bill, "You know you don't ask JB questions so, just write me another." And turning to the boss, Ed said, "JB you can have my shirt."

Ed Wheeler (center) at site of the Camp 7 machinery shed where six Linn tractors were lost in a fire. Late spring 1922. There are still visible remains of Camp 7 are scattered around the base of the valley between Ice Cave and Canachagala mountains. Courtesy John Todd (The John B. & Scudder Todd Collection)

"We could all see the old pipe quiver as JB chuckled like he had put one over on Ed. Then he turned to Bill and told him to make out another check for Ed for $400. JB handed Ed a little black book and told him to look inside and said, 'Ed, someday you may be needing this.' Ed put the black book proudly into his pocket."

After listening to Scudder a while I felt like I knew these lumberjacks. Ed Wheeler was a cook, L [unrecognizable] Roux, Johnny Pinochle was a foreman, and Mrs. Mally Irish another cook.

Ed Wheeler was a tall man with a drooping moustache and few wisps of reddish hair sticking out from under his white chef's cap. He was from Canada.

"Spring came early this one year," said Scudder, "and JB had to round up the crew from hotels and get them ready for camp and get Ed Wheeler sobered up as he was one of the first to go in. As Ed was being hoisted up on the back of the company truck loaded with potatoes, JB came out of the office in his shirt sleeves. He grinned at the woebegone cook, who being [unrecognizable] and had pleaded all morning for one last quart of whiskey. He got only an unresponsive grunt from JB. After the truck was completely loaded and Wheeler uncomfortably settled on a bag of potatoes, JB handed him a bottle and said, 'Wheeler, this has got to get you into camp tonight.' Wheeler gleamed and said, 'Well put your little hand in mine,' and reached for the bottle.

History-loving pals Jean Benjamin (Lt.) and Mary Teal. Courtesy Lyons Falls History Association

Adirondack TIM-Berrr!

Chapter 41 | William J. O'Hern

REMEMBRANCE: AFOOT WITH SCUDDER TODD

There was no room for humdrum in retired the Rev. A.L. Byron-Curtiss's summer days at Nat Foster Lodge, along the shore of North Lake in Atwell, New York. His comfortable camp was in the shadow of one of Gould Paper Company's large timber operations in the headwaters of the Black River that encircled Ice Cave Mountain.

Overtime, "B-C," as he often referred to himself, became tight friends with John. B. and Scudder Todd. One unmistakable passion Scudder and B-C shared was fishing. One memorable trout fishing experience B-C recalled[5] over and over to many camp visitors was of a day of angling in the waning years of the 1920s with his partner Scudder.

Scudder had a lightened work load during the summer. That afforded The Reverend the opportunity to spend a couple of days with Todd at Gould's Camp 7. At the time, Camp 7 was Gould's main headquarters. It was nestled in the valley between Ice Cave Mountain and Canachagala Lake, whose Native name means "rocky shores." Scudder managed his duties so that B-C and he were able to spend part of several days rambling the deep woods and fishing the streams in the vicinity of Camp 7.

Whether everything The Reverend recorded was true can be questioned; J.B. Todd's grandson and great-grandson, John and Scott Todd, admitted a bit of exaggeration might have slipped in over the years.

B-C and J.B. were known to have held quite a few hand-sawing contests for the Atwell Fish and Game Club. At the club, they also ran something else that drew a lot of attention, and that was a liar's contest. All lies had to be about fishing or hunting. B-C and Scudder heard some pretty good ones.

The following is from B-C's remembrance of being afoot with Scudder Todd.

Pushing through a thick growth of bushes, crowded witchhopple and alders that lined the banks of a stream they had earmarked for fishing, both men found the intertwined plant thicket a difficult stand to penetrate. "We were forced to look for ways out over the water or wade in," recalled Byron-Curtiss.

Scudder Todd (Lt.) at Camp 7. Courtesy Lyons Falls History Association

Spying a large three-foot-diameter pine leaning out over the stream, Scudder struggled over to it, mounted the log and began an unsteady creep—careful to recognize the slippery green patches of moss, and navigating through the tangle of broken and half-rotten branches that were not at all reliable handholds. About four feet out on the log the shoulder strap of his creel became tangled with an upright branch. As he twisted sideways to untangle it, his pole caught another branch. In one unexpected instant he lost his balance and slipped off. B-C related, "First came a great

Scudder Todd found the natural setting of the North Lake country to be one of his favorite places for relaxing recreation. Courtesy Rev. A.L. Byron-Curtis

shout, followed by a loud splash. He landed in waist-deep water." B-C was concerned, but the tone of his voice showed that the happening was a very funny scene. Byron-Curtiss continued his remembrance. "Stumbling, falling, laughing, bumping into a rock I never saw, and dragging a long branch I planned to poke out over the water as a retrieval pole, I worked my way as best I could to the edge of the bank to help him. Reaching land, I kicked the ground to make a good foothold, leaned backwards, stood immobile to steady myself against Todd's pull, and outstretched the pole in my arms."

Scudder couldn't help noticing Byron's grin. Grabbing hold of the pole his partner had extended to help him haul himself out of his cold bath, Todd yanked hard enough to tip B-C forward and into the stream. Then, looking at B-C, he cursed: "Sorry Reverend, but damn your comic rippling and a footbridge anyways!"

"We were wet anyway, so we proceeded to fish by standing waist deep in the water. In no time the trout began responding well to our attractive offering of 'garden bait,'" B-C said.

Eventually the chill and discomfort became too great. B-C shouted over to Scudder, who was working downstream but

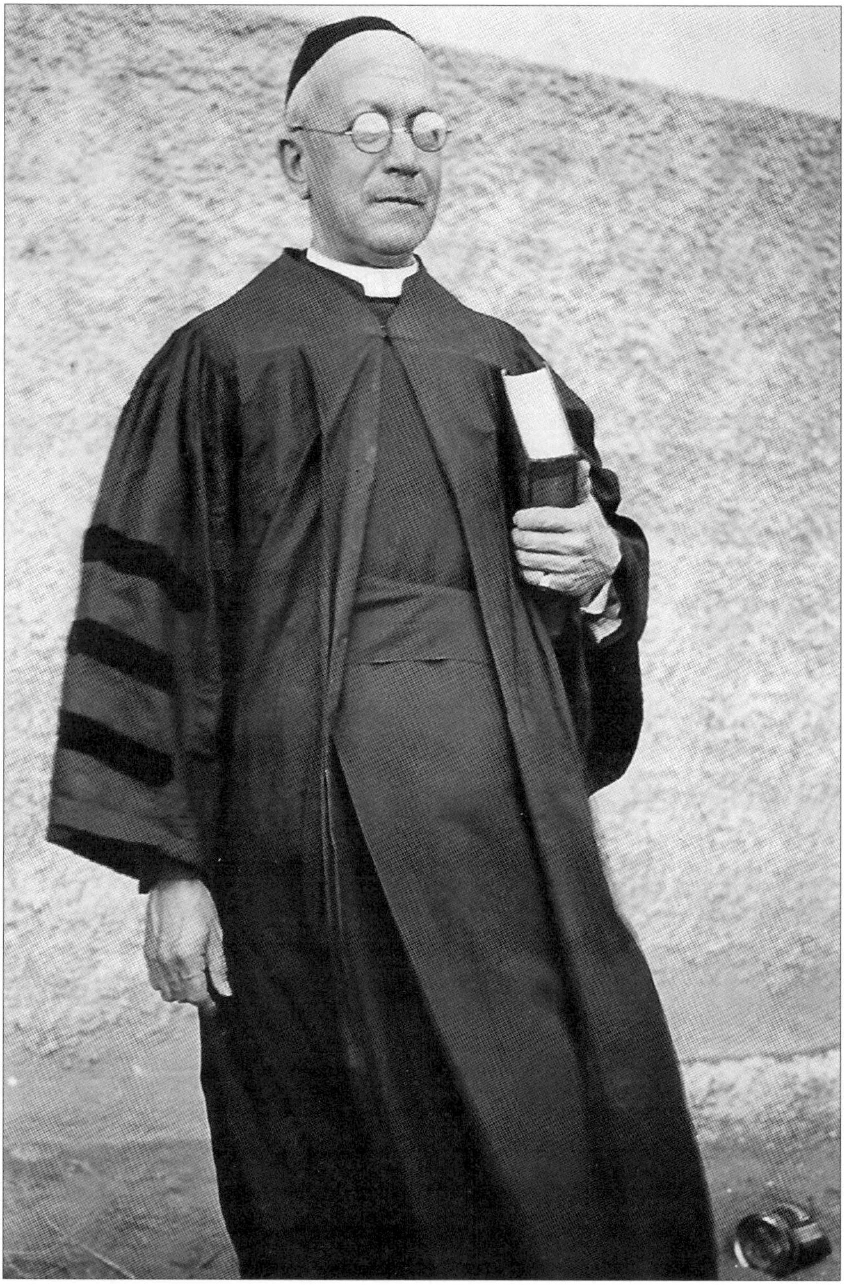

The Rev. A.L. Byron-Curtiss was an Adirondack preacher, a social philosopher, a political activist, and a believer in living as ascetically as possible. He was also a thief, a fish hog, a tippler, a scofflaw, and a nature lover. These are the elements that make good reading and a fascinating character. His story is told in the biography *Under an Adirondack Influence: The Life of A.L. Byron-Curtiss 1871–1959* by William J. O'Hern (The Forager Press, 2008). Courtesy Jeb Brees

A.L. Byron-Curtiss and Scudder Todd spent many enjoyable hours visiting over fish fry meals at The Reverend's Nat Foster Lodge at North Lake. Courtesy Thomas and Doris Kilbourn (The A. L. Byron-Curtiss Collection)

within earshot, "Todd, I love the forest as much as you value the precious timber. I'm going to start a fire." He clambered out of the water as he called a warning that was meant to be a parting salvo: "Stay off the bridges."

Byron-Curtiss had a fire going in no time. Soon Scudder, with chattering teeth, joined him, holding out his shaky hands to the heat.

The close friends laughed about the day's experience. Todd nominated The Reverend for "Hero of the Day," and their little fishing adventure became fodder for amusement in their many chats in later years.

Spring-fed Hardscrabble Lake was a favorite fishing destination for Scudder and The Reverend.
Photo by the author

Atwell Fish & Game Club, Atwell, N.Y. The annual summer club gathering near the foot of North Lake continues to this day as it did in Scudder Todd's day. Courtesy Bruce and Mary "Chick" Koenig

Adirondack TIM-Berrr!

Chapter 42 | Boyd W. Moffett

MICHAEL GLEASON, A MAN OF MANY TRADES

Among multiple old newspaper clippings Mary Teal had saved over the years in the Lyons Falls History Association archives is an interview with Michael Gleason conducted by Boyd W. Moffett titled "Moose River Section Once Center for Big Tanneries." The article I discovered was just the beginning. There were more articles, and I followed them down a trail to the past.

After some research, I learned that Boyd W. Moffett of Black River, long-time editor of The Farm & Garden, the Watertown Daily Times *weekly supplement, had interviewed Michael Gleason in 1940. The paper published six interviews then, and reprinted them in 1976. I obtained permission from John B. Johnson, the newspaper's CEO and co-publisher to include four of the interviews in this book.*

It's a rare treat for me to read first-person accounts by anyone who lived long ago. It is through their eyes and recorded words that one experiences vicariously a past time and place.

Gleason's remembrances began with the Black River Canal. This man-made waterway was built largely by Irish immigrants. A historic bike, hike and X-C path follows along the many locks that are still extant today, including a five-lock combination in the Lansing Kill Gorge, and four-lock combination just north of Boonville.

The canal brought a wave of prosperity to the Black River Valley. Thomas C. O'Donnell's Snubbing Posts *(North Country Books, 1972) tells the existence of the canal made it profitable to harvest the softwood forests of the western Adirondacks (Lewis and Herkimer counties). In winter and summer alike, legions of loggers invaded the forest wilderness, and sawmills sprang up on streams throughout the region.*

Timber, sawn lumber, and other wood products (pulpwood, firewood, shingles) were by far the most important commodities shipped on the canal, accounting for more than 90 per cent of the tonnage in the early years. In 1866, 29,000,000 board feet of lumber, 135,000 cubic feet of timber, and 10,000 cords of wood were shipped on the canal, destined primarily for the Capital region, the Hudson Valley, and New York City.

A canal boat at Gould Town along the Black River Canal. *Snubbing Posts* by Thomas C. O'Donnell (North Country Books, 1972) is an excellent source of canal history. Courtesy Lyons Falls History Association

Virgin spruce from the area was instrumental in building the Port of New York. Giant spars—often more than 70 feet long—were towed through the Black River Canal on multiple cribs. These water-resistant spars became the pilings for New York's wharves and docks. One important by-product of the lumber industry was hemlock bark, some of which was used by local tanneries, but most of which was shipped to tanneries in New England, where the hemlock forests had been largely cleared.

The Black River Canal made history. For the first time New York's North Country could get its goods to outside markets. Especially lumber and farm produce. Courtesy Black River Canal Museum

I like to think that if Michael Gleason was alive today, he would be a most enthusiastic interpretive volunteer guide at the Black River Canal in Boonville, N.Y. (http://www.blackrivercanalmuseum.com)

In another article I found, Michael Gleason reminisced about working in the tanneries along Moose River, but I learned he had also been a Black River canalman, had operated a hotel, was postmaster at Carthage, a shoe merchant, and also Jefferson County Sheriff.

Boyd Moffett's interesting interviews with Michael Gleason are a plum for local history, for they collected and documented facts about earlier times that otherwise would have been lost to the passage of time. The interviews also preserve the character of Michael Gleason, who cut quite a figure a century ago.

The first article in the series tells about Gleason's days as a 16-year-old steersman on the Black River Canal.

★★★

"Canal Days: A Hustling Life"

By Boyd W. Moffett

For over a century the Black River Canal was a busy thoroughfare, serving as the leading route by which materials from this section, chiefly lumber, were transported to outside markets.

At Rome, the southern terminal, the canal linked with the Erie barge canal to form a direct route to New York markets via Albany and the Hudson River.

Although abandoned now for a number of years, portions of the old canal locks still stand and are visible from the state highway between Carthage and Rome. In many places the canal bed has been filled with dirt to provide a sub-base for the highway.

The Black River Canal joined the Erie Canal at Rome, N.Y. Its life span ran from 1850 to 1922. In that long corridor of years folks who ran the boats, tended the locks and kept the canal in running condition, made the most of this early transportation system before the age of the automobile.
Courtesy Black River Canal Museum

As early as 1821, boats were operating on Black River. At that time the river was declared navigable to Lyons Falls, then known as High Falls.

However, the river was not seriously considered as a suitable waterway prospect until about 20 years later. Although the canal from Rome to Boonville was completed in 1868, the route north in Lyons Falls was not rushed and it was November, 1855 before the first boat moved into Black River above Lyons Falls.

Michael Gleason, who as a boy worked as steersman on the canal and later was a hotel operator at Moose River and Carthage, as well as postmaster at Carthage for 28 years, recalled his experiences on the canal.

"I first went on the canal as a driver for three months with Thomas Flynn, whose home was in Cohoes," Mr. Gleason began. "When I was 16, I was a steersman, the youngest boy known to handle the tiller.

"Some boats on the Black River Canal were 100 feet long, 14 feet eight inches wide and about seven and one-half to eight feet high. They were capable of carrying 85 to 90 tons of produce.

"The cabin, located at the rear of the boat, projected about two feet above the deck. Here the captain and his wife slept. There were cooking quarters and bunks for the drivers and steersman.

"The horses were stabled in the prow. Each boat carried two teams. One team worked six hours pulling the craft, while the second team rode in the prow.

The George Weaver canal boat docks at a Forestport sawmill to take on lumber.
Courtesy Black River Canal Museum

"Boats on the Erie Canal were slightly larger," continued the former canal driver and steersman. "They measured 100 feet long and 20 feet wide and carried about 240 tons. They were much slower than the Back River boats, however.

"The Black River Canal was four feet deep and from 50 to 60 feet wide. Boats drew about three and one-half feet of water.

“There were 100 locks between Rome and Lyons Falls. Seventy of those locks were located between Rome and Boonville. Between Boonville, the summit of the canal, there were two sets of three locks and one set of five locks. Above Boonville there were three sets of four locks. Then there were two locks in Black River, and one at Bush’s landing and one six miles above.

“Approximately 1,000 boats plied the canal during its boom days, with a driver and steersman paid about $30 per month.”

Life on the canal provided a bustling day’s work, according to Mr. Gleason.

“There was a difference in the Black River and Erie barge canals,” he said. “The Erie Canal ran day and night. The Black River Canal, when I first went on, ran daytime only.

“They used to tie two boats together, fastening them with lines tied from the bow of one boat in the stern of the one ahead. One man would then steer from the rear. One pair of horses would draw the two boats and would go about as fast as if they had only one. Black River boats started this idea and after a few years the Erie boats copied it.

A boy leisurely fishes The Basin, Lyons Falls, N.Y. Markham’s Mill is in the background behind Huzzy’s Hotel. Courtesy Black River Canal Museum

Following the Black River towpath south today from Boonville to Pixley Falls brings to mind memories of former days along the same route. Courtesy Black River Canal Museum

"The boats started at Beaver Falls, then left Lyons Falls from a sawmill. They had about 20 boats to Albany and made the trip in about twelve days, down and back, going with a big load and coming back empty. Black River boats were smaller and faster than Erie boats. When they had two boats lied together they ran day and night and changed crews every six hours. Steersmen and captain started at 7 a.m. and at 1 p.m. they changed the crew, steersman and driver of the teams. The ones who came on at 7 in the morning came on again at 7 p.m.

"The lumber district in Albany where they unloaded was about three miles long and a quarter of a mile wide," continued Mr. Gleason. "The lumber came from all over the country. Much of it came in from Oswego and Buffalo and the northwest. They would pile the lumber up as high as any building in Carthage.

Port Leyden's Lock 96. A number of the Black River Canal locks exist today to investigate north and south of Boonville, N.Y. Courtesy Black River Canal Museum

"Lumbering was a big thing in those days and the canal was a busy place. When I went on the canal they paid 29 cents a bushel for carrying wheat from Buffalo to New York on Erie boats. I was also on the canal when they carried it for six cents a bushel from Buffalo to New York. When they were getting the high rate they were going pretty fast. Lumber was transported at so much a thousand or so much a trip.

James Murray visits with lock tender Everette (last name unknown) by the side the tender's station. The Black River Canal operation was a kind of family or neighborhood affair. Courtesy Black River Canal Museum

"The season usually opened the latter part of April and would go well through the first of November. We made 15 trips down and back in a season."

"Was there any rivalry along the canal to see who would get through first?" Mr. Gleason was asked.

"Oh, yes," he replied. "Once I drove down to Boonville where there is a place called Bull's Run. As we were coming back, I said: 'There was a man living in that house and his name was Stewart Keyes. He had two sons who boated when I did.'

The Black River Canal at Lyons Falls, N.Y. Courtesy Black River Canal Museum

"Just as I made the remark, a man walked out on the porch. My wife said that he probably wouldn't remember me, but I figured I could talk with him just the same.

"'Who lives here?' I asked, and he replied: 'Ed Keyes'

"I said: 'I used to boat it when you did.'

"He immediately replied that he remembered I had worked for Jared Randall. "I said: 'I thought all the people had forgotten me down here.'

"But he replied that all the people knew me and just then his brother came out and said, 'You were the only human being, Mr. Gleason, who could see in the fog as well as in regular weather. You made one more trip every year because you could see in the fog.'

Canal near Port Leyden. A work crew loads a barge. Tons of sand, blocks of limestone, timber, potatoes, shingles, barrel staves and other agricultural and industrial products accounted for a high annual percentage of tonnage from year to year. Courtesy Black River Canal Museum

"I don't know what there was about it and I don't know why, but I could see the whole outline of the canal in the fog.

"The canal was really a hustling life," Mr. Gleason added. "A lot of people thought it was a tough life, but it wasn't. It wasn't a drunken life. Men on the canal boats had to be sober. It was dangerous if you didn't have your senses about you."

★★★

The interview I found in the Lyons Falls archives brings together information about the once- thriving tannery district around the Moose River, where thousands of hides were transported from New England for processing. This interview was the third in the series published in the Watertown Daily Times.

"Moose River Section Once Center for Big Tanneries"

By Boyd W. Moffett

"The Moose River section of the Adirondacks," wrote Moffett, "situated about 15 miles northeast of Port Leyden, was for a number of years a thriving tannery district. Thousands of pounds of hides were brought from the New England states each winter to be processed at Moose River tanneries.

"After you left the canal, didn't you work at Moose River?" Moffett asked his interviewee, Michael Gleason.

The Lyons Falls History Association maintains an extensive museum pertaining to Gould Paper Company history, logging, the Black River Canal and local history in the back portion of The Falls Pharmacy in Lyons Falls, N.Y. Courtesy Black River Canal Museum

"Yes, I drove team and drew bark," replied the man who has seen many trades during his 75 years.

"Bion Carter was head at the Moose River tannery. I drove a company team and took bark out of the woods. There were about 500 teams drawing bark that season and the jobbers came up to the woods to buy it.

"Hemlock, as you know, grows about three or four feet through on the stump. They would take off a ring about four feet long and then peel bark off and then fell the tree. A man with an iron spud would peel the bark off. He had to do that when the sap was in it, too. They would peel it off the tree and spread it out where the tree was cut down to dry and cure.

"I never did any of that work but I watched and saw how it was done. They piled the bark up when it was cured, rough side up. Then they cut roads out and piled the bark along the roads. The horses from the canals were taken up there as soon as the snow came, to work in the winter drawing bark. They worked until about April when the roads softened up and made it difficult to get into the woods.

Lyons & Snyder Tannery at Moose River Settlement was 630 feet long. Trace remains of the vats are still visible. Courtesy Town of Webb Historical Association

"They drove the bark out to a tannery and put it in stacks and ground it up fine. There were big vats about 16 feet in diameter and six feet deep at the Moose River tannery, and those were filled with ground bark and hot water run into the vat. When they drew the water off, the juice from the bark was used to tan the leather.

The Lewis-LeFevre Tannery was one of many industries that once dotted upstate New York. *Hides, Hemlocks and Adirondack History* by Barbara McMartin (North Country Books, 1992) is an excellent resource on how the tanning industry influenced the growth of the region.
Courtesy Lyons Falls History Association

"Hides were brought from Boston to Port Leyden by train. There they were put on sleighs and wagons and brought to Moose River, about eleven miles. They were tanned in the liquor they got out of the bark and then fished out of the vats and put through the sweat pit to finish the operation. Sole leather was processed in the tannery there.

"Of course those plants all wore out after a while, but they had tanneries at Fine and Houseville and there was one in Carthage years ago. They woke up, after they got the bark all skinned out of the country, that they had only gotten about ten per cent of the juice out of the bark. They had wasted most of it because their water wasn't hot enough."

★★★

Other than this interview conducted by Moffett in 1940, there are very few sources about Lyman R. Lyon and H.D.H. Snyder, Jr.'s Moose River Tannery. Today the site that developed at a ford in the river between McKeever and Port Leyden is known as Moose River Settlement. If one carefully walked around the site of the former tannery settlement today, they would still see the depressions where vats were once located.

A Beaver Falls tannery woods crew. Courtesy Lyons Falls History Association

McMartin's book about the Adirondack hemlock bark tanning industry provides an excellent history and footnotes to other sources about the tannery once located along the Moose River Road. Moffet's interview is not among the sources in her bibliography. A close inspection of The Town of Webb Historical Society's framed photograph of the tannery shows the huge vat building and other buildings associated with the tannery, including a boarding house, a blacksmith shop, a sawmill, and a hide house. Also interesting is a large photograph of the Lyon & Snyder mammoth 630-foot tannery at Moose River that is part of the Town of Webb Historical Association collection in their museum in Old Forge, N.Y.

★★★

Close by the Moose River Settlement was Abner Wood Lawrence's popular hotel that could accommodate twenty-five guests. The large building was first known as Lawrence's Moose River Hotel, later, under Carney's ownership it was called the Moose River House. Michael Gleason worked at the Moose River Hotel when it was owned by a Mr. Carney. In this fourth interview in the Watertown Daily Times *series, Boyd Moffett talked with Michael Gleason about his job at the Moose River Hotel.*[6]

Moose River Hotel Houses Lumberjacks and Tourists

By Boyd W. Moffett

This is the fourth in a series of six articles on early northern New York history, as recalled by Michael Gleason, former canal-man, hotel operator and Carthage postmaster. The article today describes the Moose River Hotel.

When lumbering was at its peak in the southwestern part of the Adirondacks, the hotel at Moose River did a thriving business. During the winters it housed the logging crews. Summer trade was composed of tourists and wealthy down-state residents who had summer homes along the Fulton Chain.

Jim Higby stands beside a carriage that transported guests over the rough, unforgiving Moose River Road to the hotel at Moose River Settlement. Courtesy Lyons Falls History Association

"I worked at Moose River driving team one winter, and Bion Carter said to come back the next fall and he would give me a better job," said Michael Gleason. "I weighed bark and leathers that winter.

"When it was spring I hired out to the hotel. We had guests up there that went up the Fulton Chain. There were tourists in the summer and in the winter we had the men who worked in the woods.

A group of Beaver Falls tannery bark pilers. Courtesy Lyons Falls History Association

"The logging crews, despite their reputation were not rough or crazy unless they had a reason for it. I went to work for John Carney, who conducted the hotel. That was my first hotel work. He had been there six years. It was a temperance house, but Mr. Carney got a license shortly after that. If I had known that I probably wouldn't have gone to work for him. We didn't do much of any business in that line, however. The people going through were not drinking people. There was no bar-trade to amount to anything.

Sleigh loads of hemlock tree bark. The bark was an essential ingredient used to tan animal hides.
Courtesy Lyons Falls History Association

“I did the chores, took care of the horses and the outside work. The first of May we heard there was a party coming to go to their camp at Fourth Lake. They were the Louis Lawrence family of Utica. Mr. Carney said: ‘You needn’t pay any attention to them. They haven’t spent a cent here.’ I had the idea if you kept a hotel you should pay attention to people.

“About 11 that morning they put the horses up in front of the hotel. Mr. and Mrs. Lawrence were on their three-seated wagon. I went inside, got a chair, took Mr. Lawrence’s hand and helped him down. He smiled and thanked me very nicely. Then I helped Mrs. Lawrence down. They were pleased. No one had ever paid any attention to them there before.

A Beaver Falls tannery crew of workers. Courtesy Lyons Falls History Association

“The driver drove up and changed the packs to a buck-board to go the 13 ½ miles through the woods. They came by stage lines. When he was changing the packs he looked rather slow, so I helped him. Mr. Lawrence was walking up and down. When we got the packs tied on, Mr. Lawrence called out and said they had better stay for lunch. They had lunch and the fellow hitched up to his buck-board and left his wagon there. They thanked me for what I had done.

"Mr. Carney said 'What! Mr. Lawrence had lunch here?'

"He said that was the first lunch they had had there since he had operated the hotel.

"They were in and out of the woods about every two weeks. I knew when it was time for them to come out and was anxious for them to stop again. When they drove up Mr. Lawrence called out: 'We'll have lunch here again today, Mr. Gleason.' They always stopped after that.

Loggers often frequented the Moose River Hotel. Courtesy Lyons Falls History Association

"Once the Lawrence family was going through to camp and they had Mr. Lawrence's father with them. There were four men from Old Forge who came out to Moose River, fixed up a wheelbarrow and were going to carry the old gentleman through to the camp. They got started about 9 in the morning and the old fellow was tired even then. They had planned to have the men carrying Mr. Lawrence change every ten minutes.

Tourists who enjoyed vacationing in the area often hired camps to be built for their seasonal visits.
Courtesy Lyons Falls History Association

"Mrs. Lawrence called to me and asked if I could go with them. I said I didn't know as Mr. Carney was there all alone. She said: 'Well, if we hired Mr. Carney's team wouldn't you go along to drive them?'

"So, they did that. When we got five miles they stopped. One of the men carrying Mr. Lawrence was really sick. It was suggested he drive my team and I told them I'd help carry. We carried one mile and it took 40 minutes. After we got to Old Forge we put him on the boat and took him to camp."

★★★

In another interview, the fifth in the series, Gleason explains how lumbering and tanneries kept men occupied during the winter and how they worked as guides for wealthy tourists during the summer. Michael Gleason remembers a time when transportation was only by foot, wagon and over the Fulton Chain of lakes and tells of how a seemingly incidental good deed won him an election.

"Life Was Exciting at Moose River [Settlement] in 'Good Old Days'"

By Boyd W. Moffett

Life at Moose River "in the good old days" was far from dull, it was recalled today [in 1940] by Michael Gleason, as he sat at his home at 118 North School street and reminisced of the days when he worked in the woods and operated a hotel in that section of the Adirondacks.

The lumbering and tannery industries kept men occupied during the winter seasons. In the summer there was plenty of opportunity to hire out as a guide for parties coming up the Fulton Chain of Lakes on vacation trips.

Moose River Hotel. Bert Morehouse, the proprietor stands far right. Courtesy Lyons Falls History Association

"The fellows who came to Moose River in the fall to work in the camps were a rougher 'lass,'" said Mr. Gleason. "We didn't have any trouble with them, however, when Mr. Carney was there. Along about Christmas time when the men came back in I could see they had been drinking, so I closed the bar room. I told Mr. Carney that we would have to have one idea of running the hotel. We decided to close the bar at 10 every night and after closing at 10 on Saturday nights, we didn't open again until Monday mornings.

An angler tries his luck in the Moose River. Courtesy Lyons Falls History Association

"Mr. Carney sold out after two years to Charlie Barrett. He and his family had operated a hotel at Old Forge. He was a good-natured fellow."

"Were there many camps in the Moose River neighborhood?" Boyd asked Mr. Gleason.

Roughing it. Courtesy Lyons Falls History Association

One mode of travel over the muddy, rock-strewn Moose River Road, Brantingham, N.Y.
Courtesy Lyons Falls History Association

Possibly a church group from Boonville enjoying an outing at Moose River Settlement.
Courtesy Lyons Falls History Association

"Oh, yes," he answered. "At that time it was necessary to pass through Moose River to get up to Fulton Chain and there were numerous camps along the route. They went by saddle horse and buck board. In one day, I have seen as many as 40 saddle horses go through to Old Forge. People came from New Jersey, New York City and Pennsylvania. Many came up from Syracuse and the cities along the Mohawk Valley.

A cozy Adirondack camp. Courtesy Lyons Falls History Association

"Guides did the cooking and took care of the camps. They used to get pretty good pay, too; they received $10 per day. They had a boat and would carry it from one lake to another. The only way to go from Old Forge to Fourth Lake was to row up there.

"They didn't want it any different then," said Mr. Gleason, chuckling. "The guides got big money that way."

"One time when I was at Moose River," continued Mr. Gleason, "I had to get to Port Leyden to summon a doctor for a little girl at Moose River who was critically ill. I had to go through a cut where the snow had melted and there was enough water there to drown the horse. On the way back I followed the doctor, and his horse was frozen after going through the water.

"The results of the trip were brought out in the next election, strange as it may seem.

"Mr. Carney, for whom I had worked at the hotel, was a staunch Democrat. On the average, only seven Republican votes were cast at Moose River during any election.

White-tailed deer hunting season drew hunters to the Big Woods. Courtesy Lyons Falls History Association

"On this particular year, we were voting for governor. Then there were the various town office elections and it promised to be a stiff battle all around. I had introduced different candidates around there, not thinking the people would consider their qualities and vote for them.

"I had the Republican ballots on Election Day and Mr. Carney had the Democrat ballots. Mr. Carney went across the street and stayed there from the time the polls opened until they closed. People came asking for ballots, so I told them I had the Republican forms and Mr. Carney had the Democratic.

"The Republicans got the majority that year. People said they voted for the Republicans because I had indicated they were friends of mine. I learned later that they said the reason they had voted for the Republicans was because I went out that night to get the doctor from Port Leyden for the little girl when they thought no one could get through."

A guide-baked slapjack outdoor luncheon at Lone Pine Camp. Courtesy Lyons Falls History Association

★★★

Speaking of elections, a 1926 Watertown Daily Times *article reported that Gleason, who had been Jefferson County Sheriff from 1918 to 1920, had announced his candidacy for nomination in the September 1926 primary, on the Republican ticket. The article explained, "Although the laws of New York prohibit a sheriff being candidate for re-election as his own successor there is nothing to prevent a citizen who has held the office in earlier years from accepting nomination and election."*

Michael Gleason was a man who served his in his community in a variety of ways, and one who was clear about his feelings regarding alcohol. As county sheriff when Prohibition began, he may have had more exciting adventures than are recorded in this chapter. Gleason's life was like many of those in the Adirondacks who did whatever job they could find to make a living, but Gleason seems to have had an extra dose of ambition. He seems to have had a great deal of influence on his employer, Mr. Carney, and his stints as shoe merchant, as sheriff, and as Carthage postmaster for 28 years show his leadership in both civic and government endeavors.

Stony Lake, Glenfield, N.Y. Fishing continuous to attracts anglers to the Adirondacks.
Courtesy Lyons Falls History Association

Jay O'Hern (left) and Dick Ulrich in front of Hemlock Mercantile building at the Black River Canal Museum in Boonville, New York. The popular seasonal exhibit has a life-size canal boat, a blacksmith shop and interpretative exhibits and a research room. Information about the canal is found at www.blackrivercanalmuseum.com. Courtesy Dick Ulrich

Adirondack TIM-Berrr!

Chapter 43 | William J. O'Hern

PERK AND SCUDDER

Born Donald Walter Joseph Perkins in 1896, "Perk" first took aim at a deer in 1905. By age 9 he had become a lumberjack, skidding logs with a team of horses. In 1910 he began his career at the Adirondack League Club (ALC) as a bellboy. In 1912 he became a bona fide guide, and in 1920 began full-time employment (June through Labor Day) at the ALC.

Perk's mountain justice (game wardens called it outlaw behavior) regarding hunting was first shaped in tandem with his upbringing. Families prepared throughout the summer for survival during the long arduous winter. If things really got tough after a family's cows, pigs, ducks, and turkeys were eaten, deer were sought. In Perk's opinion, "the best venison to eat was killed between June 15 and December 14," I learned from him when I interviewed him in the early 1980s. I wish now I had asked what the normal hunting season was. I just accepted his manner of speech indicated some taking of deer meat was out of season.

During the Great Depression, North Country natives experienced hard times. Perk could earn 75 cents for the hind quarter of a deer. "Sneaking an occasional hind quarter or two out of the League Club even in broad daylight was not uncommon; it was survival," he told his biographer, Ed Levine.

Older woodsmen were his mentors. Born in Old Forge, Perk was recognized by the old-timers as a kindred spirit. Common to many natives, Perk's outdoor work, activities, and sense of fun were driven by the ominous and uncertain economic ups and downs of the rural north country community as well as by the thrill of breaking rules.

In the fall of 1920, armed with on-the-job experience gained from years of working at his father's Third Lake lumber mill operation, Perk entered employment with the Gould Paper Company, a giant in the timber industry. Working in the woods, he met Scudder Todd, Gould's lumbering operations boss.

Both men were successful fishermen and hunters.

Scudder learned of Perk's woollier ways, including poaching (compliments of the League Club). The mountain man had no problem bagging a buck or two every now and then somewhere on the League's 96,000 acres "at night with the aid of a telescopic sight and a little lighting." The reality that killing deer on ALC property was illegal did not stand in Perk's way. His sources for venison were often millionaires. Levine said a $50 fix from a source for venison was "a drop in a bucket of water." Old Perk "knew which palm to slide" the bribe into. No ALC guard at the club gate "ever saw" Perk go in at night, nor did they observe him leaving "with a fresh kill."

Byron-Curtiss wrote of his first official visit to the camp in *Adirondack Stories of the Black River Country* by William J. O'Hern (North Country Books, 2003). His lengthy memory began:

> **Monday morning, August 16, 1926, Scudder Todd and I boarded his power boat and rode to his company's landing near the head of North Lake. From there we tramped the remaining eight miles over the rough tote road to lumber camp 7 of the Gould Paper Company. John B. Todd, superintendent of Gould's forest operations and Scudder's father, had invited me the previous year to be a guest of the camp while we were on a fishing trip together. This was my first opportunity to avail myself of Todd's hospitality. I planned to use the camp as my base from which I would leave to search for the often talked about but rarely seen Ice Cave and the snow and ice on the mountain of the same name. Camp 7 was positioned at the northern side of its base in a valley between Ice Cave and Canachagala Mountains.**
>
> **On my arrival, I found the camp so unusual and possessing so many varied departments and enterprises new to me for lumber camps that I tarried there all of one day....**

The Reverend's full account of Gould's camp is a rare historical insight into the logging camp that has now vanished into the memory of all who once worked there. Courtesy John Todd (The John B. & Scudder Todd Collection)

Donald "Red" Perkins in his Riverview Drive yard in Old Forge, 1976. As he relaxed in his chair Perk enjoyed passing on knowledge. Here's one opinion regarding doe seasons he felt cause a huge reduction in the white-tailed deer population.

> ***One buck can take care of 50 does if he can catch them. But kill one doe and you've lost three deer. The more does you kill the less chance a herd has of multiplying.*** Photo Courtesy Town of Webb Historical Association

If you looked at any number of old timers who lived between the 1890s and the 1930s, you'll positively find a few frayed sepia-tone photographs of the woodsmen dressed in woolen clothing down to the socks and long underwear with rifles and fishing rods prominently positioned, looking about as roughneck as any woodsman has a right to appear—the great Adirondack sports hero, as filtered through the popular novels and folklore of the day.

To Perk, their bold ways seemed to sum up the mountain justice that often came hand in hand with natives' ideals of rugged individualism. Opposing regulation was just his modern-day way of stating he opposed anyone who messed with his freedom.

Perk was also known to have a lot of fun. He and Scudder found a special freedom together; adventure was a part of their lives.

Scudder Todd. Courtesy Lyons Falls History Association

Grandfather Scudder's stories are a part of Scott's life. "I still think of my grandfather," Scott Todd told me, "and each time I'm hunting near Old Forge, Scudder's spirit reminds me of this special tale. It's a true story that Scudder told me about the ALC when I was a boy."

The tale shows that Perk and Scudder considered themselves exempt from ALC rules.

From left, Robert Goodsell, Red Perkins and Pitt Smith stand next to a successful day's deer hunt.
Courtesy Town of Webb Historical Association

★ ★ ★

No Trespassing
Property of the
Adirondack League Club

So read the enameled metal posted signs. But Perk didn't care.

"Scudder, probably because the Adirondack League Club leased a huge chunk of land from the Gould Paper Company, gained permission from the club to hunt on League property. I don't remember if he had been given permission to take friends also but that is what he did." Scott didn't think his grandfather would have made light sport out of allowing friends to trespass and poach on ALC posted land, but he obviously did make an exception with one buddy.

"Grandpa made arrangements with a few friends and when deer hunting season began they met near Old Forge Pond and drove together to the club, going in through the South Shore Road gate.

"Well, as Scudder put it, his friend Perky 'hadn't had any venison in a while and was dying for a good buck.'" Perky was a marked man. He had traveled extensively throughout the League's preserve. He knew firsthand how the rules were being enforced. Perk held a guide license from the State of New

York Conservation Department. He was licensed to act as a guide for hunting, fishing, and camping parties. He knew the state laws and club's rules and for the most part he upheld them. However, not unlike other turn-of-the century Adirondack natives, Perk opposed outside influence. He didn't always agree with newly-decreed government regulations that the state imposed. And, like some locals, he resented the wealthy private preserve. Their posting of thousands of acres didn't sit well with him.

Perk guided for the ALC. He considered himself a servant. He never lost his temper with an employer. It was common knowledge that any employee who made an inappropriate remark or had an 'outburst of nastiness' would lose their job. Perk always said, 'You had to be very careful how you talked to club members. All they had to do was say that so and so wasn't wanted at the club any more, and that was the end of your career. You had to be damn careful. You were always the underdog.'"

Perk told Ed Levine there were plenty of times when he "would have gained a great deal of satisfaction by kicking one of the members in his or her behind." But he "trained himself to smile instead during difficult moments."

"'Some of them were sarcastic, especially when they got full of scotch. The minute they got to drinking, they got ugly," Perk shared with Levine.

Perk's retribution came when he was deep in the preserve. He knew that the farther one got back in the woods, the less the laws were observed.

"Scudder was fully aware that his friend Perk was an outlaw poacher," Scott continued. "He had been banned from the ALC."

"After some coaxing, Scud agreed to smuggle Perky into the club, hidden inside the trunk of the car. Scudder waved to the gate keeper as he passed and that was all there was to entering.

"'Well,' Scudder said, 'we all got bucks that day including Perky. On the way out, the bucks were tied all over the car, all except Perky's. We hid his rather large buck in the trunk with him.' Anyway, the gatekeeper was Mr. Carmen. I worked with his son Daryl, who was on the Webb Police Department when I was a Trooper in Old Forge."

As Scudder's vehicle exited the club's gate, "Carmen noticed the back of the car was squatting low and demanded that they stop and open the trunk. When the trunk was opened Perky and the buck were discovered."

"Carmen demanded Perky climb out and bring the buck over to the office. Once that was done, he started scolding Perky."

"'I know you're banned from the club,' Carmen chided. 'I'm taking this buck and reporting you.'"

"Carmen's words provoked Perk. A violent struggle resulted between Carmen, Perky and the buck. In the end Perky got the upper hand and broke away from Carmen, who was pulling at the large animal, which looked much too big for Perk to carry easily over his shoulders."

The sign Perk and Scudder considered themselves exempt from. Courtesy Robert J. Elinskas

"Now according to Scudder, Perky, in a single jerk, lowered the animal to the ground, grabbed hold of the rack, and started drawing the buck over the snow as he took off running alongside the beast as fast as he could toward the South Shore Road. Carmen took off after him in hot pursuit. Scud and his buddies jumped back into the car and followed their friend. Carmen was not about to let Perk get away any more than Perk was about to be nailed with the animal.

"Well, the road to Old Forge was covered with a hard-packed layer of snow and ice and the gatehouse is at the top of a long hill. When Perky crested the top he jumped right on the back of that big buck and rode it all the way to the foot of the hill, laughing all the way."

"The scene was hilarious. Scudder and his party were all laughing. My grandfather said, 'Old Perky was riding that buck just like a toboggan, using the antlers to steer.'" To add indignity to the strange and funny scene, "Carmen fell half way down the hill. By the time he got back on his feet, shook off the pain, and regained his composure, Perky and the buck were out of sight."

"Perk was not about to be found with the evidence in his hands. The illegal shooting took place on the Adirondack League Club preserve. Perk was out of bounds and he knew it. Perk needed to conceal the evidence. The local rumor mill held that the buck hung in every freezer in Old Forge over the next few days while the ALC searched for it."

If truth be told, the longer it took for the authorities to search for the evidence, the more popular Perk became. In the barrooms from Old Forge to Boonville, patrons were talking about Perk. There were any number of whoops and hollers of joy for brave Perk, who took on the wealthy establishment.

Jake's Maple Diner, Old Forge, N.Y. Owner Jake Berkowitz stands in the window.
Courtesy Town of Webb Historical Association

His outlaw status was getting so much publicity and gaining him such popularity that others might have thought about committing a similar trespass as they downed their suds. After a week of investigation, the buck had not been found and a new incredible question began to circulate: "What if Perk's innocent?" He wasn't, but first he had to be proven guilty. The case was finally dropped. The ALC knew the charge would not hold up in front of the local justice of the peace unless the buck was discovered. To Perk's clever credit, Scudder bragged, "they never found it."

Scott found this part of the story ironic: "But for all the deer Perky put away while doing for a meat-hungry family, he had a natural dislike for the taste of venison. Perk has said on more than one occasion that despite all the fishing and hunting he did over his lifetime, he was '…not fond of fish or venison. If there was nothing else, I ate it. We lived on venison for a time because we didn't have anything else and we couldn't afford anything else.'"

"Years after hearing this story as a boy," Scott continued, "I was a state trooper stationed in Old Forge in 1978. Ed Levine had recently written *The Adventures of Red Perkins, Remembrances of an Adirondack Guide*. It was a small book about Perk's Adirondack exploits."

Levine met Perk at Jake's Maple Diner, owned and operated by Jake Berkowitz, when he arrived in the Adirondacks in the winter of 1975. The former newspaper man said "the locale at once entranced him." Over the course of the winter, Perk and Ed became fast friends. In his foreword, Levine had this to say about his newfound buddy: "Most folks called him Perk. Some knew him only as Red because of the color of his hair. Those closest to him used his name, Donald. For more than three-quarters of a century he has been up to his ears in a heady love affair with the Adirondacks.

"He was a hard worker. He was and still is a true friend. He was and still is a firm upholder of morality, although his friskiness got in the way at times. He never stopped being young at heart, and this is his most refreshing quality."

"I found Perk living in the first home on Riverview Drive along the Moose River in Old Forge," remembered Scott. "I was in uniform when I went to his place to speak with him. Before I left, Perk told me my appearance had alarmed him. His initial thought, seeing me at the door, was that I had come with a warrant for him. We had a nice visit. I asked about the toboggan buck story my grandfather told about him. He didn't deny it. In fact we both laughed about the story, which he confirmed as the gospel according to Perky."

★★★

I shared with Scott my familiarity with Perk. I had read about him in The Barkeater, a magazine that featured Adirondack sporting stories. The article elevated Perk to local celebrity status.

It appeared on the newsstand the year I began researching the history of the Moose River Plains. I was a total stranger when I knocked on his door. I remember he had country music playing on the radio and that he warmed quickly to me. "Sure I know about the Plains," he said. He seemed genuinely interested in talking to me and sharing his knowledge of the wilderness.

As the time passed, I realized I had not brought along enough tape cassettes. Perk's head was a treasure chest of tales. "Dump the gun and let's get the hell out of here quick," were the last words recorded on my single cassette.

Both Scott and I were lucky to have been able to share Perk's memories and laugh with him as he looked back on his past. The men and women who had rich memories of their pastoral homeland in the early days in the Adirondack Mountains have all passed on. It's a shame only the surface of those stories has been scratched and recorded. There are so many other tales of living in the mountains that have not lived on.

November 28, 1976. Red Perkins at age 80. Courtesy Town of Webb Historical Association

Adirondack TIM-Berrr!

Chapter 44 | William J. O'Hern

MORE ABOUT "PERK" PERKINS

There weren't many limits to Perk Perkins' escapades.
—Mart Allen

It's true. Donald "Perk" Perkins Sr., first a logger and then a caretaker and guide for the Adirondack League Club in Old Forge, N.Y., was a colorful character.

Perkins was known for voicing strong opinions. One he freely expressed many times was about the careless lumbering by the big companies that he said was nearly the downfall of the Adirondacks. He held that much of the land that was cut over around the turn of the 20th century had still not fully recovered by the 1980s. He said, "Franklin Roosevelt attempted reforestation during the Great Depression, but the forests never did amount to much."

Donald Perkins, as was the case with many Adirondack guides, started out logging with his father. His father Joseph operated a small sawmill at Third Lake, and Donald's job was skidding logs with a team of horses.

By the time that Forest Ranger Mart Allen arrived in Old Forge on December 3,1958, Perk's exploits were well-known. It's been said his legendary status began to develop in 1914, when at the age of 18, he performed a truly amazing feat as part of his job as and Adirondack League Club (ALC) caretaker. The story goes that the foreman of Little Moose Lodge at the ALC told Perk he could earn $15 by delivering a Parsons guide-boat to the president of General Electric, who owned a camp at Honnedaga Lake.

After rowing the boat across Little Moose Lake, he hefted the 87-pound boat and carried it nine miles, mostly uphill, to Honnedaga, where he left it.

Since he had a date that night to go square dancing at White Lake, and he didn't want to miss out on the fun, he RAN the eighteen miles back to Little Moose Lake! Because he was too tired to swim the mile across the lake to the lodge, he skirted the lake's shoreline, which added two and a half miles to the trip. Perk's total journey consumed forty and a half miles, and he accomplished it in nine hours!

In Perk's later years he spent the majority of his time working on projects around his yard on the banks of the Moose River, and at Jake's Diner, where he caught up on the local news.

It was most likely there that Mart Allen not only first met Perk but also began to pick up stories about the old days.

The following story is Mart's heartfelt remembrance of Donald Perkins. It originally appeared in Mart's long-running weekly *Adirondack Express* column "To Make a Long Story Short" on August 25, 1995.

★ ★ ★

I personally had the privilege of knowing Donald Perkins Sr. There is no question in my mind that there never was a more interesting character to emanate from the Adirondacks!

He was known as "Perk" to all but his wife and possibly his best friend, Reg Villiere. He was "Donald" to Reg, and you sensed a mutual bond that was not to be invaded by outsiders using Perkins's given name.

Some of their escapades became known to me directly from one or both, and others from their many friends and acquaintances. Many of the disclosures came in later years after they had mellowed. I sometimes felt they were disclosed as an offer of repentance.

They were poachers par excellence and, like Willie Sutton, operated where the loot was plentiful. In their case, this was the Adirondack League Club. The Club bore the brunt of many of their indiscretions. They had access through their guiding and caretaking work, and you could say it was like "giving the rats the keys to the cheese factory."

The Club was very different in its security, which I am sure presented a challenge that spurred them on. A 24-hour watch was maintained on both entrances to the Club throughout the deer season. This proved to be a minor inconvenience to them and others.

The deer [they took] were stored in some unsuspecting owner's icehouse until the season ended and the Little Moose gate was unmanned again.

There was always a ready market for venison. George Elthorpe related one episode: Late in the winter Perk had a customer for a hind quarter of

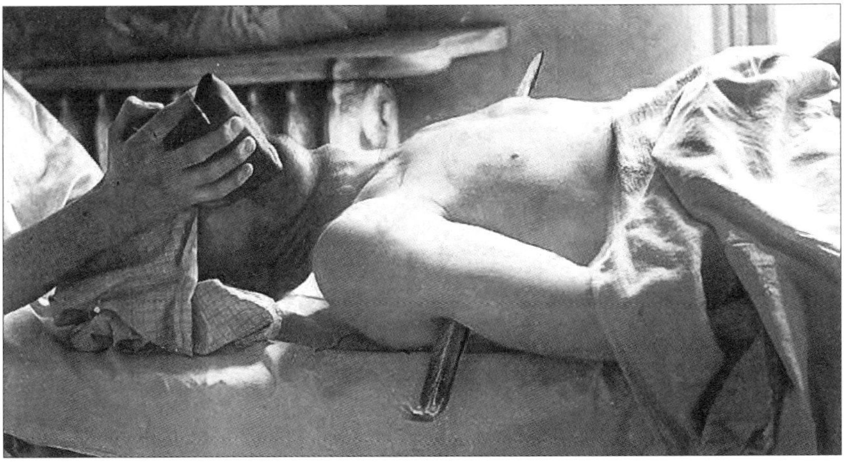

George M. "Cobby" Lanz, age 38, lies in the hospital before the massive splinter was successfully removed. Perk, who said he was a teenager in 1908 at the time, reminisced about the horrific accident that became a matter of some medical history during the author's meeting with him.

The following story of the Thendara, N.Y., sawmill accident is from the author's unpublished *Adirondack Timber*. It reports background and details of the sawmill accident in Thendara, N.Y.

> The Old Forge area had two mills, one of which was run by the Pullman brothers, who operated largely in spruce. Their spruce production included many quarter-sawn spruce fiddle butts for the Breckwold mill at Dolgeville.
>
> Dr. Stewart W. Nelson of Old Forge, who was a native of Taberg and graduated from Boonville High School, lived in Old Forge since 1897. In the early years in that community, he made many medical calls in neighboring lumber camps, including one which stood on the present site of the theatre in that community. Peter Landry, who clerked later for the Finch, Pruyn Company, was the camp clerk. Some camps in Dr. Nelson's early years were a few miles from Old Forge; others were north and south of Old Forge along the Adirondack Division of the New York Central Railroad.
>
> Most of those medical calls were made on men who were ill or had been injured on the log jobs. A few of them were to vaccinate against smallpox and quarantine men who were ill with it. In one case along the Adirondack Division, the call involved the vaccination of the entire camp of forty men.
>
> Dr. Nelson experienced an unusual accident which took place at the Pullman Brothers mill in 1906. George "Cobby" Lanz, who was the edgerman in the mill, lifted a spruce edging which was stuck on the saw.
>
> As it came free, the swiftly-revolving saw caught it again and sent it like a bolt of lightning. The thirteen-foot edging pierced Mr. Lanz's chest and came through on the right side of his back, also piercing his right arm. Members of the mill crew carefully sawed both ends of the thirteen-foot piece so Mr. Lanz could ride in the baggage car. He was treated by Dr. Nelson, who accompanied him to St. Elizabeth's Hospital in Utica on the train.
>
> After careful examination, Dr. Hyland, a prominent surgeon on the hospital staff, decided to remove the edging through the back and proceeded to do so. George Lanz recovered and had many useful years of service. His son, Frank Lanz, was an experienced printing pressman at the Willard Press in Boonville. Frank reported his father fully recovered from the mishap—passing at the age of 78 in 1944. Photo Courtesy Town of Webb Historical Association

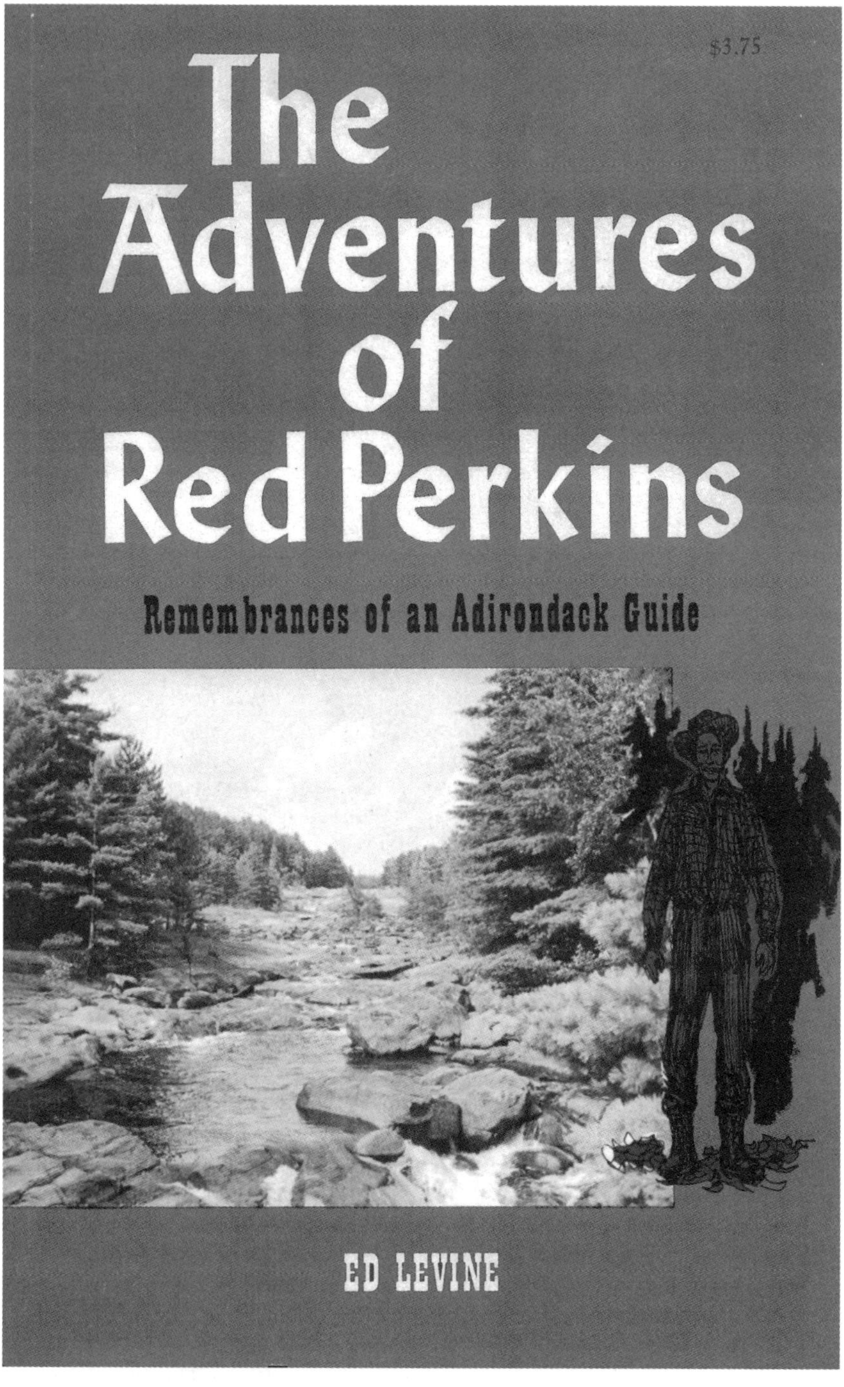

The out-of-print book *Adventures of Red Perkins* by Ed Levine (North Country Books, 1976) is a classic tale about an Adirondack guide and logger. Author's collection venison. He had none available, but remembered a hind quarter of bear George had hanging.

Bill Lawrence, a Club member they were guiding, had killed an old boar bear during the season and George had saved the quarter for just such an occasion.

To make a long story short, the quarter ended up in the trunk of the customer's car in the Knotty Pine parking lot and Perk chalked up another of his famous stings. I would really have enjoyed being there when they tried to eat that quarter of "venison."

This was mild for Perk, who once fed a nasty little neighborhood dog to his poker buddies.

They all enjoyed the meal, which was not complete without Perk informing them of what it consisted. The owner, a man named Pete White, soon learned of the dog's fate and never spoke to Perk again.

Jake Berkowitz was a loyal friend of Perk's, but it did not stop Perk from making him one of his victims.

Jake told me that Perk supplied him with some lake trout for which he paid Perk in cash. At the end of the month, Jake received a bill for the same fish from Marks and Wilcox's Market. Jake had a good laugh and always felt it was worth every penny he paid.

Perk did not always emerge unscathed from his escapades and he was known to run afoul of the law on more than one occasion.

★ ★ ★

Late in Perk's life he did not hold back his worries about the changes in the attitudes of people and his concern about the future of the Adirondack Park. Perkins lived long enough to see he had outlived the majority of the local old-time loggers, people he had guided, ALC workers and many old-time millionaire ALC members. He died on Sept. 27, 1986.

Now 91 [in 2019], Mart Allen often looks back at his career, folks he knew, and old snapshots with fondness, sharing some of the same concerns Perk did. Mart has enjoyed a rich and varied life, and continues to live at his home along the banks of the middle branch of the Moose River.

Adirondack TIM-Berrr!

Chapter 45 | William J. O'Hern

MARJORIE NELLENBACK

Blaze orange-jacketed deer hunters were heading into the surrounding Tug Hill upland when I visited with Marjorie Nellenback on a brisk, cool autumn day in 2017. Marjorie had enjoyed my book *Adirondack Logging* and followed up by writing me. Her short letter reported:

> *I am a lumberjack's daughter. I grew up in Swancott Mills. My father worked for John Hogan for years and I have a picture of my father in a Linn tractor and three or four other pictures. I live in Ava, N.Y. right on Route 26. There is a sign out front that reads Nellenback's Antiques. If you are interested in talking to me, give me a call.*

Swancott Mills was once a thriving community. Photo donated by Ed Fynmore. Courtesy Lyons Falls History Association

Marge stands by her front door in Ava, N.Y., June 2018.The first time we met, I asked if her "Beware of the dog" sign hanging in the front window was because of her collectable antiques. "No," she replied, "I tell everyone to never mind the dog. They better just beware of the owner. I know how to use a gun." Photo by author

Over a century ago, the area north of Camden, N.Y. (that included Swancott Mills) had been lumbered for hemlock bark, not its wood. The bared logs had been left in the woods to rot while the bark was shipped to tanneries[7] for processing leather. The Costello tannery in Camden stood where Teelin Motors was established in the 1930s, and there was a good-sized tannery in Altmar, besides those in Florence, Osceola, Redfield and other places on Tug Hill.

David Swancott established Swancott Mills in1867. He was the grandfather of Mrs. Mary (Dick) Burke, who operated Hills Fine Jewelry in Camden. Mary lived at the lumber camp until she reached high school age.

Swancott Mills School, 1905. Photo by Ed Fynmore. Courtesy Lewis County Historical Society

Water power was used to run the saw mill at Swancott Mills. According to the *History of the Town of Lewis 1805–1883*, by Franklin B. Hough, the original mill "was built by Mr. Herman, and afterwards owned by David L. Swancott." In addition to the mill there was also a broom handle and paddle factory at Swancott Mills.

The mill also shipped out railroad ties, lathing and raw lumber.

Swancott Mills was in the western part of the town of Lewis. It was entirely destroyed by fire on February 7, 1907. The mill and community was rebuilt in 1919 according to the *History of Lewis County, N.Y. 1880–1965* by G. Byron Bowen. Bowen's history tells:

The Hogan homestead in Redfield, N.Y. The boy by the fence is John Hogan. The farm is no longer there. Courtesy Marjorie Nellenback

The mill had employed about thirty men, and David Swancott of Lee Center was the owner at that time. …the Tug Hill Co. with principal offices at Swancott's [sic] Mill in the town of Lewis filed a certificate of incorporation…for the purpose of dealing in timber and timber lands, stumpage and real estate of every description…. In 1965 this property was owned by Joseph and Chester Kwasniewski. A large new mill was built and the business was known as the J. & C. Lumber Company.

In 1953, Mrs. Burke described the location to *Lumber Camp News* correspondent Mary Ruth White,[8] formerly news editor of the Camden *Advance-Journal* newspaper. She described the now-vanished community this way. "The lumber camp was a complete village with a school, general store, boarding house, company houses for the married lumbermen and dance hall. They even had a baseball team. The tract was sold in 1920 to the Gould Paper Company." Nothing now remains to show what a complete community once occupied the site.

Gordon Gould stands by his modified Model A Ford snowmobile. Courtesy Ernest Leigh Portner

Ninety-year-old Marjorie Nellenback has carried a soft spot in her heart for her childhood home at Swancott Mills and the logging activities she grew up around. Yet even as she shared cherished memories, she made it clear that she would not, even if it was possible, want to go back to her childhood to face the problems of that time without the knowledge that she had gained along life's way.

Marjorie should not want to leave the present, even for a moment, lest she miss some exciting antique road show, or a thrilling partridge hunt or other opportunity of the time in which she lives.

Marjorie is a no-nonsense person, an active antique dealer, a life-long hunter and an example of the generation of Tug Hill natives who faced and lived through challenging times. A sign prominently displayed in her front window announces that she willingly and capably defends her turf with firepower. As an example of her inner toughness, Marjorie, sick as she was, incredibly went partridge hunting literally hours before her scheduled surgery for a collapsed colon. That's grit!

Nellenback's remembrances of growing up a logger's daughter on Tug Hill provide quite a contrast to today's 21st-century way of living. And while they are a collection of memories that recapture the past, they disclose her personal home life—typical of the late 1920s and 1930s when there was no television, and radio was in its infancy. When children arrived home from school, there were chores to do. Marjorie never mentioned children whining about having nothing to do (probably because her parents would have immediately thought up something).

Teamster Conrad and his tobacco-chewing horse. Courtesy Marjorie Nellenback

One of her weekly chores was helping her mother bake. It was typical to make a week's supply of bread, cookies, doughnuts, pies and cakes. And there were other responsibilities she learned to help with, such as churning butter and turning the handle on a hand-operated meat grinder to turn out hamburger and sausage; canning; being familiar with caring for animals; and learning to butcher animals they raised.

These were just some of the everyday activities that were part of being a logger's daughter.

Marjorie remembered: "My father worked for the Gould Paper Company. The Goulds lived nearby. Gordon Gould used to ride his horse past our house. His dog always tagged along. We had a dog that was half police and half Eskimo Spitz. Our pet and Gould's dog always fought. Our dog always managed to get the best of Gordon's dog by rolling him over. That made him mad because his dog could never win a fight. I remember he would ride by about every other day—that was during World War II. I was about 12 when the war began. Gordon knew Jack Hogan, dad's boss. Gordon had very little personal contact with my family. He was a big shot in the Gould Paper Company.

"I recall there were some families named Swancott who lived in Swancott Mills. My family's house was two and a half miles west from Swancott Mills along the West Leyden-Osceola road. The Abbotts once operated a general store. In my day the store was gone but there was a dance hall behind Freeman's Hotel. It was a popular place. Most of the Swancott Mills people walked everywhere because they didn't own cars. All our neighbors used to go to the dances. There was always a big crowd there and of course the bar room drawed 'em in too.

Marjorie Nellenback recalls that this picture of her parents, Grace and Bud Rocker was taken just before her father started walking to the store in Osceola. Courtesy Marjorie Nellenback

Howard Wieman operated this bulldozer during the two years Gould's work crew developed the access road into the Moose River Plains. Courtesy Harold Linck

"Howard Wieman and a teamster who worked for Hogan named Conrad, but who everybody called 'Red,' used to attend the dances. Red chewed tobacco, and often shared a plug with his horses. The horses liked the tobacco. It was a treat for them. They'd chew it right along with Red. Red was a short, round, heavy guy. Howard was a big and powerful fellow. He used to lift Red up over his head and twirl him around on the hardwood dance floor. Oh how those fellows used to raise heck at the dances.

"They used to have good western musicians there. My mother told me, 'When you reach 12 years old, your father and I will take you to the dance,' and when that time came my parents asked Becky Hogan if she'd drive my mother and me to Camden to buy an outfit for me to wear.

"Loggers, people in the community and those from around Fish Crick and gals towards West Leyden—why, people from all over and from all the back roads attended. Who'd know how popular the place used to be back then, because just about all the remnants of what was once Swancott Mills is gone today.

"I didn't live just in Swancott Mills. My father moved our family more than a dozen times before I attended high school. Each logging job might last one to four years. Dad always built a little camp for the family on the log jobber's property. The buildings were small—one main room to cook and live in heated by a wood stove, and a kitchen all fueled with wood, and two bedrooms. A curtain separated my parents' bedroom from us kids. All the kids slept in one room sharing beds. There was no running water. I could show you today the creek we carried water from to the house.

A Linn snow plow kept the Osceola-West Leyden Road open in winter. Courtesy Ernest Leigh Portner

"We cooled our perishables in an old boiler pan that was sunk in a bottom-fed cold spring. There was no refrigeration or electricity. A large lid held down with a rock protected the contents from bears, raccoons—well any animals from getting the meat, eggs and homemade butter. We heated with wood."

Bud Rocker on a dozer. Marjorie said her dad, like so many oldster, had many skills.
Courtesy Marjorie Nellenback

Marjorie handed me winter scene of her mom, Grace and dad, Bud. She said it was a mid-winter day the picture was snapped. The couple was standing on the road that lead to the Osceola –West Leyden Road when they lived in Swancott Mills, She remembered, "When our pantry ran out of flour and sugar, Dad would strap on a pack basket and walk six and a half miles to the grocery store in Osceola to restock the essentials. We raised pigs and chickens, made our bread and butter, and canned vegetables raised in the garden.

Swancott Mills has long been a destination for hunters. Photo by Ed Fynmore. Courtesy Lyons Falls History Association

"Dad didn't just work in the woods. He drove Linn tractors and worked as a mechanic; he'd repair big tractors and worked on all sorts of mechanical equipment.

"I didn't hear many logging stories—you know we lived the life, so it wasn't something the family heard around the dinner table.

"One time he got hit in the face with a big log hook and one other time when he was riding a load of sleighs piled with logs as it went downhill one of the sleds got stuck. Dad went between the loads to see what was wrong. All of a sudden he saw the sled on the uphill side begin to slide toward him. All he could do was drop down flat and hope it would slide over him. But that wasn't the case. Dad didn't get one foot entirely out of the way. His leg got caught and that injury laid him up for a good month.

"The accident was hard on our family but back then our house was owned by Hogan so there was no rent and we didn't have electricity, and so we had really just groceries to buy. Otherwise we lived like everyone else. We just got by. People today couldn't live that way. You could say we lived on nothing—because actually we didn't have a thing other than a place to live in, a dishpan to wash up dishes, a fry pan, and food enough to get by.

"Hogan, Dad's boss, had a smoke house to cure our pork. We'd smoke half a pig and the other half we ate fresh. We always butchered them in fall when cold weather came on. Kept it hanging in a little building and it would freeze and whenever you wanted a piece of meat you went out and sawed it off. I never saw any black bears come around; they were up in northern Osceola."

By the end of World War II loggers throughout the country had developed more interest in forest conservation. While Gould had always been a leader in this movement, by 1946–47 men who worked on logging jobs, in the sawmills and in all branches of wood-working industries were beginning to realize the importance of a steady harvest of logs.

Marjorie Nellenback, like other Tug Hill natives is familiar with deep lake-effect snow.
Courtesy Marjorie Nellenback

In New York State, the *Lumber Camp News* was one publication among others in many parts of the country that printed articles about intelligently managed forests. Loggers and large companies like Gould realized that in order to do this they needed look to those who owned and controlled forest land beyond the companies.

Professor Unger of the New York State College of Forestry at Syracuse University reported that "Most of our forests are in private ownership. There are four million small owners and operators, about three million of which are farmers, and they alone own approximately one-third of all private forest land."

Professor Unger was engaged in public relations work and public education in forestry and felt that, "while in the past, owners and operators have been accustomed to harvesting the original forests without any thought of the future, today [1948], not only through the urging of employees but through government agencies and others who have an interest in public welfare, scientific forest management is gradually being achieved."

Many states, like New York, had set up systems for assisting the private owner in placing his forest land on a continuous production basis.

A panoramic view of Swancott Mills. Photo donated by Ed Fynmore. Courtesy Lyons Falls History Association

Forest conservation progress had been slow, Unger said, but it had been steady, protecting the forest against fire and other destructive enemies through reforestation, in-field service and information dissemination.

But Professor Unger stressed, "we must attain a still greater appreciation of the value of the forests and how to manage them before a sufficient supply of the various kinds of wood and stabilized employment in the industry is secured."

When Marjorie and I find a common time to take a nostalgic car ride back into the Tug Hill forest of Lewis County, and to walk to sites long familiar to her, I hope those dreams and memories that were once a young girl's and are now a woman's will expand to include even more.

An unidentified man stands near his Swancott Mills homestead in 1905.
Photo donated by Ed Fynmore. Courtesy Lyons Falls History Association

Through the years, Marjorie carefully kept her favorite Swancott Mills family pictures in her photo album, and as she sat and remembered at her Ava home kitchen table, she would put up a hand and say, "I can see everything so clearly even now."

As her mind raced from subject to subject, the cassette tape recorder preserved a flood of memories that poured out.

> We had a small garden; it wasn't much because half the time dad would come in, say "Hogan is done" and we needed to move on to so-and-so—like Highmarket, Michigan Mills or whatever. Whenever my father walked to the store it was only for staples: lard, sugar, flour, rice, maybe some canned peaches…
>
> We lived so differently than kids do today. We had playing cards for entertainment, but not much more. Kids played outside. In

Marjorie's remembrances of growing up "Tug Hill strong" could easily become a full-fledged book.
Author's photo

> the winter the snow was so deep we shoveled holes in snow banks to hollow out caves and lit a kerosene lantern inside. The heat hardened the inside walls. We'd all go in there to play. That's all we had…. We'd move in Hogan's truck…We had hardly any clothes, a decent outfit and school clothes. Mother did a lot of sewing by hand. She cut and hand-stitched dresses for the girls and shorts and shirts for the boys' outfits—five of us in all. When there was enough money I remember someone drove us to the movie theater in Boonville, it was probably Shirley Temple or something, and when we lived in Lyons Falls I remember we walked all the way to Port Leyden to see a picture show—a Saturday western, probably Roy Rogers or Gene Autry. It might have cost a dime or quarter to get in. I don't remember.
>
> All the logging families' fathers around us all worked for Jack Hogan. Hogan employed large crews at camp 4….
>
> Dad followed Hogan to about the beginning of the war [WW II], then Hogan and McDermont went into the Gould Paper Company. We moved back to Swancott Mills three times. We lived a good distance off the road. Dad would be gone all week and only return home on the weekends.
>
> Mom managed the family by herself and kept a loaded .22 rifle, and she knew how to use it.

A majority of the small houses Hogan built for his employees are now privately-owned camps. Marjorie said she could lead me right to the one that was her home eighty-three years ago. "It's a fair distance off the West Leyden-Osceola Road, but there's a gate along the dirt track that blocks the private portion of the road," she explained.

My cassette quickly filled with her logger daughter memories. They served as a seal to her past. I told Marjorie she could quickly fill a yellow notepad with what she remembered for her grandchildren, and how easily it could become a full-fledged book of remembrances: *Rings of a Logger's Daughter's Family Tree*, it might be titled. It would be a true product of Tug Hill told in personal details of simple living. Histories of an area wrapped unforgettably in personal reminiscences are some of the best stories of a homeland, because they offer unusual charm.

During Marjorie Nellenback's childhood it was a common practice for people in Swancott Mill's to walk to distant Osceola for supplies. Photo by E. Clark. Courtesy Lewis County Historical Society

But for the time being I'll look forward to Marjorie's guided tour back to where the community of Swancott Mills used to be and where David Swancott first bought prosperity to The Hill.

Where cellar holes fill with large trees now,
And red-tailed hawks still sail,
A girl of the forest and mountains
Still dreams and tells her tales.

Her old trails threaded the woodland,
Deep through the spruce, hemlock and pine;
Coursing a way to Fish Creek's source,
And crossing The Tug's wide spine.

—W.J.O.

Adirondack TIM-Berrr!

Chapter 46 | Ken LaFrance

KEN LAFRANCE RECALLS LIFE IN A LUMBER CAMP BEFORE CHAIN SAWS

I quit school at 16 years old (in 1949) and lied and said I was 18 and got a job in the woods with my father. Later on, the boss told me if I hadn't been with my father he'd have never let me go in there at 16.

The first year we didn't stay in camp. We'd get up at four o'clock in the morning and walk two miles to catch a ride. And then we'd get in the back of a pickup truck and ride another, probably, eight miles. And it was cold. And the same thing reversed at night.

The logging as such, the big logs, was pretty well done up in this neck of the woods. So we were cutting pulp (near Duane) for the St. Regis Paper Company. And of course it was all done by hand. As a matter of fact, on the job I saw my first chain saw. Didn't impress anybody very much. To begin with, the guy couldn't get it started. And once he got it started it didn't seem to cut much faster than the handheld bucksaws we were using.

We used to cut two cords of pulp a day. That was the going amount everybody did. When we first started in the morning, (my father and I) would go in the woods. And we would fall a lot of trees, just keep knocking them down. Then he would get a horse and he'd start limbing them up and hauling them out. And then I would saw them up. I cut them up myself with a bucksaw—four-foot pieces. And with any luck at all, at the end of the day, we'd have two cords. And for that we each got eight dollars. Got eight dollars a cord for cutting pulp. And it was hard work, no two ways about that.

We were cutting along the side of a river. I guess they call it the Everton River. They would load (lumbar) on big long double sleds. They'd haul probably two or more cords on a sled. And they would just follow down—on the ice it was

Peeled pulp stacked and waiting for the spring runoff. The bark was peeled by hand spud. When the river was right, logs went tumbling down. Photo by Dewitt Wiley. Courtesy Leigh Portner just easier going, while the ice was good. But when it got toward spring and the ice was bad…they had to haul through the woods out to the road.

The next year when we went in, we went up here on what's called the Blue Mountain Road (near Santa Clara). And we stayed in a lumber camp there. We were, I guess, probably 15 miles back up in the woods. Mostly in the winter the only thing that went up through there were the bigger trucks that were loaded coming out. They did plow it, but that was a bad road. There was a lot of ice and some big hills. It was tough going. Trucks were stuck often and we stayed right in there.

Typical lumber camp in Ken LaFrance's days in the woods. Courtesy Bruce Koenig

I can't tell you the exact size of the camp. But the first winter there were about 40 men staying in there. We had a stove made of just a steel barrel, one on each end (of the room), for heat. For water for washing up we had a pipe that ran from the spring on the hill, ran into the camp through the wall—that wasn't warm water. And the camp was only made of single boards covered with tar paper. And in the middle of the night it would get mighty cold when the fires went out. Nobody would get up and take care of the fire, so when the fire went out it got cold. But in the early morning, about 3:30 or four o'clock, there was one old guy who would get up and start the fires and get things going. I think everybody else got up around four. And breakfast was served by five.

We ate good, I'll say that. We always had a good cook. (They stayed) right there. They had a little room. … The cooks didn't last long because it was hard work. You were working a lot of hours and they were older people. Usually, if they could get them, they'd get a woman and her husband and he would take care of the fires and things like that while she did the cooking. And our breakfast consisted of almost the same thing as every other meal, except we would have eggs for breakfast. Everything else was the same; meat and potatoes. Because we ate, say, about 4:30, five o'clock in the morning and you didn't get anything else to eat until noon. So you filled up pretty good for breakfast.

Six cylinder Linn tractors had been replace by Caterpillar crawlers by 1949. Courtesy Leigh Portner

It wasn't very glamorous working in the lumber camp. The first couple of days that I was there in winter I got up in the morning and I couldn't find my socks. They had wires where we strung up our socks and mittens and wet

A good camp cook kept loggers returning to the same camp year-after-year.
Courtesy Lyons Falls History Association

clothes and such. And I told my father, I said, "Somebody's taking my socks every night." And he said, "Well, that's normal in a lumber camp. First ones up get the best socks." So, after that, I was up early and I got a decent pair of socks. Not necessarily my own, but I did get something that didn't have holes in them.

You didn't keep a lot of clothes or anything like that. You'd keep an extra set in case you got wet. Outside of that, you didn't keep too much stuff in there. And for the most part they didn't bother anything else. Mostly, it was socks and maybe mittens. We wore buckskin mittens with liners in them. And they were warm. They kept you warm. My biggest problem was keeping my feet warm. My feet always got cold.

(In the spring, the blackflies) would carry you away. And they didn't have the good stuff, like they have today, to keep them off. My father wouldn't put anything on. He said, "You get sweating good and they won't bother you." Well, I never got to sweating that good. They used to make (repellent) with pine tar and citronella and, I don't remember, some kind of oil base. It kept the flies off good, but you'd be all black, putting it on. And you'd smell like a pine tree for weeks afterward.

The old lumberjacks went out twice a year, spring and fall. They'd work all winter. When spring comes, they would draw their money and head for town. They'd put them up in the Riverside Restaurant or the hotel that was (in St. Regis Falls) at that time and they'd stay until they spent all their money and then catch a ride back in. They were in awful shape when they came back in. They could hardly walk. Some of them, that's all they would do is walk up and down the road, try to get in some kind of shape to get back into the woods and go to work again. I don't think any of them lived to be awfully old. A lot of the lumberjacks weren't married or anything, they were alone. So that's all they worked for was to get enough money to buy a pair of pants and shirt, and maybe a pair of boots if they needed them, and then drink it up.

The "Barnsmell" boys was a good-humored expression given to these unidentified lumberjacks.
Courtesy Indian Lake Museum

One guy, he would go back out at night after supper with a lantern and saw pulp that he had skidded out during the day. Night after night he would do that. Mainly so he would have more money when spring or fall came and he went to town.

He died drunk. And he wasn't very old, either. I worked with him a little bit, we were good friends. And sometimes at night we'd go out—and we weren't supposed to, but him and I each had a fish pole in camp. Because it was all on private land, we couldn't have guns or fish poles or anything like that. But we snuck a couple of them in there and some evenings, if the guys were wanting to have a fish feed, we'd go out and catch enough trout to feed everybody went. Some of them would only haul four cords on a load. And it would take them all day to go over there, deliver it and come back, and if they were hurting for money, which they usually were, they would come back in the middle of the night, we'd load them up and they'd go again. And there were trucks broke down all the time. I used to pity those guys out there on a 30-below-zero night working on a truck. They'd have a pail of oil burning and set it under there to keep things warmed up a little bit. And it seemed like the same guys broke down all the time. But they all ran old trucks, anything they could get that would haul a few cords. Fix it up, get it so it would go down the road, and then fix it when it broke.

I never saw too much (trouble in camp). The only problem we had at all, once in a while some of the men would go out and get drunk and come in the middle of the night, noisier than the devil. And then there would be a lot of yelling about "shut up," people had to work the next day. But that didn't

1940 sprinkler wagon pulled by a cat crawler was used to ice winter roads. Courtesy Leigh Portner

A typical truck load of nice hardwood was a familiar scene to Ken LaFrance by 1950. Courtesy Bob Fallon

happen very often, because they had to walk to get out to the barroom. Out to the barroom (at the end of Blue Mountain Road) was about 12 or 14 miles… and sometimes when they left camp they wouldn't have two or three dollars in their pockets between them.

In the evening, all of the guys, some of them were singing songs and some playing—we had one guy who could play guitar. He would play guitar and everybody would sing. It was kind of a happy bunch in the evening. Hard to believe that men that age would act that way, because the majority of them were in their 60s that were in camp. So it was kind of enjoyable. I wish I had copied down some of the old songs that they sang, because they were lumbering songs, about people who were killed and this and that, different ones. At that time I knew most of them. Not anymore. Too bad. Probably aren't too many people who know them, either. It's too bad to see something like that go, part of the culture just threw away.

Chapter 47 | William J. O'Hern

John Gymburch Remembers His Logging Days

John Gymburch Sr. and his best friend, Alec Mondrick "were two totally different people," Gymburch's son John Jr. told me as he began to describe his father's experience in Gould Paper Company's Camps 1 and 2 in the Adirondack woods deep in Moose River country. "Alec was always 'up for any challenge' and wanted to live life to the fullest. Dad was a quieter, solemn person who was the 'wise old owl' that would watch, learn and let things come to him."

John and Alec were 18 years old in 1938. Their teenage years spent growing up during the Great Depression were typical of other young Americans. John was born in Hudson, New York but his family traveled around a lot looking for work. Raised on a farm in Lee Center, New York. John had recently graduated from West Leyden High School. His parents just barely made a living. Farmers were especially hard hit by the Depression. Farm prices were so low that yearly revenues often barely paid for operating costs. No one had much money to buy produce like eggs. Sometimes farmers felt they almost gave their products away. Even those lucky enough to have avoided mortgages or other debts were still cash poor.

During the early years of the Depression, the Gymburchs found it difficult obtain enough money to buy a sack of flour to make their own bread. They raised a garden, canned vegetables and bottled fruit. They did pretty much everything for themselves; they hardly ever bought anything. "It was awful hard times," John Sr. told his son.

Lee Center, N.Y. was a close-knit society. Struggling neighbors seldom went unnoticed. In that day and age, if your neighbor was having problems, you were supposed to be over there helping. You'd take your horse and machinery and help them put in their crops or whatever needed to be done.

John Gymburch and Alec Mondrick left their parents' farms to seek opportunities for decent wages and full-time employment in the logging woods of Herkimer and Hamilton counties.
Courtesy Lewis County Historical Society

Farming was the only trade John knew, but the experience had taught him to work hard. The hard times of John's Depression years later became favorite stories to tell his son.

"In the late 1930s, work was scarce in Lee Center," recalled John Jr. "My dad and his friend Alec heard that Gould Paper was hiring for their logging

McKeever was once a bustling center for logging. Courtesy Town of Webb Historical Association

Many men found employment in logging camps during America's Great Depression.
Photo by Dewitt Wiley. Courtesy Leigh Portner

John and Alec Mondrick's experience working with horses on their farm proved valuable in the logging camp. Courtesy Lewis County Historical Society operation," 20 or maybe 30 miles east of McKeever. There were three logging camps that housed perhaps 200 lumbermen who worked at a pace which only the strong could stand as they raced against the weather in one of the seasonal phases of the Adirondacks' great and old-time industries—logging.

"For the most part they looked at it as an adventure to go work in the woods and experience life," continued John Jr., who had only a sketchy idea of exactly how the fellows reached McKeever after first hitching a ride to Boonville and eventually to their destination.

John quickly learned Prince sensed when it was time to quit work and head for the barn.
Photo by Dewitt Wiley. Courtesy Leigh Portner

"I would have enjoyed visiting the site of the camps where Dad worked, but in reality I know there wouldn't have been anything left," he said. "Just the same, the thought of retracing Dad's steps would take me back to those days where he was a small part of a mixture of many nationalities" known as 'jacks—characters known from Maine to Oregon, for lumberjacks form a fraternity of their own. There were those with homes and families to whom they sent most of their earnings, and others with no place to call home but the woods.

"I remember one road adventure our family took nearly every summer was to head up to Old Forge for a day trip," John Jr. recalled. "Every time, we crossed the bridge over Moose River on Route 28, just past the turnoff that leads to McKeever and what remains of a cluster of Gould's buildings. Dad parked the car off on the shoulder of the road in sight of the abandoned mill, and we all piled out to look upstream to a distant spot Dad pointed to as he began to reminisce. 'There's where I worked for a couple of winters when I was young.'

"One year, Eddie Kornmeyer from the Georgia Pacific mill in Lyons Falls had an old map in his truck that showed the old Gould Paper job sites on it. As we studied the map spread out on the hood of Eddie's truck, Dad pointed to the sites and showed me where he had worked. Eddie and Dad had a good visit over it while discussing old times."

In 1938, Roy E. Bird was Gould's woodlands manager. Bird had recently succeeded Gordon Gould when Gordon took over as president of the Gould Paper Company following the death of his father, Harry. Bird's office was at McKeever. Bird listened to the boys, asked a few questions, and recognized immediately they were not lumberjacks and had no particular skills for the logging profession. But because they had grown up on dairy farms, and had had a good exposure to using tools and knowledge of many forms of physical work, including a limited familiarity with logging, they were hired.

A Linn tractor draws a sleigh load of logs along the Indian River. Courtesy Bruce Koenig

"Dad said Bird told them that being that they were 'green' to the commercial logging business, he would pretty much start them out as spare or miscellaneous laborers—filling in wherever they were needed," John Jr. explained.

Camp 2, Indian River. Courtesy Bruce Koenig

"One of the earlier stories that Dad told me was about when they were on 'firewood detail' for the camp. Firewood detail involved skidding small hitches of wood from the woods to a landing. Typically Dad would hitch up a log to a single horse, slap the horse on the rear and send him down to the landing where Alec would unhook the horse and send him back up the trail for another hitch. Normal quitting time for this work was around 3:45 p.m., and it seldom went past 4:00 p.m. On one particular day the boys decided to work a little past four o'clock to get ahead on the firewood. At 4:15 p.m., John hooked up the hitch, slapped the horse on the rear and sent him down to the landing. When the horse, who was named Prince, got to the landing, he thundered past Alec, hit the main haul road and continued into the horse barn with the log in tow and turned into his stall. The camp cook heard the commotion and went to investigate. When he saw the horse eating his hay while still hooked to the log, he broke into a fit of laughter. He then suggested to Dad and Alec that they cut up the log and split it into firewood before the rest of the camp found out. Apparently, some horses know that quitting time is 3:45 and not 4:15!"

John and Alec were not lumberjacks but they knew how to use a variety of tools.
Courtesy Lewis County Historical Society

After being signed on, John and Alec were told to report to Herb McGee, the foreman at Camp 9. McGee was the boss of The Landing, a site on the Canachagala Stillwater where logs were piled on the frozen south branch of the Moose River until the spring river drive. McGee and Hugh Dowling worked Gould's annual spring log drives when the river was high. It was only much later that John realized that in meeting the landing boss, he had briefly known a logging legend. McGee was a Canadian who had come to work on the river drive for the Gould Paper Company in 1916. He spent most of his life in the Moose River country. John recalled the man's hands were "hard and calloused." McGee worked with bare hands no matter how cold the weather was. In 1940, the year John left the woods, McGee was given the foreman position of Camp 3.

It took great care and skill to load logs into a sleigh. Courtesy Lewis County Historical Society

At McKeever, it just so happened the boys were in luck. There was a conveyance outside Gould's headquarters that was heading into Camp 9. There wasn't anything memorable about the ride other than the roar of the gasoline engine, the grinding of gears, the narrow, somewhat rutted roads and dizziness from the constant swaying of the truck's body.

"Times were definitely tough at the end of the Depression," John Jr. continued. "Dad's parents' farm fed the family, but money for paying the taxes and any extras was hard to come by. To supplement the family income, my dad and his older brother Mike ran trap lines together. When Dad was eight years old, he caught his first mink in a borrowed trap. The local fur buyer, Grover Tuffy, gave him a crisp $20 bill for the raw fur. After that Dad was hooked. He took the $20 and bought more traps, flashlights and batteries so he could check his traps at night. Along with the trapping, he worked odd jobs in the neighborhood. Most of the extra money bought boots, gloves and winter clothes for the other kids in the family.

'Jacks walk across planks to span mud on their way to the cookhouse.
Photo by Dewitt Wiley. Courtesy Leigh Portner

Logging opened up clearings. The limbs left behind were used for firewood.
Photo Dewitt Wiley. Courtesy Leigh Portner

"Dad said he was confident as he rode in the back of an old truck until they reached the logging camp far up the Moose River that he would be able to handle anything the 'bull of the woods' directed him to do. When Dad and Alec reached Camp 9, McGee directed the boys to the main haul road that led out of camp toward the Indian River and their final endpoint beyond Little Indian Lake." Somewhere beyond the river, they were told they'd come upon Hugh Dowling. Dowling was the superintendent of the Gould operations along the Moose River. Known as the 'the bull of the woods,' he oversaw all activities throughout Gould's extensive Moose River holdings. Dowling would direct them to two camps a few miles beyond the log bridge that spanned the Indian River.

"Camps 1 and 2 were fairly remote," John told his son. "Our ride in the truck for part of the trip had saved us time and foot leather, but then we walked the rest of the way, eventually in the dark."

Dowling told them it didn't matter which of the two logging camps they reported to. Charles McVey was foreman of Camp 1. He had worked for Gould since 1917. Levi Godin was foreman of Camp 2, two miles beyond Camp 1. They'd be working at one camp or the other as needed.

As John Sr. remembered, the first things he recalled seeing parked outside Camp 1 were a big square water tank on runners and a Linn tractor "with a number six painted on a metal tag that was mounted on the front of the grill."

By the time John and Alec came into the lumber woods, major changes had come to the logging operations. Decades earlier, little machinery had been in evidence. Skilled woodsmen cut the trees with crosscut saws and peeled the pulpwood logs with spuds. Later in the season, trees were skidded by horse power and cut into logs for the winter haul. Skidways were located along the winter roads where there was easy access to streams.

Early mechanical changes came first in the transportation of logs. Difficulties involved in the long team haul caused logging operators to seek a better solution. Inventors and manufacturers came to their rescue.

John was a crack shot with a rifle. His accuracy brought deer meat to the kitchen time after time.
Photo by Dewitt Wiley. Courtesy Leigh Portner

An early response to the need for better transportation facilities came in the form of the steam log hauler.

With the development of World War I, British inventors applied the moveable track idea to the construction of a tank, which became a very effective weapon of war. After the war, many of these tanks became available for the logging industry.

One day, on a log job in the northern Adirondacks, John E. Johnson, the operator, and DeWitt Wiley, who was the logging superintendent, decided to build a road and drive a truck directly to the log pile on the side of the hill. This opened up a new method of transportation from the log job directly to the mill. The change to truck transportation was hastened by the use of the bulldozer, which made better roads possible.

For several years, few developments came except in the field of transportation. Trees were still cut with the crosscut, peeled with the spud, skidded with the skidding horse, cut into bolts with the bucksaw and moved to the landing with horses and Linn tractors.

John and Alec were on the cusp of more change. By 1938, spruce was still being harvested, but Gould had also begun to cut hardwood, transporting the logs on trucks over hardened roads to the mills. It was one of those roads that the teens followed into the Indian River country.

John Sr. repeated his long-held memories of his logging-camp years throughout his lifetime, staple stories his son enjoyed hearing. To avoid forgetting the accounts, late on the night of February 7, 2017, John Jr. wrote them down. He said he had heard the stories so often, he could vouch for the accuracy of what he remembered.

JOHN GYMBURCH SR.'S LOGGING CAMP MEMORIES

"Life in a logging camp had a certain 'pecking order' that went along with it. At night the old-timers were huddled around the pot-bellied stoves with the younger guys out toward the walls. At some point in your career someone would say 'Hey John, why don't you move up next to the stove and pull up a bench.' From that point on, you were considered one of them and with it came a higher level of respect. If an older guy liked you, he would allow you to do something that would just about kill you; then they would show you the right way to do it. One such example was loading sleighs at the headers. Typically a header had two vertical support posts that propped up the horizontal skids that the logs were piled on. To load a sleigh, two men would crawl under the header and chop away at the verticals until they heard a pop. At the sound of the pop, the experienced guy would grab the newbie and press him up against the dirt bank while the logs above thundered onto the sleigh. During his time at the camp, John never recalled anyone being injured while loading the sleighs. The key to everything was having two people who worked well together and watched out for each other.

"Much has been written about the food in the logging camps. My dad said that depending on what was going on, some camps fed three meals a day and some fed only two. He said that if the cook liked you, he would fix something up for you to take with you. Typically, it would be salt pork or fried eggs on thick sliced bread. (This sandwich would be wrapped in waxed 'butcher paper' that you would fold up in your pocket and reuse several times.) The road crews (known as road monkeys) worked at night watering the road and putting dirt/straw on the hills. A meal or snack would be brought to them on the job.

During the spring river drives a number of logs became beached or jammed between rocks. Men who walked the shoreline looking for these straggling logs were called "river pigs."
Courtesy Lewis County Historical Society

"When the camp found out that Dad was a hunter, he was sent to the deer yards to bring some fresh venison into camp. Some of the deer that were shot in February and March yielded very poor quality venison, but the cook was good at 'doctoring' the taste up and making it go a long way. Breakfasts were always the favorite meal of the day. The food was always good and you could have as much as you wanted. The coffee was always strong and it had a tendency to give you a caffeine 'jolt' to start your day."

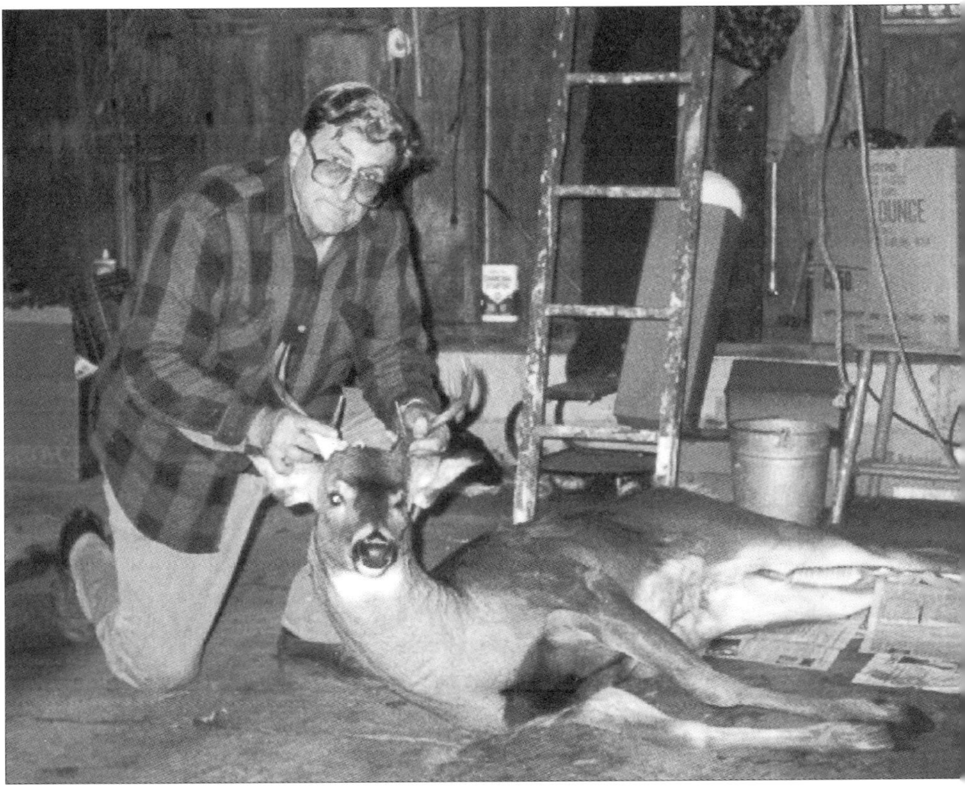

John Gymburch Sr. never lost interest in deer hunting. Courtesy John Gymburch Jr.

"The camp cook saw an innocence in Dad and took him under his wing. When it came time for the 'boys' to go into town, the cook would tell Dad 'There's enough trouble in this world without you going looking for it; stay here and tell me about this farm of yours.' Having a cook taking a liking to you had its advantages. Peeling potatoes, carrying in wood for the cook stove and a few other menial tasks was a good trade-off for a thicker sandwich or an extra snack during the day. Those men worked so hard and burned so many calories that anything extra in their stomachs kept them healthier and gave them an edge. My dad used to joke about the CBS show 'Survivor' being based on life in a logging camp. Everyone that went home with their limbs intact was the grand prizewinner."

"As you can imagine, injury and illness were a part of everyday life in a Moose River Plains logging camp. One of the famous 'cure-alls' was a product called Sloan's Liniment™. Sloan's was used on cuts of all sizes (I hear that this stuff burns like fire!), rubbed into sore joints and most importantly as a treatment for lame horses. Whatever ailed man or beast, Sloan's was the answer. Usually it was kept in the horse barn and everyone used the same bottle. Another 'miracle-cure' was Vicks VapoRub™. This product was also used to treat cuts, to rub on your chest during a cold, and some would even eat it to treat certain stomach ailments. Later on in the spring it was applied liberally as a form of bug-dope to ward off the black flies. (Many of the logging camps on Tug Hill actually had mounds of the purple bottles that were discarded after they were emptied.)"

"Many of the loggers couldn't read, so John and Alec would read their letters from home for them. Some wanted their letters read in private, while others had theirs read in front of the group. If letters were in short supply, some of the better ones would be recycled several times before the logging season was over. To the men, old news was still better than no news.

"Every once in a while the men would be allowed to go into town to experience some night life. Generally they all returned in the same condition: empty pockets, a big head and a few extra scars to wonder about. The Hulbert House in Boonville still has floors with holes from the corked (calked) logging boots. Usually in the wee hours, the foreman would collect everyone up, pay for any damages, throw a horse blanket over the men and return to camp. These men knew how to work hard and play even harder. (John and Alec sent most of their pay home to help out with raising their siblings back on the farm.)

"When the logging season was winding down, many of the woods crews were released while the river drivers were doing their work. Everyone said that they would stay in touch (which they never did), wished everyone luck and waited for the next logging season to come. For many of the hard-core loggers, the woods was all they knew. For these men, working on farms or in the mills was torture for them until the following November.

"The second year, Dad and Alec worked on a 'cleanup crew' along the river following the Moose River log drive. This was very difficult work because some of the logs were wedged into the rocks really tight and others were 'stranded or beached' some distance from the water. The younger men would do this work; most seasoned 'jacks wouldn't because they considered it 'too low.'"

Following John Gymburch's time in the logging camps, he took a job at Revere Copper & Brass in Rome, N.Y. Shortly after that, World War II began. John and two of his brothers were drafted into the Army. He served nearly four years in the European theatre. When discharged, he returned to work at Revere, where he worked for 42 years, retiring in 1981. (In those days your time in the service counted toward your work years.)

John's son concluded: "Dad always said that working in the camps prepared him for what was to come in the war years. I remember him saying that his time in camp taught him how to get along with others, it taught him that life wasn't easy and the most important lesson of all, don't ever feel sorry for yourself because there just isn't time for it. Life in the camps was very tough, but once you were accepted into the group you felt like you were part of something that was bigger than its individual pieces. Occasionally when a problem occurred, it was usually settled by making a trip behind camp and 'hashing it out.' Generally that meant having a 'discussion' during a wrestling match. By the next morning, neither party remembered what the scrap was about and life went on.

"By design there was a fair amount of competition between the crews as to who could put up the most wood in a day. Peer pressure among the crews was pretty intense.

"Most of the foremen were tough characters, but generally they were fair to their workers. Dad told me that one of the foremen had a harsh saying for a crew that was slacking off. On many occasions the boss would say 'You boys want to rest? You can rest when you're old. Now back to work!'

"Dad never recalled any issues of theft in his camp. No one had very much, but what was yours was yours. He thought that everyone knew the consequences of messing around with the wrong person's belongings. Among friends, a few practical jokes were played, but they were never very serious. For the most part, there just wasn't time for it."

Thanks to John Gymburch Sr.'s penchant for telling stories about his days spent in the logging camps of the Adirondacks' Moose River Plains, and thanks to his son's excellent memory of those stories, first-hand information of a kind not found in typical historical records is preserved for those who are curious. They are especially meaningful to people interested in The Plains and whose parents or grandparents worked in the camps and whose stories have been lost to time.

Adirondack TIM-Berrr!

Chapter 48 | Bill Hill

A CENTURY, A FIRE AND A SAW

Former logger Bill Hill listened in his imagination to the voice of an early 20th century Adirondack forest.

Not, on this day, to cheerful mountain songbirds or to the raucous chorus of blue jays, or to the hounding buzz of black flies, or even to the love-struck chorus of frogs in a nearby vernal pool he prudently avoided. He listened instead to the way-back sounds of logging before there was any engine-powered machinery.

Up until after the turn of the last century, logging was done first with teams of oxen, and later with horses. Horses could pull a load great distances, and because moving logs across rough terrain was difficult, loggers often built skid trails of wood planks or corduroy poles to smooth the way over wet terrain.

Bill pictured the pleasant image of a logger and a team of horses—rather than the gear-grinding mechanized skidder with its unpleasantly noisy motor. A logging operation with horses was much slower, and its affected area smaller, with less disturbance to the forest than harvesting with today's mechanized equipment. A good team of horses offered a logger lots of control for logging in partial cuts, moving timber around trees that were left to grow without damaging them.

From the gee and haw command of the teamster to the horses, to the clear ringing made by hammering a steel wedge that echoed through the forest, Bill heard it all in his mind. He knew the distinctive thud of a double-bitted ax and the sound of the gliding, slicing whizz and swish of a four-foot two-man cross cut saw as the concave-backed felling saw moved back and forth, conforming to the arc made by a sawyer's arms as he sawed.

Bill's way of work was different from more modern ways. He knew that even though the tools and machinery he relied on to the make a living were technologically advanced, the times were changing, and new ways threatened his one-man logging operation's survival.

Logging a hundred years ago seemed so pitifully simple, he thought on the day that his operation stopped. He can still revisit that past because of something he found one day among the layers of needles and leaves that had formed a soft carpet over the forest floor.

This is Bill's story.

★★★

I had always been around logging of some sort. My dad often cut trees for lumber and firewood, so I had been involved in it since I was a youth. In high school I took a two-year vocational (BOCES) forestry/conservation program. I followed that with a one-year certificate conservation program at Community College of the Finger Lakes in Canandaigua. I got away from working in the woods for a few years; then in the early 1990s I started to sell firewood again, and slowly worked back to logging. I had always enjoyed the woods, and it seemed like a great time to dive in full time. After the ice storm (1998), I had a lot of opportunities to do salvage cuts around the area. I bought an old, ugly C4 Tree Farmer skidder, and an awful old JD log loader. I eventually upgraded to better, but even older, gear.

Bill Hill said, "I did this kind of work for a good many years, although I had more modern trucks. And yes, it was a tough way to make a living but I never enjoyed any job more." Courtesy Bill Hill

In the early years of the twenty-first century, I was logging a white pine job in the northwest Adirondacks in St. Lawrence County. It was quite a tough job. Skid trails had to be built by an excavator; the skid was a mile and a half each way, and the only level spots were swamps. Nothing came easy here.

The property belonged to a hunting club, and the members told me the story of the area I was logging. The spot next to a small lake on the club had burned in a large forest fire at the beginning of the twentieth century. After the fire, it had never been logged and had grown back to a decent stand of pine. I know that there had been logging there before the fire, as they had shown me photos of horse teams hauling wagon loads of sawn lumber out of these woods. I also was shown a circular sawmill blade that leaned against a tree. It was a tradition to bang the blade on the way by when hunting deer.

As I was skidding near the lake, I noticed something on a large boulder that looked out of place. When I made my way over to it, I found a cross-cut saw. The wooden handles had obviously burned off, and I imagined it had been through the forest fire a century earlier. The blade had formed around the rock from the heat, and the steel had actually blistered. Nearly a hundred years had passed, and now I was cutting timber on the same ground as this logger, before the forest fire destroyed everything. Was he logging when the fire came through, leaving his saw behind in a rush to get away? Or had he simply forgotten his saw? These are not questions that will ever be answered—so I guess you can come to your own conclusions. I straightened the saw out, and now it sits on the wall in my garage.

Much of the timber on that job was pretty rough and bully (with lots of limbs and therefore lots of knots) where it had grown next to the lake. While I was cutting the job, a local sawmill contacted me looking for pine logs of this type. The mill had a large order for Adirondack siding lumber (the bark left on one edge, with a heavy contour). The siding was for what would become the "Wild Center" [formally the Natural History Museum of the Adirondacks] in Tupper Lake a few years later.

This job also involved a good share of misery. The skid was long and rough, and even after you got the trees to the landing, you were still well over a mile from the nearest paved road. It was because of the remoteness that these trees had grown untouched over the course of a century. I can say pretty safely that I was the first mechanized logger to ever make sawdust by that little Adirondack lake.

Though I know I wasn't the first person to log any forest I worked in, I would often feel like it. It is wonderful to spend your day in a place where it is hard to see a trace of civilization; the solitude of the woods has always agreed with me. I would see more animals than people on any given day.

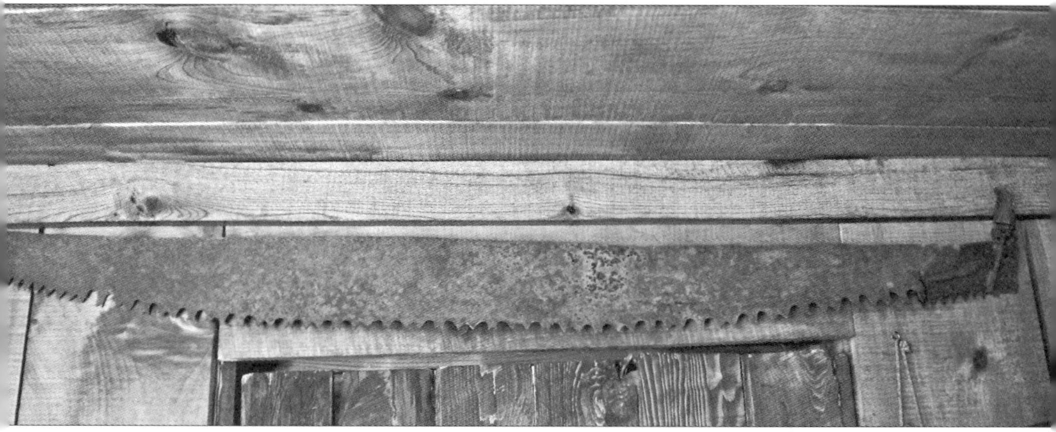

Bill Hill's fired-scoured two-man saw hangs on his wall as a daily reminder of the days that gave him so much pleasure. Courtesy Bill Hill

I have since stopped logging professionally. The economics of a one-man logging operation just didn't make sense any longer. Chainsaws and cable skidders are now nearly as antiquated as the horse teams and crosscut saws. Feller bunchers, whole tree chippers and grapple skidders are now the norm. It was hard and dangerous work, but I never have had a job that I enjoyed nearly as much, before or since. I never walk past that crosscut saw without a moment of reminiscing. I still spend as much time in the woods and forests as I can. Now I carry a camera instead of a chainsaw.

★ ★ ★

Bill's rescued logging artifact can no longer be properly sharpened, nor can it make deep cuts or produce thick shavings that carried out the sawdust and prevented the saw from binding. Instead, it hangs in a prominent position among other tools as a reminder of the days when logging was not so fantastically complicated and enormously sophisticated.

Bill has been driving a school bus for the Edwards-Knox school district for about a dozen years now. In the summer, he still sometimes works in the woods for a local jobber when the jobber needs an experienced hand.

Adirondack TIM-Berrr!

Chapter 49 | William J. O'Hern

LUMBERJACK PALMER'S HARD CIDER

The clapboard house has weathered over a hundred and sixty-four years of Tug Hill wind and rainstorms, deep cold, record-breaking snowfalls, and blistering heat. The white trim has been periodically repainted and wooden siding has been replaced.

But there is still an air about the place that evokes thoughts of horse-drawn bobsleds loaded with logs, of root cellars, potato bins, and kegs of fermenting fruit juice, as if their ghosts waited beneath the adjacent gnarled apple trees, in a long-neglected farmyard, watching from the rolling brush and bramble hillside. Inside the homestead, the entranceway opens into a bright, comfortable open-concept sunroom-kitchen. On the wall opposite the refrigerator stands a soapstone pellet stove. The big room opens to what might have been a parlor but now serves as a computer room and dining room. A bathroom is just before the stairs that lead to the second floor. My guess is that the inside floor plan has not changed all that much from the original. The house was marked on the Oswego County map in 1854, but no one knows its actual age. George and Michelle Stevens, the present owners just say "it dates back before 1854." Their abstract tells us it was owned by "H. Streeter" in 1867.

On August 20, 1868, Palmer Cross and Sarah Jane Moore married, and by 1889 they had purchased this simple, yet serviceable farmhouse along what was once a dirt-packed main connection between Boylston, Sandy Creek, and the virgin stands of forest in Boylston, New York.

Palmer, like so many men in those days, was a farmer but also worked in the woods. Since logging operations did not start until the late fall following harvest, he signed up as a logger to earn extra money during the winter months felling trees that were transported by bobsled to local sawmills or drawn to rivers. In the spring they would drive the logs down the rivers before it was time to plant the next summer's crop.

Palmer could chop, saw, and hew. Often log jobbers liked some logs hewed or squared because more squared logs than round logs could be piled in the hold of a ship for the export trade. It's very possible Palmer might have used his hewing talents outside the woods too, the frameworks of houses and barns were constructed with hewed logs.

A string infused with chalk was twanged against the side of the log to show the hewer how much to cut off. A highly skilled hewer cut the rounded log as smooth and straight as possible to produce flat ninety-degree sides.

Being a chopper also required keeping one's axe sharp. A wet stone was used to sharpen the metal edge razor-sharp. Water was put in a storage reservoir or water box, and as a logger turned the handle, the round-wheeled sharpening stone became wet. The water made the stone slide more easily against the steel blade of the axe.

The Palmer Cross house. Courtesy George Stevens

Since the Cross home was ideally located a short distance from the "lumber woods," an old-time term in his day, it was not uncommon for men Palmer knew, and had worked with, to stop by—and even stay overnight. Food and liquid refreshment would have been served, and it's plausible to imagine their conversation might have included planting, ripening hay, harvesting, squealing pigs, or the grandeur of the virgin forest. These were men who were conscious of the purity of the Tug Hill character. Not that they ever put it into words, but they felt some greatness within themselves as their souls responded to the silent communication with God that they found in the forest.

When Palmer Cross quit the lumber woods, he stayed active on the farm and continued to remain in contact with fellow loggers. By then his reputation for his perfected home brew was known far and wide. Palmer had nailed the art of producing hard cider. Hard cider is simply apple cider that is allowed to ferment and produce its own alcohol content. And the numbers of wooden barrels that sat in Palmer's stone-lined cellar attested to the success of his brewing operation.

When it came time for the Sandy Creek Historical Society to write the history of the town, they didn't forget the Civil War veteran who served in Company G N.Y. Volunteer Cavalry and the 1854 Palmer Cross Farmhouse that still stands, neatly painted an olive green, along County Route 15, identified as house number 1411.

The local history book states: "The simple home was a favorite resting place for the hardworking teamsters hauling logs from the Boylston woods to the Lacona sawmills, for Mr. Cross was generous with the goodly supply of cider which he annually put into his cellar. Palmer and Sarah raised a daughter, Mina, who married Edward Waggoner and a son, Sheridan Cross, who was a lumberjack and laborer—and a local character, wealthy in tall tales."

Palmer Cross died in his home in 1917. His life is just one of many Tug Hill characters who captured the essence of life on The Hill.

The old Palmer Cross homestead before the aging structure was renovated. Courtesy George Stevens

Adirondack TIM-Berrr!

Chapter 50 | Amy Feiereisel

Ross Young: Life, Love, and Logging in the Woods

This story, originally titled "North Country: Life, Love, and Logging in the Woods of Harrisville" comes with permission from the author and North Country Public Radio's (NCPR's) North Country at Work project, which explores the working lives and history of the region. To see all their stories, check out ncpr.org/work.

Logging is some of the oldest work around Northern New York. Many communities around the North Country were established around logging camps in the 18th and 19th centuries, and big money was made turning felled trees into products like chairs, paper, crates, and even matches.

Not too many people are around that worked logging before chainsaws and trucks, but Ross Young is one of them. He started working in the woods at 16, with handsaws and horses.

Going into the Woods

Ross Young was born in Harrisville in 1934, the youngest of three sons. His father had moved to the area from Canada, and his mother from Ohio.

When describing his life, Ross glosses over his childhood and jumps to 1949. That's the year he met a young woman named Delores LaFave at school. Ross was fifteen and Delores was fourteen. A year later, he says he turned of working age and started working with Delores's father, Oliver LaFave.

"Course when I got old enough to quit school, at 16, I had to quit and go to work, working in the woods, cutting pulp, logs. We didn't have any chainsaws then, so we did it all by hand."

That meant hand-held saws; Ross says he used "sweedsaws" and "crosscut saws," which had an iron frame and a pulp hook. One of his favorite memories from that time period is riding logs as he skidded them out with the horses.

"...sometimes you'd have two logs together, instead of walkin' beside the logs you'd jump right on and ride 'em."

Marriage and a Family Business

Ross and Delores were married in June of 1952, when Ross was 18 and Delores 17. They spent their first summer together living in an abandoned lumber camp, where Ross worked with his oldest brother cutting trees and peeling the pulp off spruce and hemlock logs for a local jobber named Johnny Bango. Summer was the ideal time to cut and peel the bark off trees, because it's when the bark was loosest.

Ross Young and his experienced work horses. Courtesy Ross Young

"You take what you call a spud and you'd spud all the bark off the trees. Well, you gotta get right under the bark, it's like a big chisel. Some trees had sticky bark and some had heavy bark you left the top on to draw the moisture out. The tree was cut into pulp after peeling season was over."

When the summer season ended, Ross went to work for the St. Regis Paper Company in Harrisville. He only stayed a few years before becoming restless with mill work. Ross then returned to the woods in 1955, where he ran a logging operation with his two brothers for the next 12 years.

Ross quit school at 16 to begin work in the woods. Courtesy Town of Webb Historical Association

It was just the three of them, and they started out with very little—three men, two horses, and hand tools. They got their hands on some chainsaws, but Ross says: "They didn't work so good. Sometimes they'd bind and just about kill you."

After a few years they bought a farm tractor to help "kid," or move logs, and eventually they bought a John Deere bulldozer. They delivered the peeled pulpwood to the St. Regis Paper Company in Deferiet, and the Diamond Match Company in Ogdensburg.

The trio cut and peeled trees in the summer, skidded them into piles in the fall, and took them out in the winter. That was the best time for it—when the ground was frozen solid. Ross says the bitter cold was part of the job, and remembers many a day when they'd head into the woods with sandwiches for lunch, but by the time they were ready to eat, the sandwiches would be frozen solid, and they'd have to build a fire just to thaw them out.

During this time, Ross and Delores bought and lived in a small house about 3 miles out of Harrisville, which he describes as "really being in the boondocks." There was no electricity, but he says he and Delores didn't mind.

That's how they liked it. Even Ross's off-season work from logging kept him outside.

"During all these times, when it come up the spring of the year of course, you couldn't work in the woods so easy. So then I worked in sugaring for a number of years, for Frank Mantle on the Jerden Falls Road."

Maple sugaring. Unknown man gathering sap. Circa 1930s. Watertown, N.Y.

Courtesy Jefferson County Historical Society

The former St. Regis Paper Company mill in Harrisville. Ross is currently (2019) the Harrisville historian. He enjoys sharing his local history knowledge and talking about days gone by and the many changes since. Courtesy Ross Young

Ross Young's reliable bulldozer. Courtesy Ross Young

Young's farm tractor. Courtesy Ross Young

One of the small buildings the Ross's lived in out in the boondocks. Courtesy Ross Young

Ross and Delores Young. Courtesy Ross Young

WORK AFTER THE WOODS

By the mid-1960s, Ross says the demand for logs was petering out. In 1966, Delores got a job working for the local school system as a cook, where she stayed for the next 26 years. In 1967, Ross started worked at the Jones and Laughlin Steel Corporation in Benson Mines, and the couple bought a house in town and moved out of the woods.

Ross smelted ore for ten years at J&L, then worked for Viking Snowplow until retiring in 1996. He says retirement is his best job yet. He and Delores will celebrate their 66th wedding anniversary June 27, 2018.

Ross and Delores enjoyed kicking up their heels on the dance hall floor on a Saturday night. Ross said the activity was relaxing after a week's work. Courtesy Ross Young

Epilogue | William J. O'Hern

LUMBERJACK SOULS

One-by-one the loggers I have known, and some I have worked with, have "gone on." With their passing they took with them a love for the industry and their historical connection to a whole aggregation of loggers who cruised woodlots, followed the timber, cut it down, bucked it up, hauled it to river landings, cared for horses and machinery, drove logs to the mill, sawed logs into lumber, and produced pulp from wood for paper products.

Logging still goes on today but with a difference. The logs have to be cut, skidded, chipped, and gotten to market, or mill, the same as ever. The great difference is in the change of tools used developed by new technology: Chain saws, chippers, whole tree harvesters, skidders, and trucks for hauling, while in the years gone by the work was performed by man-and horse-power.

Rev. Frank Reed entering logging camp. Courtesy of Lyons Falls History Association

Earl M. Kreuzer. Photo by the author

While the colorful old-style 'jacks, fiercely proud teamsters, inventive blacksmiths, prima-donna cooks, log-hopping whitewater men and river hogs have passed on, logging goes forward. Meanwhile, their history continues to draw attention to their times.

The idea of cutting timber to make a living appealed to those I knew, as did knowing they belonged to the ranks of those who had preceded them—all a special breed of men, and yes, some women, who pitted their skills and talents against the forest Lumberjacks and lumberjills.

A local North Country saloon where loggers swapped tales. Courtesy Town of Webb historical Association

The generation I knew were not the "shanty-boys" of old—loggers from the "pineries," the virgin timber of the Northeastern forests who practiced the old ways of traditional logging long before the new era of machinery.

A neatly dressed forester, left, stands next to a lumberjack in one of John E. Johnson's camps.

Photo by Dewitt Wiley. Courtesy Leigh Portner

I'm happy to say that among all the oldsters I've interviewed, not one shared their memories from their bed in a nursing home. All lived generally independently—with the same air of freedom they had experienced in the forests. It was their generation who knew first-hand the older "shanty boys." And it was they who passed on the memories through songs, stories and vintage snapshots, many of which I included in *Adirondack Logging: Stories, Memories, Cookhouse Chronicles, Linn Tractors and Gould Paper Company History from the Adirondack and Tug Hill Lumber Camps (In the Adirondacks*, 2016).

Earl M. Kreuzer was among the oldest 'jacks I spoke with. My memories of him come back each year as I pass the dirt road that leads to West Canada Creek at the turn-off from Route 8 just before Hoffmeister, N.Y.

My remembrance of Earl is as special as my memories of all the folks who have opened their doors to me and shared a bit of their life—stories that help to add to an understanding of a time we can know about only when history is recorded.

This memory is for you, Earl, and for all the other special souls who've given freely of their time to help preserve their era.

55-gallon barrels of fuel and kerosene stand outside one of Gould's tractor shed. It's one of the everyday scene an older logger would see. Photo by Dewitt Wiley. Courtesy Leigh Portner

★ ★ ★

Every year the trout lie sleeping in still cold pools waiting for an Adirondack winter to change to the warmth of spring. With each cycle, new people find the old footpaths up mountains, around the edges of boggy ponds and alongside streams that twist toward distant lakes and rivers. This annual freshness has a history. Earl Kreuzer, also known as the Mayor of Hoffmeister, was part of

Leigh Portner (left) and Bob Failing, two retired loggers, demonstrate to the author a lumberjack's handshake, summer 2018. Photo by the author that history. He traveled those Adirondack trails long before me, rode logs on the Hudson River and owned a general store. His father, a former lumberman, owned and operated the Henry Kreuzer Hotel in Morehouseville.

"You've got to talk to the Mayor," I was told, to get the lowdown on the logging operations in the West Canada Creek basin. "Earl knows everything from way back. Besides, he has the best collection of old lumbering stuff around."

My best memory of meeting him is the clouds of black flies and the smell of his house, best described as poorly-ventilated cigarette smoke plus old stuff, mixed with woodsmoke. I made two trips to his small cabin along West Canada Creek. The interior was cluttered with relics of another time, hunting and fishing paraphernalia, old logging tools and memorabilia. Earl told nonstop stories—one after another. I loved those stories but I never grew used to the swarms of black flies or the perpetual cloud of cigarette smoke. I snapped a favorite photo of Earl on my last visit.

"Want to see a trick?" he asked, following my comment that his well-cared-for vegetable garden did not have a protective wire fence. For the life of me I didn't understand how he protected the crops from the forest critters.

"Sure," I replied. "What're ya gonna do?"

Earl's next moves sealed him in my folklore mind as a legendary hero of the Adirondacks. Earl picked up his .410 shotgun, grabbed a handful of unshelled peanuts, sat down on a log stump at the edge of the garden, and laid the rifle across his lap. "Watch this," he said as he placed a peanut on the top of his bald head.

It was only a matter of minutes before a chipmunk appeared. Chippy darted toward Earl's motionless body, raced up his side, grabbed the nut, poked it into his paunch and leaped off on a mad dash to who-knows-where.

Earl's 90-plus-year-old body bolted to life. The years had not slowed his reaction time. As the animal scurried off, Earl raised his rifle, aimed and fired. "There!" he declared in a big way, "That's how I keep my corn to myself."

I didn't think much of the slaughter, but Earl was giving me a bit of insight into the ways of the old-time people of the Adirondacks. His behavior was simply part of his Adirondack character.

I rather doubt anyone consciously sets out to become a character. Character traits merely develop in accordance with one's personality. There's no recipe for being a colorful individual. The men and women I call characters are just unique in their own way.

George Shaughnessy washes up in a "boiling-up shed." George was one of the earliest 'jack's I interviewed. "I'm well over 90," he told me as he referred to me as a "young feller." He was boiling a kettle of beans as we talked. I commented, "That's one big pot of beans, George." Quickly he replied, "When I was in the lumber camps we never had a problem getting the likes of them eaten down.'" Courtesy George Shaughnessy

It's the unique cut of the old-timers characters that I think also holds a special spot in my hearts as well as in the hearts and minds of Mart Allen and Dan Christmas. It seems as if less individuality stands out in the trade today. And it's that lack that makes nostalgia for the earlier days more powerful.

Mart Allen's fondness for woods and water is shown by the placement of his woodsy Thendara home with the middle branch of the Moose River flowing past the backyard. Courtesy Roy E. Wires

While the lumber industry has always had its ups and its downs, New York State has an abundance of woodland and will continue to produce men and women who have an interest in working in the commercial lumber industry in some capacity, from cruising timber to marketing the finished goods.

The logging cry *Tim-BERRR!* has always had a twofold meaning in logging jargon. Since the days when choppers traveled by the light of a lantern into the woods, it has been a warning call from the feller of a tree to all within the sound of his voice to be careful because a forest patriarch is hurtling down. Bellowed in a woods-worker's tavern, it also was, and is to this day, a summons to all at hand to share in the caller's generosity to "belly up to the bar." For both reasons, that iconic word will continue to resonate in America's woods and taverns, recalling a colorful past and promising a productive future.

Postscript | William J. O'Hern

Timber Cruiser Bob Daws' Stink Lake Logging Camp Memories

When Bob Daws, 83 (2017), pitched camp each fall at a brushy tent site in the Moose River Plains, he no longer saw the myriad secondary logging roads established by the Gould Paper Company, heard the tales of how some lumberjack got hit with a log or how an old-timer came to start logging, or saw the waves of white-tail deer hunters who besieged the area in the late 1960s. The sights and sounds and the camaraderie he once shared with the lumbermen he hobnobbed with at Wilfred Dechene's Stink Lake lumber camp had long passed. But his memories of the colorful characters he knew remained rich and vivid more than sixty-two years after the lumber camp closed and the sounds of the logging operations ceased to echo through the woods.

Bob Daws (2012) holds his scaling stick. His sighting compass, map and scaler's crayon holder lay on the table. These tools were warm memories of his timber cruising days. Photo by Robert J. Elinskas. Courtesy Robert J. Elinskas

The camp, with the uninviting moniker of "Stink Lake," was once located amongst a popular and accessible collection of wilderness lakes between Inlet and Indian Lake, N.Y. Bob said once New York State purchased the single block of 50,970 acres known as the Gould Tract, the waters were heralded as a tremendous area for anglers that rivaled some of Canada's favorite fishing grounds. Some of the larger lakes included Muskrat Pond, Stink Lake, Balsam Lake, Little Deer Lake, Horn Lake, and Gooseneck Lake. These bodies of water are actually more inaccessible today than in the past.

Timber cruising crew. (Lt. to Rt.) George Tindall, Red Holley, Bob Daws and Sterling Holley lean against Daws's 1941 Ford Coupe just before entering the Moose River Plains, Limekiln gate during the winter of 1954–55. Courtesy Bob Daws

Legend attributes a tale of Stink Lake to "French" Louie Seymour. Gerald Kenwell told Utica *Observer-Dispatch* reporter David H. Beetle in 1947 that the lake may well have deserved its name, at least for a very short time, after trapper Seymour, for some unexplained reason, abandoned his morning catch of trout on the bank. Kenwell explained that while the lake teemed with trout and the water didn't smell any different than any other lake, the name intimidated fishermen and kept most away. This made the fishing even more superb for those who knew better.

Kenwell said he learned an interesting but never-confirmed bit of trivia about Balsam Lake, which is a short distance from Stink Lake, from "French" Louie by way of trapper Owen "Kettle" Jones. Kettle claimed that when putting down a trap line near the lake he observed unusual rows of earthen mounds. Convinced they were Indian graves lined on the level, dry terrain, he never further investigated, although he told Louie he wished he had taken the time to dig one up.

Today Stink, Balsam and Horn lakes are reached from the trailhead at the end of a barrier on the Indian Lake Road. Balsam Lake Trail is a 0.3-mile spur at off the old Indian River Trail 6.1 miles from the trailhead and leads to the southern shore of the lake. Stink Lake Trail is a 0.5-mile spur trail off the end of the old Indian River Trail about 7.2 miles from the trailhead and leads to a bay on the southern shore of Stink Lake. The trail to Horn Lake is on the opposite side of the spur to Balsam.

Gould Paper Company's Limekiln Lake gate into the Moose River Plains. Courtesy Wayne Blanchard

The Stink Lake logging camp itself is long gone, but trace remains of the various Gould Paper Company shacks that once dotted the land can still be located by someone with a sharp eye who has listened to the stories of experienced woodsmen such as Daws.

A bit of Bob Daws's personal woods-working legacy lives on through Robert J. Elinskas' *Adirondack Hunters and Trappers* book and through memories Daws enjoyed talking about right up until his passing in 2019. Years of challenging work took him through crippling buckbrush, deep snow and frigid winters, and harsh living conditions in the field.

During early winter of 1954–55, Bob began working as a timber cruiser along with his good friends Red Holley and Herb Lepke, whom he had met while studying at the New York State Ranger School at Wanakena. The young trio had been hired by Dave Hanaburg, a consultant forester. Daws said, "Hanaburg had landed a contract with the Gould Paper Company to cruise timber on 55,000 acres of property in the Moose River Plains country. The vast acreage had been cut at least once," but there were pockets that had been selectively harvested. Gould wanted to know what marketable timber remained, and this was the three cruisers' job.

Wilfred Dechene's so-called Stink Lake "bunkhouse." November 1954. Courtesy Bob Daws

Bob had no idea on that first cold November day in 1954, as he drove his 1941 Ford Coupe over the twenty-four miles of backcountry road past the Limekiln Lake gate entering the Moose River Plains going toward Gould jobber, Wilfred Dechene's camp, that forty-seven years earlier on the shore of the lake, Frank Diamond, a young law student who lived in Brooklyn, N.Y., had been camping when he narrowly escaped being burned to death.

The July 26, 1907, *Evening Recorder & Daily Democrat* described the accident: "Diamond's coat and trousers, on which he had spilled a quantity of gasoline, caught fire from a lighted match, and had it not been for his coolness and presence of mind in instantly tearing off his clothing, he would have been literally roasted to death. As it was, his body was not burned in the least, although his hands were badly blistered to the wrists."

Sterling Holley (Lt.) and Pete Goetz stand by their makeshift Carter Mudhole cruse shack near Cobblestone Brook, Winter of 1954–55. Photo by Bob Daws. Courtesy Bob Daws

If Bob Daws and his buddies had known about the accident, they might have been more careful about trying to heat up Dechene's Stink Lake so-called spare "bunkhouse" shack after enduring a week of subzero evening temperatures in camp. Daws remembered, "It had been bitter cold. There were gaping quarter-inch cracks between the wooden floorboards that allowed an uncomfortable draft to fill the interior. Believe me, it was a race every morning—jump out of our sleeping bags, dress and slip into cold boots before our socks would stick to the floor, before racing across the roadway to the cook shack that was heated by a kerosene pot burner stove. So one day Dave Hanaburg announced he wasn't going to put up with the cold any longer. We'd been eyeing the time-worn, cracked cast-iron stove and rusted, pitted stove pipe. We had not used it because it looked unsafe; besides, we had no wood.

"Following supper we cut some nearby saplings. Of course the wood was green and wet, but Hanaburg said he was going to give us a lesson on how to get the fire going in the stove. As he doused gasoline on the wood he ordered us to 'Stand back. This is what you do to get the fire going. *Woof Woof!!*' We all thought for sure the stove would explode."

Bob Daws and his crew used Gould's tarpaper Six-Mile Camp, located to the left of the current spring pipe, along the main Moose River Plains access road when they cruised Falls Pond and Wolf Lake areas. Courtesy Bob Daws

Elinskas concludes "A Year in the Woods," his chapter about Bob Daws, by writing, "Bob had worked through some tough Adirondack weather. He also had a look at and taste of logging the way it used to be with remote camps and vintage equipment."

Daws's memories of his days of timber cruising, of Dechene's camp as well as of Gould's final active logging camps, Mudhole Camp, and his own Sisal Kraft shack that he shared with fellow timber cruisers were part of his first-hand history of the Moose River Plains region.

I always look forward to enjoyed our fall camping trip in the Moose River Plains, listening to Bob share more of his memories of the south branch of the Moose River around an inviting evening campfire. There remain so many interesting back country places to explore.

It is to the credit of men and women like Bob Daws that another book about the Moose River Plains will continue to take readers on a trip back, the way it was, to one of the most popular recreational playgrounds in the Adirondacks from the 1880s to the 1960s.

ADIRONDACK
TIM-BERRR!

Appendix

LOOKING BACK THROUGH THE YEARS

McMantis Hotel, temporary home to many a logger, owned by Bill and Emily McGee, Lyons Falls, N.Y.
Courtesy Lyons Falls History Association

Adirondack TIM-Berrr!

Chapter 51 | Chip Twellman Haley

Scenic Fish Creek Club Has Long, Proud History

The Fish Creek Club, at the end of Sweeney Road, and "way off the beaten path," according to one visitor, has been attracting nature-loving members since the 1850s, when "a group of sportsmen from Rome and Camden united and decided to buy the property for a recreational retreat," according to club Vice President Jim Tracy. "Hunting, fishing—and card-playing" were among the attractions, he said, on what used to be farm land.

The original members were "prominent people" in the area, including Dr. W.L. Kingsley, James A. Spargo, A.R. Kessinger, W.E. Scripture and Charles H. Harden. The club "used to be a playground for" officials of Rome businesses. Membership has varied over the years. It stands at about 30 today, Tracy said.

The club started with about 380 acres, and expanded over the years to about 550 acres, he said. "We also have 'sporting rights' on another 1,500 or so" acres, he added. The latter property was left to the club by one of the original members who was associated with the Constable family, "one of the great landowners in the area," for whom Constableville is named.

Membership is by "word of mouth, never advertised," Tracy noted, with most new members being "a friend of a friend or of family." Membership costs $1,000 per year.

Fishing and hunting remain the major attractions of the club, along with snowmobile and ATV riding. And, of course, club members still play cards.

Dr. Edwin P. Russell, 90, [in 2018] of 200 Maple St., is a long-time club member, who has "hunted, fished, snowmobiled and snowshoed" there for years, as well as "swatted black flies" on the property. "The fishing used to be much better" in the old days, the retired general practice physician opined. The hunting is still "very good," although there are "up and down years."

The club's property includes a main house or lodge, an "old post-and-beam barn," and Fish Creek, which "runs … right through" the property, making it "almost like an oasis" in Tug Hill.

Douglas Arthur, of 204 W. Garden St., whose grandfather was one of the original club members, says the club is "just a few hundred yards from the famous Schaler Hole, widely acclaimed for its excellent fishing."

With all the trees on the site, the club takes in some "revenue from logging from time to time," Tracy said.

A farmhouse originally was located on the property, but it burned in 1911 and a new two-story frame structure was built. This house, with a wrap-around veranda, has several bedrooms, where "members stay if they want," for a fee. "We have a caretaker, a man and his wife who keep it plowed, serve breakfast, lunch and dinner, and maintain the sleeping quarters," Tracy explained.

Fish Creek Club barn raising. Courtesy Joanne Sattler

The club is open "all year-round," Tracy said, under the watchful eyes of the caretakers.

Russell said "Oh, yes," he often spent nights at the lodge, especially in the old days, "because we had a wonderful cook." He recalled Agnes Kelly as a "wonderful, old-fashioned German cook," comparable to Amish cooks in Pennsylvania. "She would have ham, roast beef or lamb" along with "potatoes, gravy, vegetables, wonderful pies … She put on a wonderful feast!"

Fish Creek Club has changed very little today. Courtesy Lyons Falls History Association

"For years, a regular crowd went up there to eat and play cards on a Sunday excursion."

The caretaker's wife would also serve a "wonderful breakfast" to the hunters before they went out in the morning, Russell recalled. That included "bacon and eggs and sausage and pancakes, sticky buns and coffee." Russell said he often put "a piece of venison and sausage between two pancakes, and carried it out into the woods for lunch."

Members visit mostly on the weekends. During deer hunting season, club members who are hunters keep the place busy.

The barn is believed to have been built around 1880. It is 80 feet long, 50- to 60-feet high, and is "an old style, with a ramp in back," Tracy reported. What was once home to livestock now stores snowmobiles and ATVs. Club members are trying to raise money to save the old barn, which has the club's name prominently painted on the outside.

MEMBERS

OF

The Fish Creek Club

ROME, N. Y.

INCORPORATED 1911

JAMES A. SPARGO	Rome, N. Y.
JOHN D. McMAHON	" "
SAMUEL H. BEACH	" "
FRED M. SHELLEY	" "
A. R. KESSINGER	" "
W. E. SCRIPTURE	" "
LAWRENCE CAREY	" "
REV. JAMES J. CARSON, M. R.	" "
C. R. EDWARDS	" "
M. J. BIRNIE	" "
JAMES H. HOOKE	" "
G. N. LEHR, M. D.	" "
F. W. BROWN JR	" "
P. H. GROGAN	" "
H. J. TELLER, M. D.	" "
W. H. DOYLE	" "
HARRY ACKLEY	" "
JOHN QUEIROLO	" "
K. E. WILLIAMS, M. D.	" "
JOHN S. WARDWELL	" "
W. L. KINGSLEY, M. D.	" "
L. O. BUCKLIN	Little Falls, N. Y.
CHAS. H. HARDEN JR.	McConnellsville, N. Y.
H. H. HARDEN	" "
WILLIAM J. MILLARD	Utica, N. Y.

Original 1911 Members List. Courtesy Douglas Arthur

Russell said the club put a new roof on the barn last summer, in an effort to preserve it. He believes the barn was moved to its spot on the property, and perhaps elevated.

Beyond the club's pasture is Fish Creek's legendary Schaler Hole. Courtesy Joanne Sattler

The barn is meaningful to Douglas Arthur, because of its connections to his grandfather, William E. Scripture, a well-known fly fisherman. "I have a photo in my collection of my grandfather with Rev. Henry Van Dyke and his son Tertius preparing to go fishing…probably in the 1920s," he explained. "In the background, you can see the same barn that stands there today. You may know that Henry Van Dyke was a noted preacher, author, U.S. ambassador to The Netherlands … .and an enthusiastic fly fisherman. So, as you can see, this little gem has drawn famous folks to the Rome area for over 100 years …"

★★★

This Sunday, May 7, 2017 Rome Sentinel *column was compiled for the Rome Historical Society by Chip Twellman Haley, retired* Daily Sentinel *news editor, with photos supplied by Douglas Arthur. Copies of Haley's book "Rome Through Our History," a collection of some of her columns, may be purchased at the Rome Historical Society.*

The Rome Historical Society, 200 Church St., is open from 9 a.m. to 3 p.m. Tuesday through Friday and 10 a.m. to 2 p.m. Saturday. Visit their Facebook page, go online at www.romehistoricalsociety.org, or call 336-5870 for more information.

FAMOUS FISHERMEN—W.E. Scripture, left, one of the original Fish Creek Club members and a well-known fly fisherman, stands with The Rev. Henry Van Dyke and his son Tertius. Van Dyke was a noted preacher, author, U.S. ambassador to The Netherlands—and fly fisherman. In the background can be seen the circa-1880 Fish Creek Club barn. Photo courtesy Douglas Arthur

Fish Creek opening into Wood Creek, now part of the barge canal.
Public Domain, Popular Science Monthly, Vol. 75, 1909

Wood Creek, the old canal entrance from Oneida Lake in 1795. The era of inland navigation canals and improvements started with the Western Inland Lock Navigation Company in 1792, which was replaced by the Erie Canal in 1820. Public Domain, Popular Science Monthly, Volume 75, 1909

Chapter 52 | William E. Scripture, Jr.

SIXTY YEARS AGO ALONG FISH CREEK

Late in William E. Scripture, Jr.'s life when he was a resident of Rome, New York, the avid life-long outdoorsman wrote of his memories which reflected his personal history about Fish Creek dating back to 1896.

His story later appeared in North Country Life *magazine as a four-part series. Scripture's remembrance is a rare, one-of-a-kind historical account of a major Tug Hill Country stream that is as popular today as it was in the author's day.*

The following biographical sketch of Mr. Scripture, who was considered one of Oneida County's prominent men and a pioneer, appears in the book History of Oneida County, New York, From 1700 to the Present Time *written by Henry J. Cookinham, published by The S.J. Clarke Publishing Company, Chicago in 1912. The book tells about the series author.*

WILLIAM ELLIS SCRIPTURE

William Ellis Scripture, who for more than four decades has been a prominent representative of the legal fraternity in Rome, and for fourteen years served as justice of the supreme court for the fifth judicial district is the subject of this sketch. His birth occurred in Westmoreland, Oneida County, New York, on the 2nd of November, 1843, his parents being Parker A. and Harriet Standish (Snow) Scripture, the latter a descendant of Captain Miles Standish. He was graduated from Whitestown Seminary in 1865 and subsequently attended Hamilton College. In preparation for a professional career he entered the Albany Law School, being graduated therefrom and admitted to the bar in 1867. He began the practice of law as a member of the firm of Hutchens & Scripture in 1868, but in the fall of the same year became the junior partner of the firm of Weld & Scripture, of Rome. He next formed a partnership with Homer T. Fowler, under the firm name of Scripture & Fowler, and was afterward associated in practice with George H. Weaver, E.M. Pavey and O. P. Backus. In 1896 he was chosen justice of the supreme court for the fifth judicial district and has won distinction in this connection. As a lawyer he soon proved himself sound, clear-minded and well-trained. He is familiar with the long line of decisions from Marshall down, by which the constitution has been expounded, as are all thoroughly skilled lawyers. He is at home in all departments of the law, from the minutiae in practice to the greater topics wherein is involved the consideration of the ethics and the philosophy of jurisprudence and the higher concerns of public policy. The decisions he has made since his elevation to the bench indicate strong mentality, careful analysis, a thorough knowledge of the law and an unbiased judgment. The judge on the bench fails more frequently, perhaps, from a deficiency in that broadmindedness which not only comprehends the details of a situation quickly and that insures a complete self-control under even the most exasperating conditions than from any other cause; and the judge who makes a success in the discharge of his multitudinous delicate duties is a man of well-rounded character, finely balanced mind and of splendid intellectual attainments. That Judge Scripture is regarded as such a jurist is a uniformly accepted fact.

Schaler Hole, past (Lt.), 2016 (Rt.), Fish Creek Club, widely acclaimed for its excellent fishing.
Courtesy Douglas Arthur

On the 15th of August, 1867, Judge Scripture was united in marriage to Miss Emma C. Goodwin, a daughter of Israel F. Goodwin of Westmoreland, New York. Their living children are as follows: Mary Standish, the wife of J.V. Holtby, of Philadelphia; Mina E.; Ella G.; Parker F.; William E., Jr.; and Vilna. The family residence is at No. 503 James Street.

Scripture's story might be the sole voice to Fish Creek life—an eyewitness version, earthy, and ultimately historical. Anglers will enjoy this memorable account.
Courtesy Edward Blankman (The Lloyd Blankman Collection)

Judge Scripture is a Republican in politics and for nearly four years served as postmaster at Rome under President Harrison. He is a valued member of the Rome Club and also belongs to the Republican Clubs of both Rome and Utica. He has been an able, faithful and conscientious minister in the temple of justice and in his private life is endeared to all who know him by the simple nobility of his character.

Sixty Years Ago Along Fish Creek, Part One

William E. Scripture, Jr., *North Country Life*, Winter 1954

The East Branch of Fish Creek rises in the town of Montague, Lewis County, and flows through Lewis and Oneida counties about fifty miles, emptying into the Barge Canal near Oneida Lake. The upper fifteen miles of the stream are easily-fishable water, where only the famous Schaler Hole and the Big Rock Pool afford much difficulty for the average fly caster.

Below Thompson's Mill, Broad Brook, Hay Bay Brook, Powlace Pond Outlet, Point Rock Creek, Furance Brook, and other tributaries serve to build up a stream having many large, deep pools. For its first thirty miles, the stream flows through wooded terrain, but its general character changes quite abruptly about a mile below Swancott Mills. Erosion has created many "cliff pools" with the wall on only one side. The walls are almost sheer, and at times in the spring and summer lovely flowers and tiny lacy ferns adorn them.

One hot day long ago, when William E. Scripture Jr. began to defer to the persuasions of age toward reminiscence, the retired lawyer, mentally materialized at the bank of Fish Creek, plying a fly rod with quiet deliberation and care. Courtesy John Chamberlain

This branch of the stream joins the West Branch at a point less than a mile from Blossvale, the two forming a stream, which is largely too deep for wading. Although a few very large trout are taken below Blossvale, I do not

A bankside angler. Courtesy Edward Blankman (The Lloyd Blankman Collection)

care particularly for the fishing here. Bass, pike, and pikeperch are found from Blossvale down to the lake.

Under a treaty with the Oneida Indians about 1803, the Indians were granted the hunting and fishing rights from the center of Fish Creek to half a mile on either side, from the southern boundary of Constable's five towns to the mouth of the creek at Oneida Lake. For many years and up to the time when I was permitted to fish the creek alone, a band of Indians, from 60 to 80 or more in number, would pitch their camp near Swancott's. Sometimes the camp would be down on the Smith Lewis meadow, and it made no difference whether the land was in grass or oats or wheat. If Smith Lewis or his father, Nicholas, or the owner of any other land where the Indians camped, objected, the headman among the Indians would listen with apparent respect and then suggest that the owner take the matter up with the Great White Father at Albany.

Scripture considered his fishing tackle objects of reverence.
Courtesy Edward Blankman (The Lloyd Blankman Collection)

I don't know what the Indians did during the years I saw them except that they gathered and "shucked" countless fresh water clams. The shell piles might cover a tenth of an acre of land. I do not remember seeing any Indian with a fishing pole or rod, but Lyman Searle, who would be about 130 years old if living, told me that as a boy he played with some of the Indian boys.

He also told me that one of the younger braves was an expert fisherman and that this brave seemed to take a fancy to him.

No angler worth his rod will be surprised at hearing Scripture's story was written, as it were, along the banks of Fish Creek, nor, that the campfires of the past had a hand in it. Courtesy Edward Blankman (The Lloyd Blankman Collection)

He said that some of the Indians often went salmon spearing in their canoes. They speared at night with one man holding the torch, another working the canoe, and a third doing the spearing. "Lym" wanted to go with them, but it wasn't until the second or third year he had known the young brave that the latter agreed to take him on a trip down the creek.

He instructed Lym in the use of the torch, telling him to be sure to do exactly what he was told to do. Lym agreed, of course, and one night the two Indians and Lym got into a canoe and started downstream.

Midway of the Sheep Pool some salmon were spotted, and Lym's friend told him how to hold the torch so that the spearer could set the spear. Lym was so excited that he did not hold the torch correctly, and the spearman missed his thrust. Without a word Lym's friend took the torch away from him and worked it the rest of the trip.

Not a word was spoken. And for the next couple of days the young brave wouldn't even look toward Lym, much less speak to him. Lym was almost a complete wreck when, about the third day, the brave called him to one side and without any apparent anger told him that he had violated a major rule of the Indians by not doing what was expected of him. He said that this particular matter was of little importance, but that the principle was the same as it would be in a major matter; that the Indians had to do exactly as agreed because sometimes it meant the difference between having food and going hungry; that in earlier days it meant the difference between life and death.

Fish Creek, Scripture's classroom. Courtesy Edward Blankman (The Lloyd Blankman Collection)

Lym said that this brave was the best fisherman in the band and was the only one who had a metal hook. One day the brave came back to camp, throwing down for the women to dress seven or eight trout. He reported that there were clouds of flies over the creek and that the trout were jumping like mad and wouldn't take the hook, although he had fouled seven or eight.

He said he would make something that would float. He cut some underhair off a deerskin, wrapped and tied it around the hook, ran his knife blade here and there across the tied hair, and had a fluffy but large fly. Then he went back to the Creek and shortly afterward returned with a great many trout. I have always thought of this as the earliest use of a floating fly in this country. I may be wrong but at least it was the earliest use of which I have any authentication.

Returned to a comparatively tranquil and ordered professional life in Rome, Scripture found it necessary from time to time to suspend work with occasional jaunts to the banks of Fish Creek.
Courtesy Edward Blankman (The Lloyd Blankman Collection)

Brook trout, of course, were the only trout in the stream until the introduction of browns, about 1896. The first brown I saw was taken on a wet fly by the late Dr. Nelson C. Scudder at Swancott's in 1897. For the next few years these were called "California trout." Rainbows were introduced later and did very well down through the gorge.

Those who saw Fish Creek at Swancott's only between 1890 and 1900 would hardly recognize it today. In those days we always stopped at the Smith Lewis place. There were no telephones up there, so we were taking a chance when, after a heavy rain, we started for Fish Creek with the horse and buggy. The Williams Bridge spanned the creek about a mile above Swancott's, and Dad would always stop the horse on the bridge and look at the creek. After satisfying himself about the stream's condition, he would drive on to the Lewis home, where after luncheon he would tell Mr. Lewis that we would be back "this day week." This meant that the stream, in Dad's opinion, would be down enough to fish in a week. Today, after a half century of timbering from Swancott's up to the source of the creek, the stream can be in flood one

When the last Norther had subsided to spring, the old song of the quest began humming in Scripture's head. Courtesy Edward Blankman (The Lloyd Blankman Collection)

day and quite fishable the following day. Today there is hardly an unwadeable riffle; then, even in normal conditions, the fording places were few.

Sixty Years Ago Along Fish Creek, Part Two

William E. Scripture, Jr., *North Country Life*, Winter 1954

For many years I had the pleasure of staying at the Widmer home (now the Rome Fish Creek Club) about four miles above Thompson's Mill. Frederick Widmer and his wife came to America from Canton Bern, Switzerland, some time prior to 1854. Mr. Widmer bought some land adjacent to Fish Creek, cleared a bit of it, and erected a log house. Here his children were born, and here he spent the major portion of his long life.

In his summer of 1939, Elmer Bernier dammed up a portion of Fish Creek back in the woods west of Constableville and floated 12,000 cords of wood to a point where they could be loaded on trucks and hauled away to the Gould Paper Company pulp mill in Lyons Falls. Courtesy Edward Blankman (The Lloyd Blankman Collection)

He had little formal education, yet he was one of the best-read men I ever knew. When he ever found time to so improve his education, I could never understand. His conversation was something to anticipate with real pleasure, and I spent a great many hours just listening to him after starting him on some subject or other. Current events, history ancient or modern, botany, ornithology, geology—he could hold one's interest with anything he talked about.

In 1867, a man named David Swancott moved into the southeast side of the Tug Hill area, about twenty miles north of Rome. Here, on Fish Creek, he built a dam and established a water-powered sawmill, around which a sizeable settlement known as Swancott Mills quickly grew up. At this place Mr. Swancott developed a diversified manufacturing enterprise. Besides lumber, he produced broom handles which supplied a broom factory in Amsterdam, and he also operated a plant which produced oars and paddles. The latter activity being entirely new, paddle finishers were practically non-existent in the area, so he imported a few from various southern states. The sawmill also put out crossties for use by the railroads in expanding their ever-growing systems. Swancott Mills boasted, besides these manufactories, a boarding house, schoolhouse, general store, dance hall, and several houses owned by the company for the use of married employees. In its heyday the place even had its own baseball team that used to play in competition with other local teams. Some sixty or more men were employed there, as well as seventy-five teams of horses for skidding and hauling logs. The businesses were carried on for many years, finally succumbing to the lack of readily available raw materials, as did many others. The tract of land, including the site of the former settlement, was purchased about 1920 by the Gould Paper Company. Courtesy Edward Blankman (The Lloyd Blankman Collection)

When he started clearing the land, salmon were still coming up Fish Creek through Lake Ontario and Oneida Lake. They spawned in the wide water just above the Schaler Hole in the beaver meadow. People came during the spawning season from all of Constable's Five Towns to get salmon to put down for winter. Mr. Widmer said that the men would come with huge barrels on stone boats drawn by oxen. They would have heavy, long-tined rakes with long handles, the points of the tines inclined toward the handles, and with these rakes they would literally rake the fish off the shallows. No one seemed to fish for the salmon.

Above Elmer Bernier's logging base camp, Fish Creek and Roaring Brook came together.
Courtesy Edward Blankman (The Lloyd Blankman Collection)

Most of the meat consumed then consisted of game, which was very plentiful, and the salmon. But in the late fifties a dam was built which prevented the salmon from getting into Oneida Lake, so the settlers lost that source of food.

The Schaler Hole is a long Stillwater in the meadow behind the Widmer house. Without question it was the most famous of any of the trout pools in a radius of many miles from Widmer's. Governors, senators, famous trout fishermen, all fished here. The Schaler Hole was something special. Big brookers were plentiful, and fishermen told of leviathans lost or only seen as they broke water.

Today there are some tremendous browns in the pool. During the daylight hours the brookers seem to predominate, but as evening comes on, one is more likely to see browns.

When hatches of various kinds of flies come on, the Fish Creek trout seem to be very "choosy." I have observed brook trout feeding greedily near the heel of a pool, while large browns were feeding just as greedily in the upper half of the pool. Three rather large hatches were on the water, the flies being large, medium, and small. It wasn't until I had changed from 10s, to 12s to 14s and finally to 16s that I moved a fish. Then in five casts I hooked five nice brook trout, but before I could drop the fly to the sixth time, the fish stopped feeding from head to heel of the pool. The large and medium flies covered the water but not a trout would rise to them.

During low water in late May, June, or August I have found it profitable to get to the stream on a morning immediately following a rain sufficiently copious to raise the water five or six inches and muddy it very slightly. I know the experts say to fish the dry fly on a falling stream, but I have had such good fishing so many times on a rising stream that I am impelled to say, with my good friend Karl, "*Jeder nach seinem Geschmach,*" or as we might say, "To each his own."

Most of the experts say that when the streams are in spate, swollen and muddied, the fly fisherman should stay at home. If you are on Fish Creek when it is in this condition, set up a couple dark buck tails on 1s or 2s and go to work. Dropping the bobber may bring results, but if you get your flies to where the trout can spot them, watch out for trouble.

Doubtless you will agree with the experts (and with me) that a blisteringly hot day in the middle of July, with the water low and clear and hardly a breath of air stirring, isn't exactly what the doctor ordered. However, under these circumstances I have moved some of the largest trout that ever came to my dry fly. (Of course, this isn't saying very much because the largest trout I ever took with a dry fly was only 25½ inches.)

During the regular cutting and peeling season, from May until August, thousands of cords of mature spruce were cut and stripped of bark. The Gould Paper Company had for years practiced a program of selective cutting, taking no trees under ten inches in diameter at the stump. The ten-inch minimum ensured another cut in the same area in roughly thirty years. However, on this job this rule could largely be dispensed with, as most of the timber was well over that size. In late summer, skidding teams were brought in and the logs were skidded to big skidways along the hauling roads. They were hauled by Linn tractors in winter on well-iced roads to Roaring Brook and Fish Creek for the spring log drive. Courtesy Edward Blankman (The Lloyd Blankman Collection)

It nearly always happened this way on Fish Creek. With not a sign of a natural fly in the air or on the water, I would tie on a large Palmer or an oversize Drake. If I spotted even a narrow ledge two or three feet under the surface of water, and if there was enough current to float and drift the fly, I would drop the fly a few feet upstream from the ledge and strip line in as the fly came down stream. More than once under such conditions, when fishing seemed more than a chance to get a good bath, I've moved big trout.

Again, when Fish Creek is low and clear and warm, a large white Palmer fished in the fastest water is often effective.

Sixty Years Ago Along Fish Creek, Part Three

William E. Scripture, Jr., *North Country Life*, Winter 1954

Seth Green, Reuben Wood, and my father, the late Justice William E. Scripture, fished at Widmer's during the seventies. Mr. Widmer once told how, after his wife had sounded the shell to call Mr. Wood to lunch, Mr. Wood came up to the house and reported a great hatch of flies on the water. He asked if he might take some feathers from some roosters. After he had secured the feathers, Mrs. Widmer brought him some red and white yarn and some light thread and a piece of beeswax. Then Mr. Wood tied some flies to approximate the real flies he had seen. Mr. Widmer believed that the pattern was later called the "Rube Wood."

In the seventies and later there was a club at Thompson's Mill, three or four miles downstream from Widmer's. This was a rather exclusive club, comprised mainly of wealthy and retired business and professional men, and its membership was said to include men from eleven or more states. I can remember seeing elderly men, their trousers cut off above the knees, wading about in the pool below the dam. Great medicinal properties were claimed for Fish Creek water.

To me that isn't so strange as it may sound. I remember having a severe attack of sciatica one June, and after suffering a great deal for a couple weeks, I begged to be taken up to my shanty at Swancott's. There on the first afternoon I managed, with help, to hobble across the flat and to the creek. I waded out into the creek until the water came up to my waist. I fished, purposely keeping in fairly deep water, until dusk, when, without help, I walked back to the camp. The next day I walked without pain, and since then the sciatica has never returned.

This exclusive club at Thompson's Mill conceived a plan to control, by lease, the fishing rights on the creek from the club property down to the Point of Rocks, a distance of 12 to 15 miles. They secured leases or options on all but a stretch of about two miles, about midway from the club to the Point. There they ran into an impasse, for they couldn't locate the owners of this land.

A Gould Paper Company logging crew somewhere along Fish Creek.
Courtesy Edward Blankman (The Lloyd Blankman Collection)

My father believed the Creek to be public inland water. When he found out about the club's plans, he started a search for the owner of the land in question and found her. He bought the land, and the club members, facing the fact that without this stretch they could not complete their plans, gave up the idea. The stream has since been open to the public, furnishing good fishing to thousands of people who never heard of the attempt to close all those miles of beautiful stream.

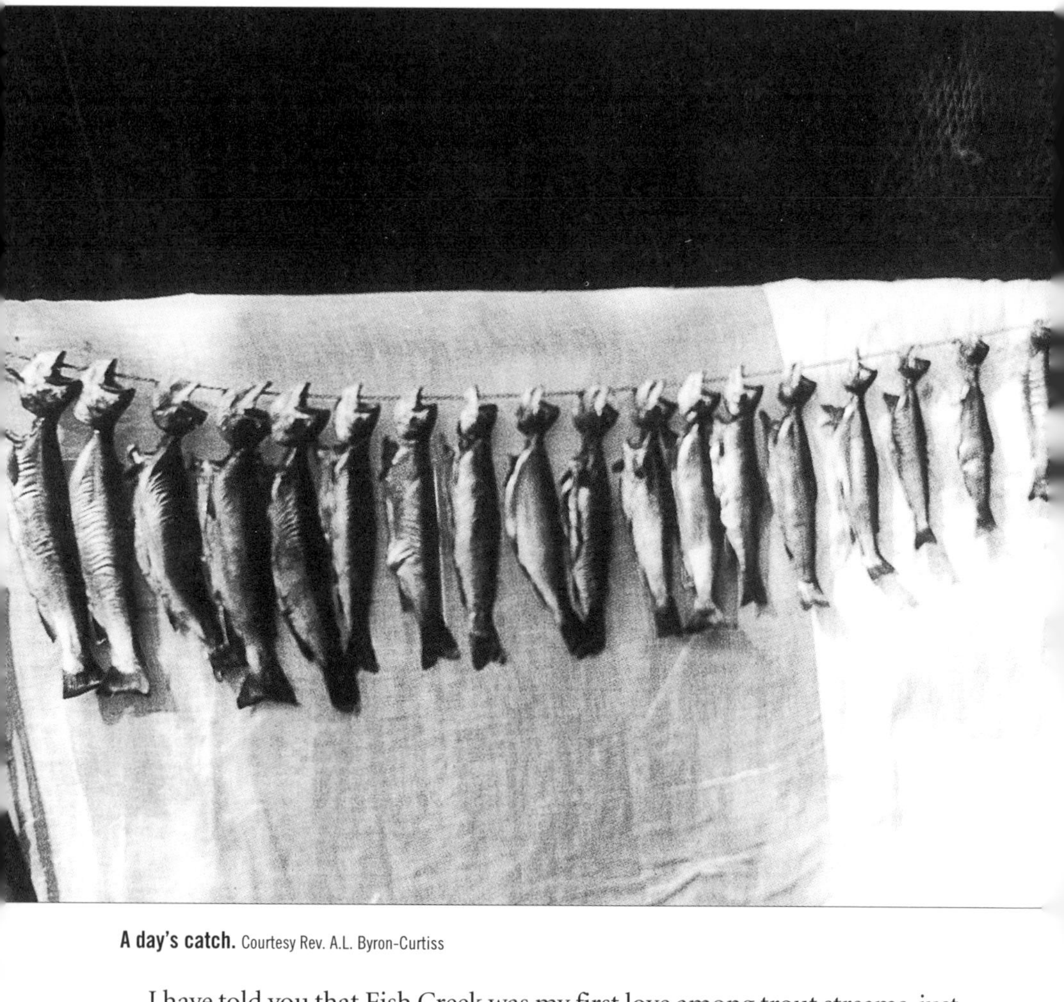

A day's catch. Courtesy Rev. A.L. Byron-Curtiss

I have told you that Fish Creek was my first love among trout streams, just as it most surely will be my last. Its waters are friendly, cheerful, and warmly embracing. The water is soft and pure and sweet. I must have drunk literally tons of it.

On the contrary, the Mohawk below Delta Dam is cold and gray and not at all friendly in appearance or feeling. Sand and pieces of shale and other things get into one's shoes.

One June Karl Karcher came up from Brookline, Massachusetts, and we went over to the Mohawk. Although we took some trout, Karl didn't like the water and, as I had extolled the virtues of Fish Creek by saying among other things that it was "friendly water," he asked if we couldn't go up there for a few days.

I arranged things at the office, and we took off for Swancott's. The next morning, we headed for the stream. Because Karl had never fished it, I wanted him to have the best of the fishing. I put him into a pool where I knew there were good trout. About fifteen feet from shore was a large log to which it was necessary to wade waist deep. I cautioned him to be careful because on the far side of the log the water was deep and there was a treacherous eddy.

I went a hundred feet down stream, waded out, and commenced casting over some shallow riffles, neither expecting nor getting a rise but giving Karl time to fish the pool. Suddenly I heard a splash upstream, and I dashed to shore and ran toward the pool. When I came within sight of the log, I could see that Karl wasn't there, but as I came nearer, I saw a rod extended above the water and an arm thrown across the log.

I stood there and laughed. My friend of about 175 pounds had changed to a man of at least 300. His long hunting coat had water cascading from it, but it was still like an oversized tub. Karl had lost his hat and the water was running down from his hair. When I could speak, I asked him if he had been hurt. His answer, which I recall with much pleasure, wasn't exactly parlor language. "Hurt?" he said. "Hell, no. Friendly water, Bill, friendly water. I'd rather drown in Fish Creek than get my feet wet in the Mohawk!"

Sixty Years Ago Along Fish Creek, Part Four

William E. Scripture, Jr., *North Country Life*, Winter 1954

Henry Van Dyke honored my family by being our guest for a week or so during two consecutive years. Our twins, Ruth and Billy, who were youngsters then, were fascinated by the stories Dr. Van Dyke told them about the Holy Land, the mountains of Japan, and the strange birds and animals of Australia.

He made a ritual of building a fireplace fire, laying each stick according to his rule and placing the fire logs just so. Our fireplace took four-foot logs, which were sometimes a bit heavy, and then he would permit me to help him. When the fire was well started, the doctor would sit before it in a large armchair, put a youngster on either knee, and tell them stories of strange lands and strange peoples.

One year the doctor, his son Tertius, Al Jones, and I went up to Widmer's (then the Rome Fish Creek Club). Dr. Van Dyke seemed to love the place. One day he and I went upstream until we reached a pool, which I knew contained some nice brookers. I suggested that he fish the pool carefully while I went up to a run, hardly out of sight from the pool. He agreed and said he would overtake me. More time than it would take to fish the pool had elapsed, however, when I became nervous and apprehensive, so I walked back to the pool. I found the doctor's rod but the owner wasn't in sight. I called, softly at first and finally with all the lungpower I commanded, but there was no reply that I heard. When I had become really scared, I heard a voice and saw the doctor coming toward me. While he was fishing the pool, he had heard a bird singing and he had left the pool and followed the sound quite a distance before he found and identified the bird, which he said he had never seen so far north.

On another occasion the doctor and I were fishing the creek below the Point of Rocks, the stretch from the Big Flat-Iron Pool to Fish Creek Dam. Dr. Van Dyke saw and identified a large number of flowers and ferns growing on the face of the cliffs. One of the flowers, according to the New York State botanist, is found only along Fish Creek.

The doctor was much impressed by the beauty of the stream. Although he had fished nearly every famous trout stream in the world, he said he had never seen a more beautiful one.

One day while the doctor was at our home, I found him before a bookcase, with one of his books in his hands. The cover was in horrible condition and some of the leaves were nicked and some were dirty. I started to apologize for the book's condition, but the doctor stopped me. "Billy, don't you know that's about the highest compliment an author can have?" he asked.

Although we had nearly all of his books, you can imagine our delight, when, a week or two after he left, we received a large package from Scribner's containing all of his prose works. On the flyleaf of each book he had written a little line or original verse and his signature.

Later, he sent to my wife a copy of his collected poems. On the flyleaf he had written "Mrs. William E. Scripture, Jr., with the grateful regards of her friend, Henry Van Dyke. May 14, 1921. Yes, any house where love abides, and friendship is a guest, is surely home, and home sweet home, for there the heart can rest."

Adirondack TIM-Berrr!

Chapter 53 | William J. O'Hern

THE ENERGY OF HORSEPOWER

During the days of old-style logging throughout the 19th and early 20th centuries, loggers skidded and hauled exclusively with oxen and hefty draft horses. These animals were steady and strong. Oxen were very slow. Draft horses weighed 1,600 to 2,500 pounds each. Their strong legs and mild temperaments made them ideal work animals.

Throughout this period, no thought was given to the future sustainability of timber. Labor was cheap and timber seemed plentiful.

Big loads earned bragging rights among teamsters. Courtesy George R. Cataldo

Anthony Coleman and Alex Compo were two typical lumberjacks who cut for years throughout the southwestern Adirondacks. The Rev. A.L. Byron-Curtiss,[9] North Lake camp owner, author of *The Life and Adventures of Nat Foster, Trapper and Hunter of the Adirondacks* and one-time minister of Christ Episcopal Church in Forestport, N.Y. knew these lumbermen. Through their deeds they developed reputations developed as colorful characters throughout the headwaters of the Black River. Bryon-Curtiss said of the men, "Their friendly rivalry was widespread in the forest, felling trees, peeling bark, skidding logs. At night, when I stayed in their bunkhouse, I noted their braggadocio was whetted by the mountain air."

Both men knew their way around horses.

Teams of horses were once an important part of logging operations. Courtesy Lyons Falls History Association

Whoa, Mac. Back! Alex Compo, a heavily-built man in thick wool pants held up with suspenders, called out commands to a pair of Belgian draft horses in full harness, directing them to step into position. *Whoa, Mac. Back!* As the animals stepped back in tandem, Compo looped a choker around a felled tree. Another command and the horses set to dragging a large log through the woodland at a quick trot as Compo jogged behind, shouting directions.

What Compo and his team were doing was typical of old-time logging methods in virgin tracts of forest. Typically, large logs were first peeled on one side and then rolled over to be skidded, with the smooth side down to make the pulling easier. Skidding tongs were used when logs were skidded individually. A logging chain was used when more than one log was skidded along a skidway. A team of horses and one man would usually skid up to 150 logs per day.

Shortly after the turn of the 20th century, machinery began to make inroads, moving logs to landings for spring river driving to mills. It wouldn't be too many more years before Compo's methods became outdated.

The Rev. Byron-Curtiss thought so much of the representative old-time loggers that he admitted, "I told many a hyperbolic yarn about those men." One tale about two lumberjacks riding over Niagara Falls became a standard in The Reverend's bag of stories. He recalled in his memoirs, "It immediately spread all through the region. The two heroes were well-known in all the lumber camps. Alex Compo was one of those men who confound the best philosophy of wise men as to formal education, for while he could neither read nor write he eventually became a jobber who oversaw three hundred men in his scattered camps. His many antics when young and his later success set me to speculating if a formal education would have spoiled him.

"Anthony Coleman spent most of his life as a lumberjack, but once or twice branched off into other occupations, still woodsy in nature. In his later years he served as the game protector for the Adirondack League Club stationed at the head of North Lake. His job was to shoo any of us freelance fishermen and hunters off the club preserve. In Herkimer County, there is a Coleman Dam built across Bear Creek located northeast of Granny Marsh or southwest of Bear Pond. It was named after him."

Those were the old days of horsepower: 1 horse = 1 horsepower; 2 horses = 2 horsepower. This energy fueled by hay and grain was replaced with new-age cutting-edge machines fueled by steam and gasoline during the early years of the 20th century.

Chapter 54 | William J. O'Hern and Fred Schneider, *Tug Hill Country*

H.H. LINN'S PRACTICAL TRACTOR

Holman Harry "H.H."[10] Linn was one of America's mechanical wizards who experimented with inventing bigger, more powerful logging machines capable of outdoing almost anything horses could do.

Linn's genius advanced ways of working and life in the woods during the early years of logging's mechanization.

Early mechanical inventors experimented to develop machinery that could replace several teams of horses. They reasoned that a powerful steam-powered tractor could haul huge loads of logs more efficiently than by team, sleigh and drivers.

Big Mike and Jerry (horses' name) ready to haul logs, 1918, Colton, N.Y. Teamster unknown. Over time tractors took the place of horses. Courtesy Colton Historical Society

Theodore B. Basselin was one such early experimenter in early steam tractors. It's likely Linn studied Basselin's early logging contraption.

Kenneth R. Proulx, Basselin's biographer, wrote of the man in his book *The Life and Enterprise of Theodore B. Basselin* (1980), "...lumber had to be transported by team and sleigh. To Basselin that method was slow and obsolete. He purchased a steam-powered sleigh for the operation. This piece of equipment...weighed approximately four tons, was powered by a seven-foot boiler which developed 300 horsepower and was capable of carrying 15,000 pounds of logs, equal to six ordinary sleighs."

There is little documentation as to how successful Basselin's steam tractor proved to be in the woods. Because of its size and weight, it certainly could not have been ideal to operate.

Approximately thirty years later, H.H. Linn of Morris, New York, developed a practical tractor that replaced horses for hauling logs. Fred Schneider tells about Linn's tractor in his January 22, 2003 column "Along the Black River" in Lowville's *Journal and Republican*.

> Linn designed his tractor with tracks in the rear and wheels in front, and unlike fully tracked machines that stop one track to turn, his was steered with the front wheels like a truck. It was an impressive hit with loggers. One Linn tractor could draw a dozen or more sleighs at one time and make twice as many trips in a day. This mechanical marvel was introduced in 1917 and production continued until 1952 and some 2,500 machines were built. In addition to logging they were used in construction, mining, and farming.
>
> For winter work in the woods the front wheels were replaced with skis and "V" shaped grousers were bolted to the tracks. The "V" shape gave the Linn tremendous pulling power and kept it from sliding sideways on hillside roads. The early models had only a roof to afford the driver a little protection and, of course, there were no heaters, but loggers were a rugged lot and dressed to withstand the cold North Country weather.
>
> Barbara Kephart Bird spent several winters with her husband, a forester for the Gould Paper Company, in lumber camps. In her book, *Calked Shoes*, published in 1952, she describes being

awakened by noise and light on her first morning at Gould Paper Company Camp Number 7. "I awoke to find myself in a shaft of intense white light. The air pulsed with weird and terrible sounds—the clank of chains, the throb of immense engines, the hoarse cries of souls in agony.

T.C. Williams' gas Lombard at Camp 7. Lombard and Linn's internal-combustion machines competed with each other as well as changed the way logging was done. Courtesy Fred Worden

"At 4:30 on that February morning… I sat on the edge of the bed and looked out of our window and for the first time viewed the impressive sight of the tractors hitching up. Each tractor was attended by a driver and a 'whistle punk,' whose whole energies were bent on being the first ones on the road."

The whistle punk was the fellow who signaled the driver as he backed up to hook up the string of sleighs, an often-dangerous job that took more than one life and limb. The origin of the term is unclear but the best information I found was that he signaled the driver with piercing whistles that could be heard over the engine noise.

When the tractor with its train of sleighs reached the skidway it pulled alongside single or double headers, where a pile of logs wait in the woods to be loaded. Logs were rolled onto its bunks first, then each sleigh was advanced and loaded. The whistle punk secured the binder chains, then signaled the driver, who headed out on the main haul road to the banking ground. There the binders were released, the logs rolled off and the tractor driver with his string of empty sleighs headed back into the woods on "go back" roads.

By the mid-1920s Linn tractors had pretty much replaced horses for hauling sleigh loads of timber, and most lumber camps had at least one Linn fitted with a water box to ice roads. Teams of horses were still used to skid the logs to roadside landings and to haul "tote" (supplies) into camps.

The first Linn tractor purchased by the Gould Paper Company. Courtesy Lyons Falls Pulp and Paper archives

One of the few Linns still in operating condition (2003) is owned by "Dutch" Buchals near Deer River. Dutch usually displays his machine at the Flywheels and Pulleys show in Constableville. The Adirondack Museum also has a Linn on display, along with a fine collection of early logging equipment.

Ernest Leigh Portner is not only an owner of four Linn tractors—one of which is in showroom working condition, but is a leading expert on the life H.H. Linn and the history of his various machinery.

This letter is a testimony from the Gould Paper Company to Linn regarding the company's purchase. It is one of the hundreds of papers Portner owns. Portner's extensive files include Linn-related manuals, photographs, documents, Linn tractor parts and Linn tractors.

FORESTPORT, N.Y., MAR. 7, 1921

Linn Mfg. Corp.
Morris, N.Y.

Gentlemen:
The 60 H.P. Linn Tractors we are now using have been the means of solving our log drawing troubles.

The grade from North Lake to Camp#7 is a rise of 750 ft. in 2½ miles. These tractors draw 2½ cords of logs on the tractor, and 8 trailer log sleighs draw from 32 to 40 cords more up this grade.

Our longest draw is about 12 miles, half of which is down grade. The roads this winter have been from 18 to 30 inches of solid ice; the lags on the track of the machine prevent any slipping.

We have used the twelve 60 H.P. tractors this winter and have had very little breakage, we carry about $5,000 worth of parts in stock in case of breaks but next winter we do not expect to carry anywhere near this amount.

On the North Lake job we have drawn 48 days using an average of six to seven tractors per day, drawing an average of 416⅔ cords per day; balance of tractors were used for sprinkling and plowing.

We highly recommend them to anyone wishing a powerful machine that will draw over iced roads larger loads than can be loaded or unloaded by a usual logging crew and outfit.

Respectfully yours,
Gould Paper Co.
J.E. Cannan, Operator
Per Wm. A. Graff

Adirondack TIM-Berrr!

Chapter 55 | William J. O'Hern

OSCEOLA CAMP COMPLETES UNUSUAL LOGGING OPERATION IN RECORD TIME

Long-time Lewis County resident John Gymburch Jr. talks about the many kinds of knowledge about the old days and ways that are still alive in residents' hearts and minds.

Gymburch's hunting camp was in Swancott Mills, so over 50 years or so he's heard a lot of stories about the local area while sitting around the wood stove at camp.

From his perspective as a hunter, he knows where many of the former Gould Paper Company's logging camps and sites were around Swancott Mills. He talks about Gould's property on Tug Hill. "I know where Gould's Camps 4 and 5 were and the locations of Elmer Bernier's camps. I know where the original Swancott homestead was located on the Creek Road. (There used to be an apple tree behind the old cellar that had yellow apples that smelled exactly like bananas!) Norm Fey Jr.'s dad, Norm Sr., has lived in that area all of his life and he has a lot of knowledge about Swancott Mills, Fey's Mill, Parson's Mill, Leisher Mill and Freeman's Mill.

"From a trapping perspective, a fellow named 'Tommy' Cullings earned a living for his family by trapping the Point Rock, Swancott Mills, and 46 Corners areas." Gymburch emphasizes, "Tommy is a very unique individual. If he likes you, he'll tell you a few interesting facts to make conversation with you, but if Tommy REALLY likes you, he can make four hours seem like fifteen minutes!

"Many things beside the annual snowfall totals make this area a very interesting place. It's hard to believe that 'once upon a time' this area had stores, schools, hotels and everything else to support a vibrant community."

John Gymburch knows that each time natives gather to talk of past times and places, the more they remember, and that before they've realized it, an afternoon has passed.

I found that to be true the day I asked John, Norm Fey Jr. and Wayne Kwasniewski about Chief Powlish after accidently stumbling across an August 21, 1919, clipping titled "Who Owns Forestport?" in the Utica *Daily Press.*

A pile of logs stacked in winter at a Colton logging camp. Over the winter loggers cut logs and piled them near the river. In spring, the "key log" would be taken out, forcing the pile to roll into the river, where the loggers could then "drive" the logs downstream. Circa 1900. Courtesy Colton Historical Society

Powliss was a member of the Oneida Nation of the Iroquois Confederacy. Tug Hill was part of their Great North Woods beaver hunting grounds. Timber became very valuable in Powliss's territory, and over time the axe of the lumberjack was heard more and more. Part of the area's folklore revolves around the investigation of the status of the Oneidas regarding Selective

Service Regulations when Karl A. Roses (sic) came into possession of some old treaties of the Oneida tribe. The newspaper article I came across told about the possible "recovery of valuable lands near the city of Oneida under a recent decision of the Federal District Court; the Oneidas have decided also to bring up their claims to other lands which have not yet been ceded to the state.

"…a short distance from the village of Forestport is a small lake, Powlish Pond, and in several of the treaties unearthed, this lake is mentioned. The Powlish family are bringing the matter up for action.

"Lyman Powliss, a well-known Oneidan who lives in Syracuse, was born near this pond and will be of aid in restoring the title for his nation. Information is now being collected from the Powliss family, now residents of the Oneida Indian reservation at Green Bay, Wisconsin."

Today's lumbermen, like Wayne Kwasniewski and Norm Fey Sr. are also knowledgeable about Lewis County's logging history and about who-owned-what and who-cut-what in that area.

They know of the big news announced on July 2, 1903, when the Cape Vincent *Eagle* told of a huge timber sale in their vicinity. The *Eagle* informed:

> An important business transaction was recently consummated in which Carthage parties were interested. A large tract of timber lands situated in Lewis county consisting of 20,000 acres of virgin forest and a one-half interest in the Glenfield-and-Western Railroad was sold by the Dexter and West Carthage Sulphite companies to the Osceola Lumber company, a large syndicate recently organized, the sulphite concerns reserving all of the spruce on the tract for use in their mills."

Years later, on November 17, 1920, the Utica *Morning Telegram*, announced another timber lot sale under the headline, "Hearst Outbid in Attempt to Buy Pulpwood Tract." It read:

> An effort by William R. Hearst to add to his already extensive timber holdings in Northern New York a tract of 26,000 acres in Lewis and Oswego Counties failed, it became known yesterday, with the announcement that the property had been acquired by the Gould Paper Company of Lyons Falls.

> The property, known as the White Preserve, was owned by the Tug Hill Lumber Company, Inc., which made the sale. It was stated that a record price was paid for the property because of the scarcity of pulpwood and the feverish competitions among the paper mills to acquire pulpwood tracts at almost any cost.
>
> Harry P. Gould…recently appointed by Governor Smith a director in the State College of Forestry at Syracuse University, is president of the Gould Paper Company.
>
> He declared that a constructive system of timbering would be used on the tract of land, which is the policy advocated by the reforestation experts.
>
> The sale was completed through John X. McDonald of the Macumac L. Corporation, Utica, N.Y.…
>
> Mr. Hearst has property adjoining the tract in question, having purchased 20,000 acres there last spring from the Dexter Sulphite Company, of which C. Clarence Campbell of Watertown is president. By Mr. Gould's methods of cutting timber, the beauty of the tract will be preserved, as only a little will be taken out at a time.

The Powlish Family Did Not Succeed

Today, what once was land the Oneidas hunted and the site of Chief Powlish's cabin, is part of Herb Kwasniewski's timber lot. Wayne Kwasniewski, Herb's cousin, works on the 30,000 acre Corrigan Tract. He tells, "The property is SFI [sustainable forestry initiative] certified and we get audited on a regular basis by a third party. We flag a 100-foot buffer along all classified streams, wetlands and vernal pools. We can have limited harvest inside these buffers, but only high-grade trees are cut if they can be extracted with limited impact. The shade integrity and water quality is a priority. Along both branches of the Salmon River there is a 200-foot no-cut buffer. We mark wildlife and heritage trees to be left in the residual stand. We are professional and we know what we are doing."

I have a feeling that Chief Powlish would find this part of Lewis County where they once hunted, trapped, and fished has remained in good hands.

The scene of the following is the former Oneida hunting grounds Chief Powlish knew well. It was recorded by an unidentified writer and appeared in an unidentified newspaper. A yellowed copy provided by Shirley Van Nest of the Lyons Falls Historical Society tells about the Gould Paper Company's "unusual" logging operation—an experimental job that was completed in record time.

Auldis LaPlatney, Ken Cring, and Buck Gerow loading logs (using a Bay City cable winch powered by a McCormick Deering motor) onto a truck bed. Winter of 1939. Harrisville, N.Y.
Courtesy Town of Diana Historical Museum

Gould's 1938 experiment required the purchase of seventeen GMC log trucks at a cost of about $1,500 each. It involved carrying 100% of the timber out of the woods on trucks for the first time. The previous year's river drive on Fish Creek had proven too costly to continue to pay the insurance on bonded Canadians. Besides this being a first-person memory of Gould's "first," the story reveals details about lumber camp life in the Big North Woods of Lewis County.

★ ★ ★

Late afternoon of Tuesday, Feb. 4, 1938, as the last logging truck, piled high over the driver's cab, roared away from the high 15-foot double-decker skidway, and began its long and slow journey over the three-mile stretch of narrow, winding temporary winter roadway through the woods to the main road, the Osceola Logging Camp, operated by the Gould Paper Company of Lyons Falls, had completed its operations for the winter season.

This date is important, not only because it is the first logging camp in this section to complete its year's work, but because it marks the close of the first phase of the most unusual logging operation in the history of the business.

In all lumbering operations it is customary to hold the logs in the woods until spring, when they are floated down the rivers in drives to the mills. But to suspend operations in the camps until the spring thaw means considerable expense and waste of time in bringing the lumberjacks back on the job after a two-month lay-off.

So, after considerable study, with the view of effecting economy and efficiency, officials of the Lyons Falls paper company set up their Osceola camp somewhat as an experimental job to last two years.

Naturally, with only the first year's operations just completed, it is a little too early to determine the exact results, although company officials have expressed great satisfaction after examining the results so far.

Jack Hogan Is Foreman

Jack Hogan, a hard-working veteran of the lumbering industry, was foreman of the camp, aided by Charlie Carr, assistant foreman, and Palmer Moore, head bookkeeper. Hogan, who started logging it back in 1920, is one of the best in the business, and really knows his stuff.

Pulpwood was cut last spring at the Osceola camp over an area of 700 acres. Most of the entire job of 7,000 cords for the year consisted of spruce, with a little hemlock.

A fleet of 17 trucks was kept on the move constantly, operating between the camp and Lyons Falls to move the pulpwood before the thaws set in, which would ruin the temporary roads in the woods which had been hastily built by bulldozer tractors of loose dirt, and then frozen.

On the average, 200 cords were moved to the mill every day, each truck making between three to four trips a day, starting out with their first load anywhere between 5 and 6 o'clock in the morning. Load per truck usually averaged between 5½ and 6 cords.

Lyman Humes and Jesse Wicks with a load of logs, Harrisville, N.Y., circa 1930.
Courtesy Town of Diana Historical Museum

A visit to the camp during the final days of the season, which a few from Boonville were fortunate enough to take, was one which will remain in our memory for years to come. For here, in the midst of great forests, was activity, activity in which time was precious. It was, so to speak, the combination of manpower and machinery against time, when at any time thaws might set in, which would in turn drop the iced truck roads out of sight and possibly hold up the completion of the job until next winter.

We marveled at the ability of the drivers of these heavily laden trucks to maneuver their loads over these winding, narrow roads which seemed to have no ending. It was estimated that there were about 12 miles of roadways about the camp, which is situated three long miles off the Osceola highway.

The loading of the trucks was done by rolling the logs off the tops of long skidways, called double headers, which stood about 15 feet off the ground. This job of rolling the logs is quite an art, we learned, and is not just a matter of manual work. It requires precision and teamwork on the part of the lumberjacks (one standing at each end of the log with his cant-hook). The log must land flat on the truck. And, strange to say, these huge 13-foot logs which drop onto the truck from the top of the double-header do not break the springs of the truck, as one might expect.

Two Boonville men, Nate Bristol and Gene Levargneux, two of the best log rollers in these parts, were on the job atop one of the double-headers the day we were in camp, and they really displayed precision as they dropped log after log. They are as good as they come.

Fifty men were on the job in camp right up until the last day. These included teamsters, tractor operators, road monkeys and just plain lumberjacks. Many of these were Boonville residents.

The oldest man on the job was Len Crouse, of Glenfield, who is still carrying on with the best of them at the age of 72 years. He is a teamster, driving the loads by sled from the skidways where the logs had been piled during the fall, to the highway double-headers, where they were to be loaded onto the trucks.

And believe me, there's a man-sized job, too. For a man must know his horses when it comes to driving a three-cord sled load through some of those narrow trails which are all up-and-down and around. Len has been a lumberjack as far back as he can remember, and he says he'll always be one for many years to come. Another old-timer on the job who is also an expert teamster is Erwin Conrad. We understand that the two, both of whom have done practically all their lumbering in this section, are bitter rivals as to their abilities atop the loaded sleds.

Self-sustaining Village

The camp, tucked away in the woods, seemed almost a self-sustaining village, although it was composed of only five main buildings. These low, squat buildings, surrounded by the camp's own highway system of sled and truck roads, with a huge snowplow and tractor for snow removal, consisted of an office and canteen building; a huge horse barn, constructed of whole spruce logs 60 feet in length; complete blacksmith and repair shop; cook house and bunk house.

Meal time. Courtesy *The Northeastern Logger*, August-September 1952.

The large bunkhouse, some 60 feet in length and 30 feet in width, was one of the finest we have ever seen, and seemed to have nearly all the comforts of home. The building housed 48 men, in spacious upper and lower bunks along the sides. A long table in the center provided ample space for the evening and sparetime activities such as reading, letter writing and cards. However, it might be well to note in this connection that lumberjacks don't find a great deal of time to "kill." Their working day usually begins long before daybreak, which is ordinarily around 4:30 or 5 am, and draws to a close anywhere between 6 and 8 pm.

“SOUP’S ON” TIME

Of course they take time out for their “three-squares” a day. And this eating proposition, which often-times brings problems to the average housewife in planning a variety of menus that will appeal to hubbie and children, is a serious part of the day for every logger in camp. The very nature of his heavy work, which keeps him out-of-doors through the entire day, demands that his system have plenty of nourishment.

And this brings into the picture one of the main cogs in any lumber camp, the cook. Demands upon the cook are heavy too. He and his assistant are on the job at 4 o’clock in the morning to get breakfast started and are seldom through with their day’s work until 8 in the evening. With the cook it is just one big meal after another. Breakfast is not simply an egg, piece of toast, and coffee, but practically everything that one could possibly think of eating for the first meal of the day. An average breakfast consists of flapjacks, sausage, bacon, cereals, potatoes, eggs, cookies, ham, coffee, etc.

Mr. and Mrs. Harvey Girard, of Springfield, Massachusetts, did the cooking for the Osceola camp this year, and from all reports they did a swell job. This couple, which is rated among the best in camp cooks, maintained one of the cleanest kitchens and dining halls ever seen. Mr. Girard has been cooking in lumber camps for over 11 years.

AN IMPORTANT INDUSTRY

With the closing of the camp on February 4, members of the crew have gone their various ways, some on vacation and others to continue work in other locations. Boonville will watch with interest the work to be started in the spring on the second and final year of the camp’s work at Osceola.

Many Boonville men are employed at the camp, and most of the camp’s business is transacted in our village, which brings to mind more forcefully than ever the importance of the lumbering industry to Boonville and its surrounding area.

Adirondack TIM-Berrr!

Chapter 56 | William J. O'Hern

CHIEF POWLISS' POND

On January 26, 1957, sandwiched between various hometown news announcements on page 9 in the *Daily Sentinel*, an attention-grabbing headline in the Rome, New York, newspaper declared *'Give it Back to Indians' Phrase No Laughing Matter.*

The article was written by Hilda Avery, a local history buff who often penned stories about her Forestport hometown. Her commentary breathed new interest into the story about Chief Powliss, and about loggers who had cut trees that had words carved into them by an unidentified person or persons. The notices read "Oneida Indian Hunting Grounds," and included "179__." (The other digit denoting the year could not be read.)

Avery's story renewed interest about Powlish[11] Pond, named for Chief Powlish, who lived in the Town of Lewis near its boundary with the Town of Osceola.

Chief Powlish's life is documented in the histories of Lewis County. They tell that Powlish died along the banks of the East Branch of Fish Creek, apparently due to an encounter with a black bear. The Lewis County history records also show that prior to his death Powlish forfeited all the property claimed as Oneida Indian Hunting Grounds west of Fish Creek to a U.S. Army officer by the name of White, after a wager over a wrestling match near Potters Corners[12] during the War of 1812.

Avery's story begins:

> When the thermometer goes below zero and the cars won't start; when the snow blows and piles into drifts that must be shoveled; when the snowplow refills the driveway just as it is cleared, the disgruntled shoveller will probably expostulate, "This country! Ought to give it back to the Indians!"
>
> The stock reply is, of course, "They wouldn't take it. Even they don't want it."

Whether they do or not, they did at one time not so long ago, and a local couple has a clipping to prove it:

While clearing out a desk belonging to the late Charles R. Hayes, a resident of Forestport for many years, Hayes's son came across a clipping with the headline "Oneidas Claim Right to Title to Forestport." The clipping is from a Syracuse paper and is dated August 10, but the year is missing. It was in an envelope with other papers [that] was marked "1924" on the outside.

"Indian Lumberjacks picturing two young men possibly Iroquois or Algonquin ancestry, likely from Akwesasne posing with axes near a felled tree. Circa 1900–1910. Harrisville, N.Y." was written on the back of this photo. Courtesy Town of Diana Historical Museum

According to the story, the Oneida Nation chieftains had sent a petition to the Indian Welfare Society to reclaim for the tribe a tract of land about 10 miles square, containing about 12,000 acres, most of which makes up the Town of Forestport (New York). They stated that when the treaties were drawn up and the lands ceded to the state this tract was not included.

It was while investigating the status of the Oneida Indian under the Selective Service Regulations that this fact came to light and they decided to reclaim their lands.

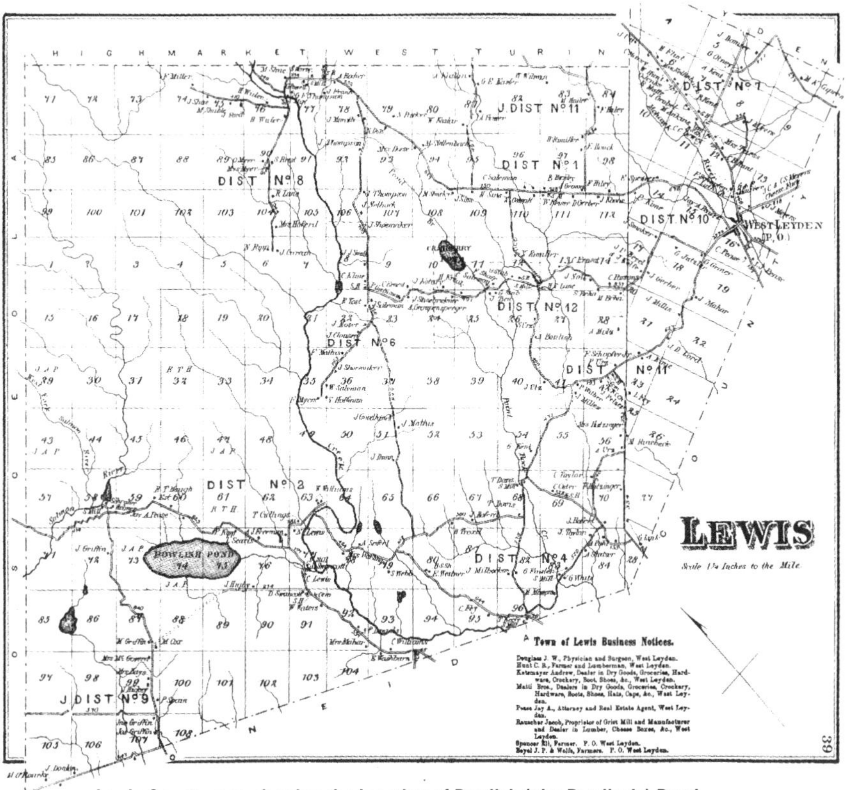

Lewis County map showing the location of Powlish (aka Powliss's) Pond.
Courtesy Lewis County Historical Society

In the early days, northern New York was occupied by the Montagnais Indians, who were given the name Adirondacks by the Iroquois. In their language the word meant "tree eaters." A hundred years before any settlements were made, the Iroquois and the Montagnais tribes roamed through the northwoods until trouble developed between them. The Iroquois finally defeated the Montagnais tribe in a battle near Lowville, practically annihilating the tribe. The survivors fled to Canada.

At this time the Adirondack country was known as Kohsaraga or "Beaver hunting country." Beaver pelts were the standard of trade. Later on, after treaties were drawn up between the whites and the Iroquois the beaver skins were often used in payment and the other tribes paid a tribute of beaver skins to the Six Nations.

In the earliest treaties no particular mention is made of this part of the country, which was the last to be settled, and it was not until Verplanck Colvin, a pioneer surveyor, showed by a map the immense wooded tract to the north that the colonists realized the value and potentialities of this land.

The clipping states that "in the opinion of the attorneys of the Indian Welfare Society there is little question that the title is still vested with the Oneida Indian Nation."

It goes on to describe a small pond near the village of Forestport which it calls Powlish Pond, and states that it is mentioned in several of the old treaties. Additional information was being compiled from members of the Powliss family on the Oneida reservation and in Green Bay, Wisconsin. The tribe was also planning to ask restitution for all timber cut from the land.

The clipping intrigues us, but it failed to give the outcome, nor could we find anyone who knew anything about it. It is quite obvious that the tribe never regained the title, whether or not it is rightfully theirs. A search of town records revealed that no papers had been served.

Numerous arrowheads found in this vicinity testify that the Indians roamed through here in the early days. They have been found on the river bank within the past 20 years [prior to 1957], and were not at all uncommon years ago when they would be unearthed while plowing.

In spite of snow and cold, black flies and mosquitoes, most Forestporters would put up quite a fight before they would give up title to their town.

John E. Clemens replied to Avery's story. Clemens provided additional information. His accounting appeared in the February 12, 1957, Rome *Daily Sentinel* under the title "Story of Powliss Pond."

I read the article by Hilda Avery concerning Powliss Pond. I wish to advise that Powliss Pond is located on the south side of the road that goes from Osceola to what is known as Swancott Mills. I superintended the construction of part of the county road through there.

Four springs head this body of water. I have driven past it all my life. The Oneida Indians lived on the land to the west of Fish Creek until they were given a reservation down near Oneida. When they moved there, Powliss, the chief, would not go. He had a trap line up the creek from Swancott Mills through the country where the four springs are. He went to run his line and did not return that night. Neighbors went to look for him and found him—three miles up the creek—near a large birch blowdown. Powliss was on one side of the fallen tree and a large bear was on the other side of the tree. The bear and Powliss were both dead. Powliss had a long-blade knife gripped in his hand.

In 1932, while I was building the road, I became acquainted with an old couple, Mr. and Mrs. Smith Lewis. They had lived there all their lives and had gone to school at Swancott Mills. Mr. Lewis was about 94 years old at that time and had lived through this history. Mrs. Lewis told me that the neighbors had sent word to the Indians about what had happened to Powliss. About eight o'clock the next A. M. the Indians began to arrive. Mrs. Lewis said she was frightened at the time. The Indians arrived a few at a time— neighbors offered to go and show them where Powliss was, but the Indians said no. The local people gathered to see Powliss and the bear when the Indians brought them out, but the Indians came back empty-handed. Some of the curious went up into the woods later to find out what they had done with Powliss. They found a huge heap of stones about four feet high but could find no place where he was buried. Local residents were satisfied that he was buried up in there….

In constructing this road, we came on a large beech tree. Years before the words "Indian Hunting Ground - 10 Mi. Sq." had been carved on this tree. The letters had spread with the growth of the tree. I notified the [Lewis County] historical society and they came and cut a six-foot chunk, including the lettering, and

> took it with them. They had us place four cement posts where the tree had been.
>
> This is my story of Powliss and Powliss Pond as told to me years ago by Mrs. Smith Lewis.

Today, West Leyden resident Wayne Kwasniewski reports the land that encompasses Powlish Pond is part of his cousin's property. Kwasniewski said, "I don't know where the concrete posts are that Clemens mentioned. In 1957, when I was about 14 years old my cousin and I were at the J & C Sawmill in Swancott Mills and two geologists stopped and asked my uncles if they knew where Chief Powliss's cabin was. My cousin and I took these guys around Powlish Pond, but could not find any remnants of his cabin. The geologists probably were not looking in the right place anyway.

"The geologists told us that they had found fossilized Atlantic salmon scales along the East Branch of Fish Creek; that is why the Oneidas came to the Tug Hill Plateau, to spear salmon. They were smart enough to live in the Mohawk Valley."

Wayne Kwasniewski's memory of the appearance of the geologists and their interest in Powlish Pond adds an interesting fact to the saga of Chief Powlish and the vast Tug Hill timberland that has long been valued by numerous timber companies.

The story of Powliss Pond was made more interesting to me because the body of water is on Wayne Kwasniewski's cousin's property. It's part of Tug Hill's historic White Tract. Wayne is steeped in its history. He can tell all about the Gould Paper Company's acquisition of the wild virgin parcel, what log jobbers cut timber and where, the species of trees found, where the various logging camps were located, and so much more.

To further my interest in Chief Powliss, I contacted Oneida tribal historian, Loretta Metoxen and tribal historical researcher, Josh Gerzetich. Both individuals are very knowledgeable about their reservation and Oneida history.

> **Shekolih:** You state that somewhere it says Chief Powliss forfeited Oneida land. This is (was) n illegal land transaction. During this time period the Oneida were governed by nine elected Chiefs and all of them had to meet in council and come to a consensus before any business could occur. Therefore, Chief Powliss even if

he was a condoled Chief did not have the authority to forfeit, sell or give away Oneida lands.

Lahnehtakete: Josh Gerzetich, Historical Researcher Oneida Cultural Heritage/Oneida History Department

Following the additional information, I provided, Gerzetich replied:

Shekolih Jay: I am sorry I was unable to find anything about Chief Powless in our records. We have several Lyman Powlesses' but they were all born here in Wisconsin. We do not have very good records for events that happened in New York. I did talk to someone here who remembers hearing about a story similar to the one told in the newspaper clipping you provided about the bear but does not recall names or places.

You have to understand that Oneida was never a written language (and) because of this there are a lot of spellings for names and Oneida words. Powless is the spelling most used today. Our records here really only begin when we arrive in Michigan Territory in 1823. I am thinking that you might have better luck contacting the New York Oneidas but again we did not write stuff down. Records, pictures, accounts like what you are looking for are rare.

All of that territory in New York was ours. We had about six million acres just in that state. The State of New York made something like 26 treaties with the Oneida and their allies. Twenty-five of those treaties were ruled illegal because of the Non-Intercourse Act passed by George Washington in 1790. Washington feared the rapid loss of Indian lands and did not trust the states to act fairly or in anyone's best interests. The non-intercourse act states that only treaties that have a federal representative are legal and almost all the treaties with New York have no federal representation and are therefore illegal. This was proven in a 1985 Supreme Court test case. This case has since been reversed somehow by a lower court for "laches" from what I am told. There are whole books written about this subject and case.

So, I cannot confirm his existence or even his title as a chief. We have two types of Chiefs condoled and what are called Pine Tree Chiefs. None of them have the authority to unilaterally make decisions or decide items for the tribe. Our government is the oldest continuing form of democracy in the world and is based on consensus of all 9 chiefs for the Oneida and all 50 for the Iroquois/Haudenosaunee Confederacy. The treaties usually refer to landmarks like creeks, streams and lakes for their boundaries. I am unfamiliar with them and usually have no idea which ones to look at. I know the 1788 treaty with New York is a big one and under much controversy as our people believed it to be a lease and not a sale.—On^kiwah

Oneida Nation tree truck museum exhibit. Courtesy Lewis County Historical Society

While I was initially hopeful some additional information would surface regarding the Native American known in Lewis County history as Chief Powliss from the Oneida Nation in New York, nothing came to light. However, Josh Gerzetich's correspondence did shed a bit more light on a location I've long heard mentioned that I frequently pass by on my way to Fish Creek.

Acknowledgements | William J. O'Hern

THANKS TO ALL

The people and organizations who helped me in this historical book are mentioned in the text, but it is important to acknowledge everyone for their assistance—whether large or small—for without their help *Adirondack Timber Cruising: Logging Tales and Lumbering Days Memories Including Mart Allen's Recollections* would not exist.

My deepest thanks to all the people who contributed to this undertaking. I extend my gratitude to: Mart Allen; Douglas Arthur; Wayne Blanchard, Director Indian Lake Museum; Edward Blankman; David Brown; George Capron; Dan Christmas; Dr. Eliza Jane Darling, Hamilton County historian; Robert J. Elinskas; Amy Feiereisel; John Fram; Mark Fridenen, Town of Clifton historian; Christine Godfrey, Jefferson County Historical Society; Goff-Nelson Memorial Tupper Lake Library; John Gymburch Jr.; Chip Twellman Haley; Charles E. Herr; Debbie Haehl, Northeastern Loggers Association, Inc.; Hamilton County Historical Association; Betty Hoag; Wayne Kwasniewski; John B. Johnson; Joe Kelly; Bruce Koenig; Katherine K. Lewis, director of the Goodsell Museum, Town of Webb Historical Association; the Lyons Falls Historical Association; Larry and Mary Meyers; Jim Plumley; Ernest Leigh Portner; Joanne Sattler; M. Lisa Monroe, Editor *Adirondack Express*; North Country Public Radio; Sandy Pascucci, Woodgate Free Library director; Dr. Jerry Perrin, Manager/Curator Lewis County Historical Society; Ellen Rocco, WSLU station manager; Sandy Pascucci, Woodgate Library; Kristy Rubyor, administrative assistant, Town of Webb Historical Association; Edwin "Doc" Russell; Bob Sauer; Joanne Settler; Mark Slosek; George Stevens; Jack Swancott; Dick Ulrich; Shirley T. Van Nest; Cristopher M. Warren; Mary Jane Watson, Colton Historical Museum; Donald Wharton; Justin White; Roy E. Wires; and Ross Young, Town of Diana Historical Museum.

I would also like to acknowledge, posthumously, Robert Adner; Barbara K. Bird; Lloyd Blankman; George Cataldo; George Glydon Cole; Bob Daws; Bob Failing; Jim Fynmore; Eric Johnson; Doris and Tom Kilbourn; Earl M. Kreuzer; Harold Linck; Dorothy Payton; Donald Perkins; William E. Scripture Jr.; George Shaughnessy; Dante O. Tranquille; Fred Warden; Howard Wieman; Lawton L. Williams; and Dick Wood.

I would also like to thank my friend Mary L. Thomas who worked as my initial editor. Neal Burdick also listened and added valuable insight. Neal edited the final draft. His constructive comments and observations tightened and focused the story.

A special thanks goes to my wife, Bette. Words will not do justice for all the time she spent traveling with me to chase down material I felt was potential historical matter for the development of this book. She is a wonderful companion on any adventure, and I hope she had as much fun as I did.

Any omission in acknowledging the assistance of anyone who helped with this project is an unintentional oversight.

Permissions | William J. O'Hern

History Is Made to Be Shared

For permission to reprint portions of Barbara Kephart Bird's *Calked Shoes, Life in Adirondack Lumber Camps* (Prospect Books, 1952) and Bird's original story "I Married a Forester" that appeared in 1951 and 1952 issues of *North Country Life*, grateful acknowledgement is made to attorney Cristopher M. Warren, great-grandson of Barbara K. Bird.

For permission to reprint Mart Allen's logging-related "To Make a Long Story Short" columns from the *Adirondack Express*, grateful acknowledgment is made to M. Lisa Monroe, Editor of the *Adirondack Express* and to the author, Mart Allen.

"A Summer Cruise in Highmarket" first appeared in *Highmarket "As you Were," Two Hundred Years of Tug Hill* by Matthew J. Conway (privately printed, 1977); grateful acknowledgment is made to Matthew J. Conway.

For permission to reprint portions from *The Central Adirondacks, A Picture Story* by Jim Fynmore (Prospect Books, 1955), grateful acknowledgment is made to the author and to his son Ed Fynmore.

For permission to use "Rita Chiasson," a Living Traditions Oral History Project (MS 18-007), Adirondack Experience Library, interview conducted by fieldworker Tom Carroll on June 19, 1996, grateful acknowledgment is made to the Adirondack Experience and to Ivy Gocker, librarian at the Adirondack Experience.

"Life in a Lumber Camp" by Ken LaFrance first appeared in the November–December 2013 issue of *Adirondack Life* magazine. Grateful acknowledgment is made to the author and Annie Stolie, editor of *Adirondack Life* for permission to reprint the article.

The story titled "North Country: Life, Love, and Logging in the Woods of Harrisville" by Amy Feiereisel comes with permission from the author and North Country Public Radio's North Country at Work project. Grateful acknowledgment is made to the author and to NCPR.

For permission to reprint "Brandreth (Lake) Station compiled by Charles E. Herr, author of *The Fulton Chain, Early Settlement, Roads, Steamboats, Railroads and Hotels* (HerrStory Publications, 2017), based on "The Mac-a-Mac Railroad" in *Logging Railroads of the Adirondacks* by William Gove (Syracuse University Press, 2006), grateful acknowledgment is made to the author Katherine K. Lewis, director of the Goodsell Museum, Town of Webb Historical Association and Kristy Rubyor, administrative assistant, Town of Webb Historical Association.

For permission to reprint "Scenic Fish Creek Club Has Long Proud History" by Chip Twellman Haley (Rome *Sentinel*, May 7, 2017), grateful acknowledgement is made to Chip Twellman Haley, Douglas Arthur, and the *Daily Sentinel*.

The story "Sixty Years Ago Along Fish Creek" by William E. Scripture Jr. comes with permission from the author of *North Country Life* publisher George Glyndon Cole. Grateful acknowledgement is made to the author and publisher.

Endnotes

Chapter 1

1. The Biltmore stick is a tool used to measure various tree dimensions, such as diameter at breast height and height. It looks much like an everyday yardstick. A Biltmore stick is considered to be only marginally accurate. https://en.wikipedia.org/wiki/Biltmore_stick (Note on Page 16)

Chapter 2

2. See Chapters 51 and 52. (Note on Page 27)

Chapter 3

3. The case was brought by the W.S. DeCamps in Fulton Chain (Thendara today) who won $1,805 in damages from those crossing their land. (Note on Page 29)

Chapter 31

4. *Adirondack Logging: Stories, Memories, Cookhouse Chronicles, Linn Tractors and Gould Paper Company History from Adirondack and Tug Hill Lumber Camps*, William J. O'Hern (2017, In the Adirondacks), documents Life and Times in the Early Years of Logging's Mechanization. (Note on Page 212)

Chapter 41

5. There are numerous references made by the Rev. Byron-Curtiss to Scudder and his father John. B. Todd in *Under an Adirondack Influence: The Life of A.L. Byron-Curtiss 1871–1959* (The Forager Press 2008) and *Adirondack Logging: Stories, Memories, Cookhouse Chronicles, Linn Tractors and Gould Paper Company History from Adirondack and Tug Hill Lumber Camps* (In the Adirondacks, 2016). (Note on Page 331)

Chapter 42

6. Further information about Lawrence's Moose River House can be found in *The Fulton Chain: Early Settlement, Roads, Steamboats, Railroads and Hotels* by Charles E. Herr (North Country Books, 2017). (Note on Page 350)

Chapter 45

7. *Hides, Hemlocks and Adirondack History* (North Country Books,1992) by Barbara McMartin is an excellent reference book on how the tanning industry influenced the growth of the Adirondack North Country region. (Note on Page 380)

8. Mary Ruth White married Thomas Henry Matteson in 1953. She later became the society and feature writer on the staff of the *Binghamton Press*. (Note on Page 381)

Chapter 53

9. See *Adirondack Stories of the Black River Country* (2003, North Country Books) and *Under an Adirondack Influence: The Life of A.L. Byron-Curtiss 1871–1959* (2008, The Forager Press). (Note on Page 480)

Chapter 54

10. See *Adirondack Logging: Stories, Memories, Cookhouse Chronicles, Linn Tractors, and Gould Paper Company History from Adirondack and Tug Hill Lumber Camps* (2016, In the Adirondacks). (Note on Page 482)

Chapter 56

11. Powlish is often spelled Powliss in newspaper articles and Lewis County histories. (Note on Page 497)

12. Potters Corners is the junction of State Routes 26 and 12 D north of Constableville. (Note on Page 497)

Index

Tim-Berrr!

More Logging Industry Books by William J. O'Hern

"Tim-berrr!!" Can there be a more captivating expression in logging language, echoing through the forest? Probably not to the lumberjack. There are old-time "jacks" who found their experiences ideal, or at least unforgettable.

The following logging books by author William J. O'Hern take readers on a journey back in time and document stories about logging and its history.

Life in a North Woods Lumber Camp

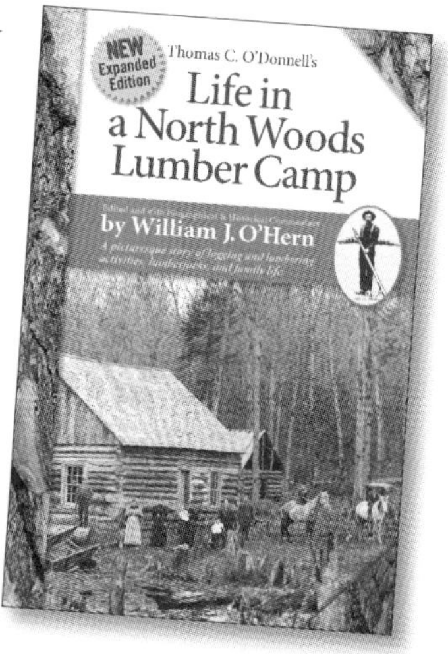

Life in a Northwoods Lumber Camp is a character-driven first-person, true-life rendition of George and Alice Vesta O'Donnell's family life in the O'Donnell Lumber Camp during America's timber operations of the 1880s–90s. The picturesque logging history sparkles with hilarious adventures, wry descriptions of troubles and triumphs, and stories about amusing camp characters from a personal-experience standpoint. 150+ historic photos powerfully illustrate lumber camp life.

Salt pork was handed out in huge chunks for breakfast, lunch, and dinner, and the day's supply of bread was laid out in a stack in the morning. "When you were hungry," George Lanktree recalled, "it was an A-1 meal, but I guess it wasn't up to the grub today." Courtesy of Pat Payne

Bog River, 1915. The truth is there were heroes and heroes' widows left with children and bleak futures. No compensation. No Social Security. It was a high risk game with 'jacks gambling their families' future and inviting watery graves for themselves. Special Collections, Feinberg Library, SUNY College at Plattsburgh B-2-13

Adirondack Logging

Adirondack Logging: Stories, Memories, Cookhouse Chronicles, Linn Tractors and Gould Paper Company History from Adirondack and Tug Hill Lumber Camps is a groundbreaking history of the timber business' modernization. Teams of heavy draft horses were replaced with tractors on skis and tracks.

The Adirondack Mountains are rich in legend, folklore, tradition—and at one time great virgin stands of the finest softwoods and hardwoods in northeastern America. The imperially tall, straight white pine, the northern black and red spruce, the white cedar, balsam fir, basswood and hemlock were all softwoods that made their way to the mills riding the rivers declared public highways for floating logs. It was not until roads were built and mechanical logging equipment of the early twentieth century came along that the old-style horse-drawn methods were replaced. In the 1920s, harvest of weighty hard woods began.

CURRENT TITLES
by William J. O'Hern

ADIRONDACK LOGGING
Stories, Memories, Cookhouse Chronicles,
Linn Tractors and Gould Paper Company History
from Adirondack and Tug Hill Lumber Camps

SPRING TROUT &
STRAWBERRY PANCAKES
Borrowed Tales, Quirky Cures,
Camp Recipes and the Adirondack Characters
Who Cooked Them Up

ADIRONDACK MEMORIES
AND CAMPFIRE STORIES
Edited and with
Biographical and Historical Commentary

ADIRONDACK WILDS
Exploring the Haunts
of Noah John Rondeau

THE HERMIT AND US
Our Adirondack Adventures
with Noah John Rondeau

ADIRONDACK KALEIDOSCOPE
AND NORTH COUNTRY CHARACTERS
Edited and with Biographical
and Historical Commentary

NEW Expanded Edition

Thomas C. O'Donnell's
LIFE IN A
NORTH WOODS LUMBER CAMP
Edited and with Biographical
and Historical Commentary

ADIRONDACK ADVENTURES:
Bob Gillespie and Harvey Dunham
on French Louie's Trail
By William J. O'Hern and Roy E. Reehil

NOAH JOHN RONDEAU'S
ADIRONDACK WILDERNESS DAYS
A Year with the Hermit of Cold River Flow

UNDER AN ADIRONDACK INFLUENCE
The Life of A.L. Byron-Curtiss, 1871–1959
By William J. O'Hern and Roy E. Reehil

ADIRONDACK CHARACTERS
& CAMPFIRE YARNS
Early Settlers and Their Traditions

ADIRONDACK STORIES OF
THE BLACK RIVER COUNTRY

LIFE WITH NOAH
Stories and Adventures of Richard
Smith with Noah J. Rondeau

ADIRONDACK CAMP STORIES
A Treasury of True Tales, Lore, History, Recreation,
and Colorful Characters of the Mountains

ADIRONDACK TIMBER CRUISING
AND LUMBERING DAYS MEMORIES

THE ADIRONDACKS
MOOSE RIVER PLAINS VOL. 1
Life Around the Indian Clearing

COMING SOON
by William J. O'Hern

THE ADIRONDACKS
MOOSE RIVER PLAINS VOL. 2
Land of Deer

THE ADIRONDACKS
MOOSE RIVER PLAINS VOL. 3
Land of Solitude and Intrigue

ADIRONDACK VACATIONLAND

ADIRONDACK ECHOES
A Portrait of Mountain Life and Tales

ADIRONDACK TIM-BERRR!

ADIRONDACK TALES FROM
THREE BEAR BOULEVARD
Following a Hermit
Through His Final Years (1950–1967)

ADIRONDACK ODYSSEYS
Adventures in the Wilderness from Bygone Days

ADIRONDACK CAMPING DAYS
AND BYGONE TALES

ADIRONDACK STRONG AND
TUG HILL COUNTRY WISE
Life on Old Time Farms

ADIRONDACK DEPRESSION
YEARS AND THE CIVILIAN
CONSERVATION CORPS

Available at
www.adkwilds.com,
in bookstores
or by phone:
North Country Books
1-800-342-7409